Published by Pearson Education Limited, a company incorporated in England and Wales, having its registered office at Edinburgh Gate, Harlow, Essex, CM20 2JE. Registered company number: 872828

www.pearsonschoolsandfecolleges.co.uk

Edexcel is a registered trademark of Edexcel Limited

Text © Gillian Dale 2010
First published 2010

13 12 11
10 9 8 7 6 5 4 3

British Library Cataloguing in Publication Data
A catalogue record for this book is available from the British Library.

ISBN 978 1 846907 28 9

Typeset by HL Studios
Original illustrations © Pearson Education Limited 2010
Illustrated by HL Studios, Long Hanborough, Oxford/Ivan Gillet
Cover design by Visual Philosophy, created by eMC Design
Cover photo © 2010 Masterfile
Back cover photos © Shutterstock
Printed in Spain by Graficas Estella, S.L.

Acknowledgements
Every effort has been made to contact copyright holders of material reproduced in this book. Any omissions will be rectified in subsequent printings if notice is given to the publishers.

Websites
The websites used in this book were correct and up to date at the time of publication. It is essential for tutors to preview each website before using it in class so as to ensure that the URL is still accurate, relevant and appropriate. We suggest that tutors bookmark useful websites and consider enabling students to access them through the school/college intranet.

Disclaimer
This material has been published on behalf of Edexcel and offers high-quality support for the delivery of Edexcel qualifications.

This does not mean that the material is essential to achieve any Edexcel qualification, nor does it mean that it is the only suitable material available to support any Edexcel qualification. Edexcel material will not be used verbatim in setting any Edexcel examination or assessment. Any resource lists produced by Edexcel shall include this and other appropriate resources.

Copies of official specifications for all Edexcel qualifications may be found on the Edexcel website: www.edexcel.com

BTEC
Level 3

edexcel
advancing learning, changing lives

D

TRAVEL & TOURISM LEVEL 3

Book 2 BTEC National

Gillian Dale

A PEARSON COMPANY

Acknowledgments

This book is for Jennifer.

Gillian Dale would like to thank the following:

For sharing their work stories
Simon Allen at Canvas Holidays
Chris Reed at Bateman's
Hayley Bevan at the Fitness Industry Association
Louisa Cutter at Jet2.com
Elizabeth Dale for Holiday Reps experiences

For tour operations information and job descriptions
Simon Allen and Lindsey Brunton from Canvas Holidays

For cruise experiences and itineraries
Francis and Wynne Bratby

And also the editing team at Pearson Education

About the author

Gillian Dale has many years experience teaching travel and tourism and running BTEC programmes. She has written several travel and tourism text books for various courses as well as units and materials for various qualifications.

She is a member of the Air Transport User's Council, an organisation which represents airline passengers' interests. She also works as an additional inspector for Ofsted and as an educational consultant and coach. Her main focus is curriculum design and programme development and her recent projects include developing courses in customer service for front line personnel who will encounter Olympic visitors, coaching programmes and e -learning seminars in project implementation and writing project proposals.

She has a Masters degree, PGCE, assessor awards and has held a fellowship at Cambridge University.

Photo credits

The author and publisher would like to thank the following individuals and organisations for permission to reproduce photographs:

Unit 11 p.**1** Pearson Education Ltd/Photodisc/Photolink; p.**3** Shutterstock; p.**7** Rex Features; p.**16** Photodisc. Malcolm Fife; p.**20** Alamy/Danita Delimot; p.**23** Photodisc. Photolink. Tomi; p.**29** Pearson Education Ltd/Photodisc/Photolink; p.**29** Photodisc. Sami Sarkis; p.**31** Shutterstock

Unit 13 p.**33** Photolibrary/Jochen Tack; p.**35** Pearson Education Ltd/Gareth Boden; p.**37** Pearson Education Ltd. Jules Selmes; p.**42** Corbis/Warren Faldley; p.**51** Photolibrary/Gunther Rossenbach; p.**61** Canvas Holidays Ltd

Unit 15 p.**63** Getty Images/Murat Turan; p.**65** Shutterstock; p.**67** Shutterstock; p.**68** Photolibrary/AIC AIC; p.**75** Alamy/Adam James; p.**77** Getty Images. Digital Vision; p.**79** Photodisc.; p.**91** Shutterstock

Unit 17 p.**93** Getty Images/Imagemore; p.**95** Shutterstock; p.**96** Getty Images/Leon Neal; p.**98** Getty Images/Christie Goodwin; p.**102** Photolibrary/Ingolf Pompe/Lockfoto; p.**119** Fitness Industry Association

Unit 19 p.**121** Photolibrary/Roy Rainford/Robert Harding; p.**123** Shutterstock; p.**126** Harriet Merry; p.**127** Alamy/Alan King; p.**128** Alamy/Martyn Vickery; p.**131** Shutterstock; p.**133** Eden Project/Tamsyn Williams; p.**139** Yuri Arcurs / Shutterstock

Unit 20 p.**27** Corbis/Image Source; p.**143** Pearson Education Ltd/Gareth Boden; p.**144** Pearson Education Ltd/Debbie Rowe; p.**147** Shutterstock; p.**150** PA Photos; p.**151** Shutterstock; p.**157** Shutterstock

Unit 26 p.**159** Shutterstock; p.**161** Shutterstock; p.**168** Tyler Olson/Shutterstock; p.**177** Corbis/Frank Guiziou; p.**183** Shutterstock

Acknowledgements

We are grateful to the following for permission to reproduce copyright material:

IRN Research for Figure 11.1 'Breakdown by destination (Passengers 000s) 2000-2009' http://www.irn-research.com/sector-specific-services/travel-and-tourism/ IRN Research – UK Cruise Market 2009, and Table 11.1 'River cruise holidays 1999-2008' from *Annual Cruise Review*/PSA(ACE)-IRN Cruise statistics, copyright © IRN Research; Iris Coates for an extract from 'Are cruise liners a viable alternative to flying' by Iris Coates, *Responsible Travel* www.responsibletravel.com, copyright © Iris Coates; TUI UK Ltd for an extract TUI Travel plc from http://www.tuitravelplc.com/tui/pages/aboutus/companystructure/ods; the Pricing Table from *Thomson Gold brochure*, p.29 'Funchal Maderia' May 2010–Oct 2010, 1st edition; and an extract from "Major changes and Our responsibility" *Thomson Summer Collection brochure*, copyright © TUI UK Ltd; Kirker Holidays for an extract about Kirker Travel, from www.kirkerholidays.com, reproduced with permission; Canvas Holidays for a screenshot from http://www.canvasholidays.co.uk/Canvas-for-Families.aspx and Canvas Holidays' children's Courier job description, copyright © Canvas Holidays Ltd; Sandstone Limited for an extract about Romanbar from www.sandstone.co.uk, reproduced with permission of Sandstone Limited; The NEC Group for Figure 17.1 'Case Study National Exhibition Centre – Birmingham' and details about The NEC Group, reproduced with permission; World Travel Market for Figure 17.3 '2010 World Travel Market Floorplan' from www.wtmlondon.com, and Figure 17.6 World Travel Market Stand Application Form, copyright © World Travel Market; VisitEngland for an extract from 'Survey of Visits to Visitor Attractions England 2008', Enjoy England; and the figure 'Length of stay of visitors to the UK' from *Britain Inbound, Market & Trade Profile*, p.16, November 2009, www.visitbritain.org/, copyright © VisitEngland; The Caterer Group for Table 20.1 'Top 100 Hotel Groups with more than 200 bedrooms in the UK, September 2007 (by number of Bedrooms) – Part I' from www.caterersearch.com, reproduced with permission; Mintel for Table 20.2 'Most important hotel facilities', copyright © Mintel 2008; Siblu Holidays for an extract from the siblu parc Le Bois Dormant brochure, 2009, reproduced with permission; Iglucruise.com for an extract from 'P&O Cruises sees 2011 booking improvement' www.iglucruise.com, 10 July 2009 by Chris Smith, copyright © Iglucruise.com; TW Group Ltd for an extract from 'Package holiday market still 'huge', says Mintel' *Travel Weekly*, 12 March 2009, http://www.travelweekly.co.uk, copyright © TW Group Ltd; and Tourism Concern for an extract from 'Tourism Concern's policy on working with industry', http://www.tourismconcern.org.uk/index.php?page=tourism-concern-s-policy-on-working-with-industry, copyright © Tourism Concern.

Contents

Unit 16 Passenger transport for travel and tourism (10 credits) is available online at the following web address www.pearsonfe.co.uk/TravelandTourismLevel3Unit16.

About your BTEC Level 3 Travel and Tourism book

Choosing to study for a BTEC Level 3 National Travel and Tourism qualification is a great decision to make for lots of reasons. Studying Travel and Tourism will allow you to broaden your knowledge of the sector as well as deepening your skills.

Your BTEC Level 3 National Travel and Tourism is a vocational or work-related qualification. This doesn't mean that it will give you all the skills you need to do a job, but it does mean that you'll have the opportunity to gain specific knowledge, understanding and skills that are relevant to your chosen subject or area of work.

What will you be doing?

The qualification is structured into mandatory units (ones that you must do) and optional units (ones that you can choose to do). How many units you do and which ones you cover depend on the type of qualification you are working towards.

Qualifications	Credits from mandatory units	Credits from optional units	Total credits
Edexcel BTEC Level 3 Certificate	20	10	30
Edexcel BTEC Level 3 Subsidiary Diploma	40	20	60
Edexcel BTEC Level 3 Diploma	40	80	120
Edexcel BTEC Level 3 Extended Diploma	40	140	180

How to use this book

This book is designed to help you through your BTEC Level 3 National Travel and Tourism course. It contains many features that will help you develop and apply your skills and knowledge in work-related situations and assist you in getting the most from your course.

Introduction

These introductions give you a snapshot of what to expect from each unit – and what you should be aiming for by the time you finish it!

Assessment and grading criteria

This table explains what you must do to achieve each of the assessment criteria for each of the mandatory and optional units. For each assessment criterion, shown by the grade buttons **P**, **M**, **D**, etc. there is an assessment activity.

Assessment

Your tutor will set **assignments** throughout your course for you to complete. These may take a variety of forms including business reports, presentations, case studies. The important thing is that you evidence your skills and knowledge to date.

Learner experience

Stuck for ideas? Daunted by your first assignment? These learners have all been through it before…

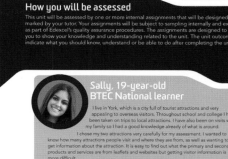

Unit 19 UK visitor attractions

How you will be assessed

This unit will be assessed by one or more internal assignments that will be designed and marked by your tutor. Your assignments will be subject to sampling internally and externally as part of Edexcel's quality assurance procedures. The assignments are designed to allow you to show your knowledge and understanding related to the unit. The unit outcomes indicate what you should know, understand or be able to do after completing the unit.

Sally, 19-year-old BTEC National learner

I live in York, which is a city full of tourist attractions and very appealing to overseas visitors. Throughout school and college I have been taken on trips to local attractions. I have also been on visits with my family so I had a good knowledge already of what is around.

I chose my two attractions very carefully for my assessment, I wanted to know how many attractions people visit and where they are from, as well as wanting to get information about the attraction. It is easy to find out what the primary and secondary products and services are from leaflets and websites but getting visitor information is more difficult.

I found out that York Tourism carry out lots of research and have statistics on all aspects of tourism. I started with their website and found a lot of useful statistics. I also gave them a call to ask some specific questions and they helped me a lot. Doing this research helped me choose my two attractions, one was the famous Jorvik Viking Centre and the other one was the River Ouse. Of course, this was more challenging in terms of appeal as I had to consider the activities that take place on the river (e.g. boat trips) as well as the events and experiences on it and along it (e.g. the York Rivers Festival).

Over to you!

1 What attractions would you recommend to a visitor in your locality?

2 Can you guess what primary and secondary products and services are? If not you will find out in this unit.

123

Activities

There are different types of activities for you to do: **Assessment activities** are suggestions for tasks that you might do as part of your assignment and will help you develop your knowledge, skills and understanding. **Grading tips** clearly explain what you need to do in order to achieve a pass, merit or distinction grade.

Assessment activity 11.1

P P P M BTEC

You have managed to get a work placement with a specialist cruise agency. This is a very prestigious placement and you are delighted. You are spending four weeks with the company. The first week was an introduction to the work and meeting all the staff. Now, your line manager wants you to take on your own project. The company has taken a stand at a cruise exhibition at ExCeL in London and has asked you to help. You have also been asked to prepare a stand display about the cruise, which should be designed to attract customers to the stand.

Use the information given in the first part of the unit and your own research to produce a wall display which gives an overview of the cruise industry. Make sure that you cover the full range, referring to the content and assessment guidance in the unit specification for the detail required.

P P P

You should include:

- Key stages in development focusing on the last 50 years, and the last 10 years in particular with a brief description of each stage. P
- The roles of stakeholders involved in the industry covering cruise operators, regulatory bodies and their links with other industries. P

- Employment opportunities – identify onboard and offshore employment opportunities with different types of cruise lines and then describe one onshore and two onboard employment opportunities available within the cruise industry. P

Support your display with explanatory notes which assess the cruise industry as it is today. Include a brief profile of the main cruise operators, identifying their parent company. Include statistical information about passenger numbers, number of ships and number and nationality of crews. Assess links with other travel and tourism industries, for example, retail agents, transport and tour operators. M

Grading tips

P Try to identify the cruise operators who are independent and those who are part of larger organisations.

P Describe the job role and responsibilities, entry requirements, working environment, terms and conditions and opportunities for promotion. Jobs could be with different operators.

M Use cruise operator websites for your research as well as newspaper articles, other websites and statistics showing the latest trends.

There are also suggestions for activities that will give you a broader grasp of travel and tourism, stretch your understanding and develop your skills.

Activity: Fly-cruise or river cruise?

Using brochures or the internet, find details of a fly-cruise and a river cruise. For the fly-cruise, choose one of the less formal cruises such as Carnival or Thomson. Describe and compare the appeal of both types of cruise in terms of:

- Itinerary and routes offered – embarkation point, cruise area and ports of call, excursions and sights, duration, days at sea, climate and any special events or themes on board.

- Type of ship – large/small, passenger crew ratio, passenger space ratio, name of operator.

Personal, learning and thinking skills

Throughout your BTEC Level 3 National Travel and Tourism course there are lots of opportunities to develop your personal, learning and thinking skills. These will help you work in a team, manage yourself effectively and develop your all-important interpersonal skills. Look out for these as you progress.

PLTS

Planning and carrying out your research to meet the brief given will help you develop your skills as an **independent enquirer**.

Functional skills

It's important that you have good English, maths and ICT skills – you never know when you'll need them, and employers will be looking for evidence that you've got these skills too.

Functional skills

Selecting and using different texts to obtain relevant information will help to develop **English** skills in reading.

Key terms

Technical words and phrases are easy to spot. The terms and definitions are also in the glossary at the back of the book.

Key terms

Vertical integration – where companies at different levels in the chain of distribution merge or one takes over the other.

Horizontal integration – where two companies offering competing products merge or one takes over the other.

Subsidiaries – companies which are more than 50% owned by another company, known as the parent company.

WorkSpace

WorkSpace provides snapshots of real-world business issues and shows you how the knowledge and skills you are developing through your course can be applied in your future career.

There are also mini-case studies throughout the book to help you focus on your own projects.

WorkSpace Hayley Bevan
Events and Sponsorship Manager, FIA

Hayley, your job title sounds very interesting. Can you tell us what it's about?
My job is to arrange various seminars and conferences throughout the year for the Fitness Industry Association (FIA). We have some Professional Development seminars throughout the year, which I organise with my team. Then there might be dinners such as our 20th anniversary dinner at the London Transport Museum.

How did you get the job?
I started with the company as a Programmes Co-ordinator, working on projects to get children active.

I managed a project called Go London that was located in Brent, promoting gym use to teenage girls. When the Manager position came up I applied and got it, making good use of my project management experience.

Are you responsible for any really big events?
The major event that I organise is an annual conference for the FIA. This year it's at the Reebok Stadium in Bolton. The aim of the event is to bring all suppliers and operators in the fitness industry together. It is a huge undertaking to organise as we have 700 delegates. It takes a year to arrange from start to finish. We need a venue that can hold the 700 delegates for two days, plus room to host a black tie dinner for 900 as extra people attend a ball on the second day. This ball incorporates an awards ceremony recognising excellence in the industry.

The event is sponsored so I have to find the sponsorship and secure the funding for the event, for example gym equipment suppliers might sponsor us. Once the sponsorship and venue are secured there is a lot of work to do arranging the marketing, invitations, delegate lists, details of programme and equipment needed. Everything has to be organised to deadlines.

Think about it!

1 What project management experience could you include on a CV or application form?
2 Have you arranged any events at school or college?
3 Have you arranged any events for friends?

119

Just checking

When you see this sort of activity, take stock! These quick activities and questions are there to check your knowledge. You can use them to see how much progress you've made and to identify any areas where you need to refresh your knowledge.

Edexcel's assignment tips

At the end of each unit, you'll find hints and tips to help you get the best mark you can, such as the best websites to go to, checklists to help you remember processes and useful reminders to avoid common mistakes. You might want to read this information before starting your assignment...

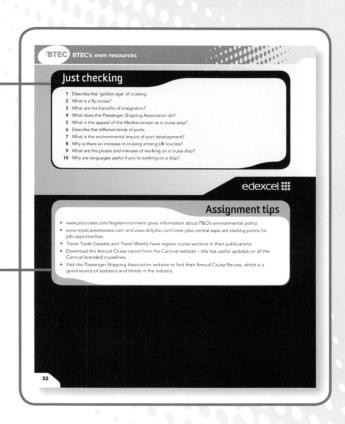

Don't miss out on these resources to help you!

Have you read your BTEC Level 3 National Study Skills Guide? It's full of advice on study skills, putting your assignments together and making the most of being a BTEC Travel and Tourism learner.

Ask your tutor about extra materials to help you through your course. You'll find interesting videos, activities, presentations and information about the world of business.

Your book is just part of the exciting resources from Edexcel to help you succeed in your BTEC course.

Visit: www.edexcel.com/btec or www.pearsonfe.co.uk/btec2010

Unit 16 Passenger transport for travel and tourism (10 credits) is available online at the following web address www.pearsonfe.co.uk/TravelandTourismLevel3Unit16.

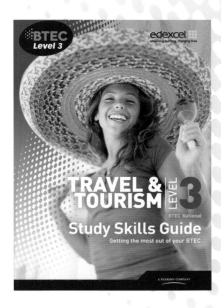

11 Investigating the cruise industry

This is a fascinating area of travel and tourism to study because the market for cruises is growing as cruise operators respond to demand for different types of cruising across all market segments. In addition, there are lots of opportunities to work in the cruise industry and it is a popular choice for young people with no family commitments, because you can travel the world as you work.

In this unit you will learn about the history and development of the cruise industry from the Titanic to today's huge liners. You can find out what kind of employment opportunities are available in cruising and whether they appeal to you. You will practise selecting cruises to suit the needs of different kinds of customer. This means you will need to know about all the types of cruises there are and what they offer in terms of facilities and ports of call. The environmental impact of cruising is an important consideration and you will find out about positive and negative impacts on cruising areas and ports.

It would be a good idea for you to collect a selection of cruise brochures to help you work through this unit. You will also be introduced to a number of websites which you should bookmark for future reference.

Learning outcomes

After completing this unit, you should:

1 know about the cruise industry

2 understand the cruise market

3 be able to select cruises that appeal to cruise customers and meet specific needs

4 understand the effects of an expanding cruise industry.

1

Assessment and grading criteria

This table shows you what you must do in order to achieve a **pass**, **merit** or **distinction** grade, and where you can find activities in this book to help you.

To achieve a **pass** grade the evidence must show that you are able to:	To achieve a **merit** grade the evidence must show that, in addition to the pass criteria, you are able to:	To achieve a **distinction** grade the evidence must show that, in addition to the pass and merit criteria, you are able to:
P1 describe key stages in the development of the cruise industry	**M1** statistically assess the cruise industry today, including stakeholders and employment **See assessment activity 11.1, page 14**	**D1** evaluate how operator, product and ship developments have increased the appeal and growth of cruising over the last ten years and increased cruise operator employment **See assessment activity 11.3, page 26**
P2 describe the roles of stakeholders involved in the cruise industry		
P3 describe employment opportunities available within the cruise industry **See assessment activity 11.1, page 14**		
P4 Identify major cruise areas available to the UK market	**M2** analyse the range of cruises and ships operating currently in a named cruise area, including their appeal to different types of customer **See assessment activity 11.3, page 26**	
P5 describe the different types of cruises available to customers		
P6 explain how cruise lines have developed products for a growing cruise market **See assessment activity 11.2, page 22**		
P7 use brochure information to select cruises that appeal to cruise customers and meet their specific needs		
P8 explain how the selected cruises will meet the needs of different types of customers **See assessment activity 11.3, page 26**		
P9 outline potential future developments in the cruise industry based on current trends	**M3** compare the negative and positive impacts of cruising on two different ports within one cruise area **See assessment activity 11.4, page 30**	**D2** evaluate how potential future developments could increase or decrease the negative and positive impacts of cruising **See assessment activity 11.4, page 30**
P10 explain how cruises impact on a cruise area, the gateway ports and ports of call **See assessment activity 11.4, page 30**		

How you will be assessed

This unit will be assessed by one or more internal assignments that will be designed and marked by your tutor. Your assignments will be subject to sampling internally and externally as part of Edexcel's quality assurance procedures. The assignments are designed to allow you to show your knowledge and understanding related to the unit. The unit outcomes indicate what you should know, understand or be able to do after completing the unit.

Kamau, 21-year-old BTEC National learner

The best part of this unit was studying all the different kinds of cruises and the places they go to. For our assessment we did some role-plays where we had to pretend to be different customers booking cruises. We had lots of brochures from sail ships and huge liners crossing the Atlantic. We had to find the right type of cruise for customers within their budgets and sell them to the customer.

One assessment was about the impact of cruise ships and it was quite hard to find information about this, but I found that some cruise companies issue statements about their environmental policy and these helped, although they were not objective sources.

I enjoyed finding out about jobs on cruise ships but was surprised at the long hours crew work. However, there were lots of different jobs to choose from and it is a way of seeing the world. This was the easiest assessment as there are lots of websites with details of jobs on board ships.

Over to you!

1 What does Kamau mean about 'objective sources'?
2 How can you check the validity and reliability of a source?

1 Know about the cruise industry

Cruising ahead

The cruise industry is the world's fastest growing leisure sector, with expansion reaching 11 per cent per annum in 2008 according to the Annual Cruise Review. The Passenger Shipping Association (PSA) reported that 1.5 million Britons took an open sea cruise in 2008 – rising from the 1.07 million who cruised in 2005. The market has more than doubled in the last decade. This growth is expected to continue as more people realise that cruising is an affordable holiday.

Most cruises are booked through travel agents, unlike other types of holiday where there is a trend towards direct or internet booking. Training courses are available to help travel agents sell cruises. They are provided by the cruise lines themselves and through the PSA's training organisation, the Association of Cruise Experts (ACE).

Have you been on a cruise? Do you know someone who has? If so, ask them about their experiences. Try to find one person each who has been on a cruise. Report back on their experiences to the group and compare notes.

1.1 History, development and growth

History

Sea travel used to be vital for trade between countries. Today freight is often carried by air but before the development of aviation that was not an option. The first routes were trade routes. Transport by a fast regular steamship service was the key to a successful trade empire in Victorian Britain. The government sponsored routes and the building of ships, and the Royal Navy was responsible for protecting the routes and their supply bases.

In the nineteenth century, steamships regularly crossed the Atlantic. The first company to operate on the transatlantic shipping routes was the British and North American Royal Mail Steam Packet Company. This later became Cunard Steamship Company, Limited. The company's first steamship was the *Britannia*, which sailed from Liverpool to Boston with a passenger and cargo service in 1840.

The famous engineer Isambard Kingdom Brunel designed the SS *Great Britain*, a ship built to provide transatlantic services. This 3270-ton ship set the standard for ocean liners for many years. It was equipped with cabins and staterooms for 360 passengers. By 1853, the *Great Britain* had been refitted to accommodate up to 630 passengers. It operated a London to Australia service for nearly 20 years. Brunel also built the *Great Eastern*. This could carry 4000 passengers and enough coal to get to Australia without refuelling on the way. It was the largest ship in the world until it was taken out of service and broken up in 1888.

Some ships were requisitioned for the Crimean War (1853–6) as troopships. This is a pattern that continued throughout the First and Second World Wars and to the more recent Gulf War.

Many early passengers on ships were migrants going to new lands and new lives. Few passengers travelled for pleasure, as journeys could take a long time.

In 1881, electricity was introduced on a passenger ship for the first time (Cunard's RMS *Servia*). By 1911, Cunard's *Franconia* had a gym and health centre on board. There were many other facilities of a luxurious standard for wealthy passengers. At the other end of the scale, those travelling in 'steerage' had basic facilities, that is, a bunk in a cabin and somewhere to eat.

Case study: The *Titanic*

You have probably seen the film *Titanic* but do you remember where the ship was going and what type of people it was carrying? The ship began her maiden voyage from Southampton to New York on 10 April 1912. On the night of 14 April, the ship struck an iceberg. The RMS *Titanic* was the largest passenger steamship in the world at the time of her launching and it was hoped that she would dominate the transatlantic ocean liner business. The owners were the White Star Line. The ship could hold up to 3300 passengers and had 899 crew. RMS stands for Royal Mail Steamer and meant that the ship carried mail. The ship was supposed to be at the forefront of technology and unsinkable. It was also extremely luxurious, as shown clearly in the film.

On this maiden voyage there were 2208 passengers; 1496 of them died. There were not enough lifeboats on board to save all the passengers – the number of lifeboats needed was calculated on the ship's tonnage not on passenger numbers. After the sinking of the *Titanic*, changes were made in ship construction and in wireless telegraphy. There was also the first International Convention for the Safety of Life at Sea, held in London. This conference led to the formation of the International Ice Patrol, an organisation that monitors and reports on the location of icebergs in the North Atlantic which might threaten ships. Following the sinking, other important safety measures were introduced, including lifeboats for everyone on board, drills, and radio communications operating 24 hours a day along with a secondary power supply, so as not to miss distress calls.

1   Summarise the impact of the sinking of the *Titanic* on the cruise ship industry at the time.

2   Find out about the International Ice Patrol today. Write a few sentences on its mission. You can find information at www.uscg.mil/lantarea/iip.

3   Choose a cruise ship that is currently operating. Find out what safety measures it has on board. Cruise brochures will help you with this.

Golden age

The period from the 1930s to the 1950s was known as the 'golden age' of cruising. Liners such as the *Queen Elizabeth* and the *Queen Mary* used to compete on transatlantic crossings for the famed 'Blue Riband': recognition of the fastest crossing. Cruising was a means of luxury travel and could only be afforded by the more affluent classes.

The *Queen Mary* was to make 1001 journeys across the Atlantic in her time of service. Queen Mary launched this liner in 1934 and it was the largest liner ever built at that time. The ship was in service until 1967.

The *Queen Elizabeth* was launched in 1938 by Queen Elizabeth, the Queen Mother. This liner did not enter commercial service until 1946 due to the Second World War.

1960s

In 1961, the 44,807-ton *Canberra* was launched. She was the largest post-war British passenger ship. Other ships at this time were about 20,000 tons. The ship was to serve as a long-distance liner on the route from Southampton to Australia. The name was in honour of the Australian capital. The ship was built by Harland & Wolff at a cost of £17 million and became known as the 'Great White Whale'. Her maiden voyage began on 2 June 1961.

The *Canberra* carried out a large number of trips to Australia. Many of these were taking emigrants from the UK to Australia. These passengers were able to buy a one-way ticket for only £10 under the government's assisted-passage scheme. By the end of the decade there were not so many emigrants and so the *Canberra* became a full-time holiday cruise ship.

1970s, 1980s and fly-cruises

Once it was easy to cross the Atlantic by air the lucrative transatlantic cruise route went into decline. Cruise operators had to find new, alternative routes, such as Caribbean destinations. Also tour operators began to appreciate the demand for cruising, and began to create cruise packages. Some operators bought their own ships and introduced cruises at competitive prices. Cruise ships at this time were smaller than today, carrying about 600–800 passengers, and cruising was very much a luxury activity.

In the 1980s, 'straight-to-the-sun' fly-cruising took off, enabling people to take Caribbean and other faraway cruises without the long ship journey to reach the destination. This meant a cruise could be taken in a one- or two-week holiday.

Did you know?

In September 2008 the *Queen Mary 2* made her 100th transatlantic voyage.

Prior to its 100th voyage, guests included Rod Stewart and John Cleese, and the first author-signed copy of *Harry Potter and the Half Blood Prince* was transported to its US debut on this ship.

Development and growth

Changing consumer demands

Growth in cruising reflects the increase in disposable income for average British people. With more money to spend, people are able to take more holidays and look for different experiences. Another factor leading to growth in the market is that for the last few years prices of cruising have been heavily discounted as more competition enters the market. During the recession of 2008–2009 a Yougov survey reported that when people were thinking about holidays they were not prepared to forego an annual holiday even if money was tight. Instead they would take fewer holidays. This shift in demand protected the cruise industry as a cruise is usually the main holiday for the year.

Needs and ages

Lower prices have encouraged first-time cruisers and changed the profile of the market. As younger people and families try cruising and enjoy it, they tell their friends about their experiences and the idea becomes attractive to a wider cross-section of society.

The average age of cruise passengers has slowly fallen. According to the Annual Cruise Review in the early 1990s, it was 60. It is now about 53. This may seem high but is explained by the large number of repeat (older) passengers who take cruises. There are an increased number of families with children who go on a cruise.

The average also reflects an ageing UK population which has more people in the 40–60 and 60-plus age groups.

Developing trends

Currently, the cruise sector is popular with travel agents as it is one of the few sectors where high commissions can be earned. Passengers are more likely to book with a travel agent than over the internet as they are spending a lot of money and are likely to need advice about the type of ship, cabins and facilities. According to Carnival's Annual Cruise Report, 83 per cent of bookings are made through agents and this is likely to continue.

More passengers – six out of ten – are choosing to take a cruise which starts from a UK port than a fly-cruise. There are a few reasons for this. The first is convenience, as passengers do not have to negotiate airports and baggage rules and can start their holiday sooner. Another reason has been the introduction of new ships by UK-based companies such as P&O. These are home ported, which means that they are based at ports in the UK.

There is a trend for less formal cruising, deliberately so as to attract younger people and families. Many cruise lines have relaxed their dress codes so that people do not have to dress up for dinner as they did traditionally on board ships.

Popular and new cruise areas

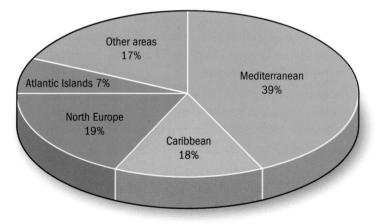

Figure 11.1: UK cruises by destination 2008

(Source: IRN Research–UK cruise market 2009)

The Mediterranean is the most popular cruise area for UK passengers, taking 39 per cent of the market. The Caribbean has increased in popularity in recent years and Northern Europe has also increased in popularity as more people take cruises leaving from the UK.

Think about it

Why do you think the Mediterranean is popular? Do you know where the Atlantic islands are? Check on a map.

Different types of ship

To cater for increased demand and to encourage growth in the market, the cruise lines are building new ships and providing a greater variety of types of cruises. Cruise ships are getting longer, wider and taller to accommodate more people and generate more revenue for cruise lines by achieving economies of scale. The average number of passengers aboard a modern cruise ship is approximately 1500, with some ships carrying as many as 5000 passengers. The average width of new ships is 90 feet, which is almost the maximum allowed for going through the Panama Canal.

In addition to getting bigger, cruise liners are growing in number. Ten new ocean-going ships were introduced in 2009. One of these was the largest ship ever built, *Oasis of the Seas*, from Royal Caribbean, at 225,000 tonnes and able to carry 5,400 passengers at double occupancy.

A further 30 ships will be introduced by 2012.

What does the *Oasis of the Seas* offer?

Bigger ships impact on ports, which have to be able to accommodate them and the large numbers of passengers and baggage that they carry. Berths have to be wider, and gangways and terminals have to be higher to meet the passenger disembarkation point.

A contradictory trend is a growth in small-scale ships which can reach smaller ports and destinations that are inaccessible to the big ships. The smaller ship allows a more intimate atmosphere without compromising on luxury. An example is the *Adonia*, a P&O vessel that can carry just over 700 passengers. Most of its cabins have balconies and the ship has a very traditional design with wood panelling and leather armchairs.

It is not only open-sea cruises that are growing in popularity. The river cruise industry is also growing. In 2010, a company called Avalon Waterways introduced two new ships, each with 65 staterooms.

New and different onboard accommodation and facilities

Did you know?

Many Royal Caribbean ships feature a rock-climbing wall, while there are ice-skating rinks on their *Voyager of the Seas* and other Voyager-class ships and a surf park on the *Freedom of the Seas*. The ships operate worldwide with a selection of itineraries that call at approximately 160 destinations.

Cruise lines vie with each other to provide more and better facilities to meet the needs of their customers and to attract passengers to their cruises. We will look at some specific cruises later on. However, many of the facilities are aimed at providing greater choice, for example more choice of dining options. Entertainment programmes are extensive and often feature celebrities.

Cruises are sometimes themed to attract people with a special interest. On some ships a series of themed programmes are offered on the same ship. For example, Celebrity Cruises ships offer themed cruises in three categories, each with its own brand name, food and beverage (Savour), intellectual discovery (Discover) and health and wellness (Renew). Passengers can participate in activities relating to the theme.

Accommodation has improved from simple berths in cabins on many ships. The most luxurious ships now have only staterooms with balconies and no bunk beds at all (except for the crew).

Mergers and takeovers

Like any other industry within travel and tourism, cruising is subject to companies taking over one another and sometimes merging. Carnival and Royal Caribbean are the biggest groups with many brands. These are brands which they have acquired at some time. Later on you will see which brands they include. Cruise lines often sell ships when they feel their useful life is over. Tour operators have also bought ships in order to enter the industry. An example is Thomson, who operate their own cruises.

Current position

Information about the current position in the UK cruise market is easily available from the Passenger Shipping Association (PSA). We have seen that passenger numbers from the UK have reached 1.5 million per year. New ships introduced will push this growth even further as more capacity is added. The PSA expects passenger numbers to reach 1.65 million in 2010.

Activity: Statistics

Find the latest statistics from the Passenger Ship Association at www.the-psa.co.uk. Look at the statistics for open cruising and see how many passengers choose fly-cruises and home port cruises. Find out which destinations are most popular.

Did you know?

The farewell cruise for a P&O ship, *Artemis*, sold out in only 17 minutes in 2009.

1.2 Stakeholders

Cruise operators

There are so many cruise operators that they cannot all be discussed, so you will look at some examples here and you will find more as you work through the unit. There are 32 cruise lines belonging to the Passenger Ship Association and you can find details of these on their website.

Well-established companies

The largest cruise line companies are as follows.

Carnival Cruises

Carnival Corporation began as an independent company in 1972. It is the giant of the sector and carries more than 2 million passengers a year. It has its headquarters in Miami. It comprises many different brands accounting for nearly half of all UK cruise sales. These brands are:

- Carnival Cruise Lines (22 ships)
- Princess Cruises (17 ships)
- Holland America Line (14 ships)
- Costa Cruises (15 ships)
- P&O Cruises (7 ships)
- Cunard Line (3 ships)
- Seabourn Cruise Line (4 ships)
- Ocean Village (2 ships)
- AIDA (7 ships)
- P&O Cruises Australia (2 ships)
- Iberocruceros (4 ships).

Some of these brands became part of Carnival in 2003 when the company merged with P&O Princess. Ten new ships are due to be added between 2010 and 2012.

Royal Caribbean

Royal Caribbean Cruises Limited is a global cruise company that operates Royal Caribbean International and Celebrity Cruises, with a combined total of 20 ships in service. The world's largest cruise ship, the *Oasis of the Seas*, belongs to this group.

NCL/Star

Norwegian Cruise Line (NCL) is owned by the Genting Group of Malaysia who also operate the Star Cruise brand. The two brands form the third largest cruise operator in the world with a combined fleet of 17 ships visiting over 200 destinations.

New companies

Tour operators have made forays into cruising over the last few years, wishing to take advantage of a growing market. The UK's major operators have cruising divisions. Thomson has a fleet of five ships. Its cruises range from the very informal to adult only.

Activity: New companies

Research some of the new cruise companies which have been established in the past five years. You could look at the Disney Cruise Line or Thomson. Why are new companies being established?

Integrated companies

As in the rest of the travel and tourism sector, a few companies dominate the market. The cruise industry is highly competitive, and is becoming more so each year. Carnival has acquired many cruise lines to form a company that now controls 40 per cent of the UK cruise market. This is a good example of **horizontal integration** (as opposed to **vertical integration** as Carnival has reached this dominant position by taking over or merging with different companies but has often retained the original brand names in order to appeal to different market sectors.

There are benefits of integration for cruise operators:

- economies of scale
- control over the supply of berths on ships
- control over distribution
- larger market share
- less competition
- established reputation.

Links with other sectors

Transport

Many cruises are fly-cruises. This means the passengers are flown to the departure port to start the cruise. As the new ships are so large, the cruise operators are able to charter planes to transport their passengers from their home country to the port. The cruise lines have special departments whose role is to organise the flights and liaise with suppliers and passengers.

Cruise lines work with **preferred partners**. Royal Caribbean works with British Airways as a preferred partner.

Key terms

Horizontal integration – two companies at the same level in the chain of distribution merge or one takes over the other. For example in 2009, TUI Travel, parent company of Thomson Cruises, took over Island Cruises.

Vertical integration – companies merge or one takes over the other at different levels in the chain of distribution, for example Thomson has an airline, a tour operation business, a cruise line and retail agents.

Preferred partner – an arrangement between companies where they promote each other's products or services.

The cruise lines also have links with other transporters, for example coach operators, to bring passengers to the ship when they are joining at a home port.

A lucrative source of revenue for cruise lines is the provision of shore excursions. The liner makes advance arrangements with local coach or taxi operators to give tours. A full-day shore excursion can cost about £100 per person. It would usually be much cheaper for passengers to make their own plans but many prefer to have everything done for them. These tours can be booked before departure or in the tour office on board the ship.

Tour operators

Tour operators such as Thomson offer cruises under their own brand name. Many tour operators offer cruises as part of their programme but do not have their own ships like Thomson. This means the cruise company liaises closely with tour operators to sell their cruises. For example, Egyptian Wonders Cruises are sold through many different tour operators including Kuoni.

Retail agents

There are many dedicated websites and travel agents for selling cruises. This is not surprising as it is this industry within travel and tourism that pays the highest commission.

Some established travel agents have their own cruise division, for example, 1st4cruising is operated by Hays Travel, an independent agent. As this is a premium market, some retail agents are cruise specialists. Bolsover Cruise Club is the UK's number one cruise specialist.

Think about it

See if you can find some cruise companies who only operate via the internet. What are the advantages and disadvantages of working this way?

Regulatory bodies

Passenger Shipping Association (PSA)

This body is the main trade association serving the cruise sector. In fact, it represents all passenger shipping interests within the UK. The PSA membership is divided into two sections: cruise and ferry. There are regular meetings to discuss matters of interest to the members.

The main objectives of the PSA are:

- the promotion of travel by sea by the public
- to encourage expansion in the volume of passenger travel, by sea and river
- to work towards the removal or prevention of the imposition of restrictions or taxes on passenger travel by sea
- to advise Member Lines to ensure that passengers travel in a safe, healthy and secure environment.

The PSA is also an important corporate contact for the media, seeking information on both cruising and ferry markets.

In addition, the organisation has the role of educating travel agents about the cruise sector through the Association of Cruise Experts (ACE). The ACE arranges in-class and online training on cruises for its agents, for example its Understanding Cruise courses. It also arranges visits to cruise ships for travel agents.

International Maritime Organization

This organisation is based in the UK. It was established in 1948 but first met in 1959. Its aims are to develop and maintain a comprehensive regulatory framework for shipping and it establishes policy on:

- safety
- environmental concerns
- legal matters
- maritime security
- efficiency of shipping.

Cruise Lines International Association (CLIA)

Cruise Lines International Association merged with the International Council of Cruise Lines (ICCL) in 2006. CLIA is the world's largest cruise association and is dedicated to the promotion and growth of the cruise industry. CLIA is a US-based organisation but it is worth noting as all the large passenger cruise lines are members.

1.3 Employment

When we talk about working in the cruise sector, remember that not all jobs are on board ship. There are many opportunities at corporate headquarters and at terminals. However, it is likely that if you are attracted to this sector then you are thinking about travelling the world as you work!

Think about it

Do you get seasick? It is worth thinking about this because you will not be able to work on a ship if you do.

On-board job opportunities

There are probably more than 150 different jobs available on a ship so we will not attempt to cover them all.

Activity: Jobs on the ocean waves

Spend a few minutes with your group discussing what types of jobs are available on cruise ships. Make a list.

You should have thought about jobs in the following different departments:

- retail
- entertainment
- engineering
- bars and restaurants
- fitness
- shore excursions
- reception
- beauty and hairdressing
- decks
- housekeeping
- tours
- medical
- casino.

There may also be openings for photographers, lecturers and florists.

You need to match your qualifications and jobs to specific skills. As a travel and tourism learner you are therefore likely to be interested in the types of position that such a course could lead to. Of course, if you have a fitness training qualification, have done bar work before or worked in a shop, you have more areas open to you. Our examples will be those most closely related to travel and tourism.

Whatever job you are interested in, you will have to speak English fluently, and many jobs require one or two further languages, so sign up for those language classes now!

Activity: Cruise ship jobs

Below are three examples of cruise ship jobs for which travel and tourism learners could apply. One requires a degree so you will be thinking ahead in this case. For each example note the role and responsibilities and the entry requirements.

Job title: Assistant purser

Department: Reception

Responsibilities:

- gives general information
- deals with accommodation problems
- deals with complaints
- carries out shipboard announcements.

Person specification: Must have customer service experience. Must have excellent administration background. Good social and communication skills needed. Must be fluent English speaker. Second language preferred.

Location: Caribbean

Salary: £1600–1800 per month

Job title: Tour assistant

Department: Tours

Responsibilities:

- gives passengers information about excursions
- takes bookings for shore excursions
- arranges disembarkation
- accompanies tours.

Person specification: Must have customer service experience. Must have travel related or cruise ship experience – one year minimum. Good social and communication skills needed. Must be fluent English speaker. Second language preferred.

Location: Alaska cruises

Salary: US $2300 per month plus percentage of sales revenue.

Job title: Customer Service Director

Department: Administration

Responsibilities:

- achieves service goals through coordinating hospitality activities
- ensures that all guest requests, enquiries and complaints are responded to promptly
- arranges necessary maintenance and repairs.

Person specification:

- good team working skills
- professional appearance and excellent social skills
- degree in Hospitality Management or Tourism Management
- cruise ship experience desirable
- fluent English, additional languages preferred
- computer knowledge: Microsoft Word® and Excel®.

On-shore job opportunities

The opportunities with cruise lines on land are similar to those of any tour operator. Some of the cruise lines are based in the USA and therefore it would be unlikely that British learners would be able to get jobs with them. Some cruise lines though have offices in Europe, for example Royal Caribbean has an office in Surrey.

The jobs you would expect to find on shore would be in:

- marketing
- finance
- human resources
- customer service
- reservations
- embarkation.

Below is an example of a position in telesales.

TELESALES – CRUISE COMPANY **OTE** 16K BASIC TO 25K

Responsibilities:

- to make outbound and receive inbound sales calls to sell cruises
- to maximise revenue by offering alternative dates, routes, classes, upgrades and other services to customers
- to participate in promotional campaigns.

The applicant must have at least 18 months' sales experience, preferably within a call centre. Must be a team player and must be able to meet performance targets.

Some homeworkers in travel sales prefer to specialise in selling cruises. They can earn higher commissions than from other sales and it is a growing market so there are many customers to target. Homeworkers are sometimes called 'travel counsellors' and may be affiliated to a large network. You cannot set up as a homeworker without a lot of experience in a travel agency.

Some landside job opportunities are available in port. The jobs available in a port are similar to those in an airport. Customers have to be checked in, their baggage has to be transferred to the ship and in addition staff are needed to run all the facilities at the terminal, such as restaurants and shops. These jobs do not require many qualifications or experience unless you are applying for supervisory or management level positions. As many of the jobs are customer facing, experience of customer service is useful.

Working environment

Shift work

On a ship, you will work long hours – it is not a 9-to-5 type of job. You might have to work seven days a week as well. You won't really be off-duty because when you are not working you are still on the ship and you have to be pleasant to the passengers. You cannot escape from the work environment or your colleagues and that can be a cause of stress.

On-board accommodation

As a worker you will not get the 'royal suite' kind of accommodation! You will get the most basic cabin on the lowest deck and you will have to share. However, as ships become more and more luxurious it is true to say that the staff accommodation also improves. Also, the more senior your position the better your accommodation will be.

It will be your responsibility to make sure that your passport, visas and vaccinations are up to date, although you will be told what is required.

Terms and conditions

Holidays and pay

In terms of travel, working on a cruise ship is a bit like a holiday in that you will have the chance to see the world. There are opportunities to visit **ports of call** and the ship will revisit the same places regularly so you will get to know them quite well. The pay on cruise ships is low for most jobs. However, there is no journey to work and even if you don't get paid much you will have food and accommodation provided. You will be able to save most of your earnings. Your contract will be for a few months and you will not be paid in the off-contract time. If you leave during the contract you will have to pay your fare home.

Key term

Ports of call – ports that the ship visits and the passengers can take a shore excursion if they wish; they have to get back on before the ship sails again!

Concessions

Sometimes departments are contracted out and that means if you want to apply for a position you have to apply to the contracted company not to the ship. Beauty salon positions are often assigned in this way. Steiner is a salon that has many cruise ship contracts.

Promotional opportunities

There is a career structure whether you work on board or on shore. Cruise companies are major employers and interested in giving responsibility to well-performing staff, like any other company.

Employers

Employers are the different types of cruise operator. Refer to the first section of this unit (page 8) for examples of cruise companies.

Case study: Matching profiles to jobs

Learner profile 1

Malika has completed a BTEC National Certificate in Travel and Tourism. She is 27 and wants to see the world. Before she returned to college to take her BTEC she worked in a bank for five years, so she has a lot of customer service experience. She also has several bookkeeping and banking qualifications which she achieved at the bank. Malika was born in Morocco, although she does have a British passport now. She speaks fluent French, Arabic and English. While studying for her BTEC qualification she worked at an airport check-in. She is sociable, charming and of smart appearance.

Learner profile 2

Greg has completed a BTEC National Certificate and wants to see the world. He has found all the details of cruise lines and recruitment on websites already as he is very good at using the internet. Greg is a fairly quiet person. He doesn't contribute much in class as he is never sure that he has the right answers. His written work is poorly produced and without depth, although he did do enough to pass the course. The other learners never want to work with him as he has little to contribute to group work. His hobby is trainspotting and he has a part-time job in a café. He went to Majorca on holiday with two friends last year and enjoyed it. There was a residential study trip to Barcelona on his course but he didn't go as he didn't want to take the time off work.

Learner profile 3

Charlotte is 19 and has also completed a BTEC qualification, the National Diploma in Travel and Tourism. She has travelled quite a lot on holidays with her family and twice with friends. She is a very loyal person and conscientious and has a lot of respect from others in her group. She is very well presented and works in a hairdressing salon in her spare time. She wants to work on a cruise ship but doesn't know how easy it will be to get a job at 19. She hasn't worked in travel and tourism apart from work placements as she has had the job in the salon for three years. The manager of the salon wants her to work full-time and complete a qualification in hairdressing.

1   Study the three profiles of travel and tourism learners and say which ones are suitable for employment on a cruise ship.

2   Explain why or why not and say what kind of job they could do.

Assessment activity 11.1

(P1) (P2) (P3) (M1)   •BTEC

You have managed to get a work placement with a specialist cruise agency. This is a very prestigious placement and you are delighted. You are spending four weeks with the company. The first week was an introduction to the work and meeting all the staff. Now, your line manager wants you to take on your own project. The company has taken a stand at a cruise exhibition at ExCeL in London and has asked you to help. You have also been asked to prepare a stand display about the cruise, which should be designed to attract customers to the stand.

Use the information given in the first part of the unit and your own research to produce a wall display which gives an overview of the cruise industry. Make sure that you cover the full range, referring to the content and assessment guidance in the unit specification for the detail required. (P1) (P2) (P3)

You should include:

- Key stages in development focusing on the last 50 years, and the last 10 years in particular with a brief description of each stage. (P1)

- The roles of stakeholders involved in the industry covering cruise operators, regulatory bodies and their links with other industries. (P2)

- Employment opportunities – identify onboard and offshore employment opportunities with different types of cruise lines and then describe one onshore and two onboard employment opportunities available within the cruise industry. (P3)

Support your display with explanatory notes which assess the cruise industry as it is today. Include a brief profile of the main cruise operators, identifying their parent company. Include statistical information about passenger numbers, number of ships and number and nationality of crews. Assess links with other travel and tourism industries, for example, retail agents, transport and tour operators. (M1)

Grading tips

(P2) Try to identify the cruise operators who are independent and those who are part of larger organisations.

(P3) Describe the job role and responsibilities, entry requirements, working environment, terms and conditions and opportunities for promotion. Jobs could be with different operators.

(M1) Use cruise operator websites for your research as well as newspaper articles, other websites and statistics showing the latest trends.

Think about it

Have you thought about what it would be like working for a cruise line? Why not look at www.cruiseplacement.com, which gives brief profiles of cruise lines and what to expect from working for them, and details of current vacancies? You could also look at a couple of other sources of information from major cruise employers, such as www.pocruises.com/careers and www.oceanopportunities.com.

PLTS

By planning and carrying out your research to meet the brief given, you are developing your **independent enquirer** skills.

Functional skills

In selecting and using different texts to obtain the relevant information, you will be practising your **English** reading skills.

2   Understand the cruise market

1.1 Cruise areas

Western and eastern Caribbean

This is the second most popular area for UK cruisers. Almost all of these cruises are fly-cruises. The appeal lies in being able to take a one- or two-week cruise in the hot sun of the Caribbean without having to sail there first. It enables passengers to fit a cruise into their annual holiday period. The Caribbean is a popular cruising area for North American passengers because of its proximity to home. The Caribbean is also suitable for year-round cruising, whereas the Mediterranean has far fewer cruises in winter. This means that there are a lot of ships operating in the Caribbean and therefore a lot of capacity available.

The advantage of going on a cruise to the Caribbean is that the passengers get to see many of the islands, visiting a different one each day. The disadvantage is that they don't get to know any of the islands very well and don't have an opportunity to meet local people. There are many islands to visit, all with different characters. French islands are Guadeloupe, Martinique, St Barthelemy and St Martin. There are the Dutch Antilles islands, the US Virgin Islands and the Spanish-speaking islands of Cuba, Dominican Republic, Cayman Islands and Puerto Rico. Former British islands are, among others, Barbados, Jamaica and St Lucia.

Activity: Cruising in the Caribbean

1   Choose a cruise around the Caribbean from a brochure.

2   Using a blank map of the Caribbean plot the route of this itinerary.

3   Choose two of the islands to be visited and describe what there is for cruise passengers to do in a day's visit.

Western and eastern Mediterranean

The Mediterranean is the most popular destination for British travellers, whether sailing from home ports or by fly-cruise. A reason for the increase in trips to the Mediterranean is the greater range of UK departure ports for cruises, especially in the south of England. Using these ports allows passengers to take a western European cruise for a week or two without having to fly. The advantage of a fly-cruise to the Mediterranean is that the flight is very short and passengers reach the sun quickly.

More than 20 cruise companies operate in the Mediterranean. It is split into four seas – the Adriatic, the Aegean, the Ionian and the Tyrrhenian and cruises take varied routes around these. Many cruises take in the Balearic islands, Spanish islands located in the Balearic sea. This is part of the Mediterranean sea located between the eastern coast of Spain, the southern coast of France, and the islands of Corsica and Sardinia. To the Northeast, the Ligurian sea is found, another popular cruise area.

The European Cruise Council reports that the most popular country for cruise ports of call in Europe is Italy. Spanish ports, including the Canary Islands, are the second most popular welcoming 2.8 million cruise passenger visits. Greece is also very popular; ports of call include Piraeus, Corfu, Katakolon, Santorini, Rhodes and Mykonos. This level of activity represents more than a quarter of a million jobs in Europe and over €10 billion direct expenditure.

(Source: www.medcruise.com/page)

Baltic and Scandinavia

The Baltic region of northern Europe has been growing in popularity for a decade. The region includes the countries of Scandinavia, Russia and Estonia. People who choose Baltic cruises are more likely to be interested in seeing the culture of historic cities like St Petersburg and beautiful scenery than beaches. Good weather is not guaranteed, although the summer months can be good and it is possible to see the midnight sun in Norway.

Over 30 cruise lines offer cruises to Scandinavia.

Arctic and Alaska

Cruise ships only visit the Arctic in the summer months as some parts become unnavigable in the winter. UK passengers fly from home to join their ships in

North America, often in Vancouver or Seattle. Visitors experience wonderful scenery at close hand on these voyages. They can see fjords, waterfalls and mountains.

Many trips include the Alaskan cities and towns of Ketchikan and Juneau. Some of the ships pass along 'The Inside Passage'. This is a narrow pass, shaped by the force of massive glaciers, through a chain of islands surrounded by mountains and forests. The islands separate the Inside Passage from the Pacific Ocean.

It is possible to take a route that goes from Vancouver to Anchorage and includes glaciers such as Hubbard Glacier in Yakutat Bay and Columbia Glacier in College Fjord.

Antarctica

A really adventurous cruise crosses the Antarctic Circle, reaching an extreme latitude at the very bottom of the world. The most popular time is January and February, when passengers can take advantage of the long days at this time of year in the area. Passengers go to explore wildlife and can expect to see colonies of penguins, great whales and hundreds of seals. They will also see thousands of floating icebergs, glaciers and dramatic cliff views. On land, passengers may see leopard seals, elephant seals and Antarctic fur seals.

Far East

This cruise area comprises two main regions:

- The Far North Asia – Japan, Taiwan, Korea and China
- South Asia – Vietnam, Cambodia, South-East Asia, Indonesia and Philippines Archipelago.

The area is rising in popularity as seasoned passengers look for new horizons. The regions offer:

- adequate accessibility to most ports
- good infrastructure at the home ports and ports of call for both cruise ships and passengers
- appeal to tourists
- good weather, calm seas and unpolluted waters.

Activity: Charting the ports

Find an example of a Far Eastern cruise and chart all the ports visited. Choose one of the ports of call and find out what the impacts on that port are. Produce your findings as a poster that can be displayed alongside your colleagues' work.

Why might people be interested in a cruise in the UK?

UK

It may surprise you to find out that a cruise around the British Isles is possible. A small ship can start at Tower Pier on the Thames and visit Edinburgh, Oban, Dublin and Waterford amongst others. It also visits Cornwall. It takes 10 days and costs an astonishing £4500.

Think about it

Would a cruise around the British Isles have a positive or negative impact?

Canaries

The Canary Islands belong to Spain although they are situated in the Atlantic. They are a popular cruising destination because of the all year temperate climate within four hours flying time of the UK. However, many cruises to the Canaries start out from Southampton.

Panama

The Panama Canal in Central America is nearly 50 miles long and joins the world's two biggest oceans, the Pacific and the Atlantic. Many Caribbean or Mexican cruises include the Panama stretch in their itinerary. Cruise passengers can travel through some wonderful rainforest on the journey through the canal and usually make a visit to Panama City. The canal is to be expanded as there is a much higher demand for traffic than was anticipated when it was completed in 1914. The aim is to double capacity and allow longer and wider ships through.

Activity: Expanding the Panama Canal

Find out more about the project to expand the Panama Canal and think about what the impact of it will be. The website www.acp.gob.pa/eng/expansion/eisa/index.html will help you.

Nile

Some cruises take place on rivers and this type of cruising is also growing in popularity.

Holidays on the Nile are primarily intended for those who want to sightsee. Sights visited include the temples of Karnak and Luxor, and the magnificent Valley of the Kings. At certain times of the year, particularly in the winter months, there can be low water levels on the Nile and the itinerary then has to change.

Black Sea

A typical cruise around the almost landlocked Black Sea might start at Istanbul and then call at ports in Turkey such as Trabzon. Sochi in Russia might be followed by Sevastopol and Odessa in Ukraine and then on to the Bulgarian port of Nesebur.

Figure 11.2: Map of the Black Sea region

2.2 Types of cruise

There are many different types of cruise available, which you will now look at.

Fly-cruise

All the major cruise lines offer fly-cruises. The prices quoted for fly-cruises include the flight with all the arrangements being made for the passenger. Flights may be charter, where the ship is large enough to warrant charters arriving from various departure airports, or they may be scheduled. The more expensive cruises often use scheduled flights because of the extra flexibility and the perception of luxury. Also included in the prices are the accommodation in cabins, all meals and usually room service, activities and entertainment on board. Fly-cruises appeal because:

- passengers can be speedily delivered to the destination region
- baggage can be checked at the departure airport and taken straight to the cabin
- regional departures are possible
- there is a wide range of destinations and itineraries to choose from
- cruises can be from a few days to a few weeks.

Fly-cruises take the biggest market share for UK travellers. However, the number of customers choosing a UK embarkation is growing and has reached 6 out of 10 departures according to the Cruise Report 2010.

The nature of fly-cruises varies according to cost and the cruise line chosen. Some have extremely good service and are very luxurious, such as Cunard cruises. Others are less formal and appeal to package holidaymakers, for example Thomson Cruises or Carnival. The type of ship and onboard facilities vary according to cost.

Round the world cruises

World cruises appeal to a lot of people but they cannot all afford the time or the money to do them! Prices start at around £10,000 per person and can be two or three times that, depending on the choice of accommodation. Also it obviously takes some time to sail around the world so work commitments might get in the way. The customer profile tends to be older retired people – with plenty of money. Have a look at the Discover Cruises website at www.discovercruises.co.uk if you would like to know more – or to plan your own world cruise.

Many facilities are provided as passengers taking the full world tour could be on board for three months.

An example of a world cruise offered by P&O is on the *Oriana*. It takes 84 days and visits 28 ports in 19 countries. The cheapest price available is just under £7000.

Mini-cruise

Mini-cruises have been developed as a means of bringing more business to passenger ferries. The mini-cruise ships have improved in the last few years and offer a good range of facilities to passengers, including cabins, restaurants, shops and cinemas. The cruise may be for one or two nights and is sometimes combined with a city stay in the middle. They depart from many UK ports including Hull, Harwich and Newcastle. Cruises to Amsterdam from Newcastle are very popular with learners, especially as the cost can be low.

The following mini-break is a cruise from Newcastle to Bergen. Note that very little time is spent in port.

River cruise

Many destinations are popular for river cruising but the Nile is probably the best known. Table 11.1 shows the relative popularity of river cruise areas.

River cruising and ocean cruising are quite different experiences. On a river, passengers are close to shore and can see sights very clearly. Often shore excursions are included in the price. This is important because passengers are unlikely to want to spend all their time on the ship, since the facilities are not as varied as on an ocean-going liner due to restrictions on space. A river vessel may carry 100 or 200 passengers rather than thousands.

Newcastle to Bergen

A mini-cruise to Bergen, the 'Gateway of the Fjords' in Norway offers an opportunity to view the country's beautiful west coast.

Take an evening sailing so that you can make the most of all the facilities on board ship. Have a romantic meal in one of the restaurants followed by dancing in a club or visit the onboard casino. There is even a cinema where you can watch the latest films.

You will have about 11 hours in port, with time to go sightseeing in the city.

Activity: Mini-cruise poster

Find an example of a mini-cruise and think about whom it appeals to and why. Present your findings as a poster for display in your classroom.

Table 11.1: River cruise holidays 1999–2008

Passengers from the UK (000s) Destination	1999	2000	2001	2002	2003	2004	2005	2006	2007	2008
Rhine/Moselle/tributaries	28.4	31.6	30.5	30.1	26.1	25.6	27.9	27.5	28.7	14.7
Danube	11.0	11.7	12.4	12.3	10.1	11.1	12.7	13.1	16.0	13.1
Russian	8.1	8.0	7.5	6.1	6.0	6.6	5.7	3.4	5.8	4.9
French (Rhone/Seine)	8.3	7.9	8.7	7.9	8.8	9.1	7.4	6.3	7.2	7.6
Italian (Po)	3.2	3.6	3.3	1.7	1.4	1.3	1.0	1.1	0	1.7
Elbe	1.1	2.1	2.2	1.1	3.2	5.4	4.7	2.5	3.8	2.8
Other European	4.2	7.8	9.5	12.5	5.5	13.9	15.3	15.3	12.4	9.1
Total European	64.4	72.6	74.0	71.6	61.3	73.0	74.7	69.2	73.9	54.0
Nile	31.4	41.0	34.5	25.5	15.8	22.7	31.8	30.1	29.0	39.4
Far East/China	1.3	3.0	7.3	18.2	11.0	13.1	6.4	8.1	8.2	6.7
Other non-European	1.3	1.2	0.8	1.3	2.0	2.2	5.7	3.5	7.0	7.0
Total non-European	34.0	45.2	42.6	45.0	28.9	38.0	43.9	41.7	44.2	53.1
Total	98.4	117.8	116.6	116.5	90.1	111.0	118.6	111.0	118.4	107.1

(Source: Annual Cruise Review 2008/IRN research for the PSA(ACE))

Activity: Fly-cruise or river cruise?

Using brochures or the internet, find details of a fly-cruise and a river cruise. For the fly-cruise, choose one of the less formal cruises such as Carnival or Thomson. Describe and compare the appeal of both types of cruise in terms of:

- Itinerary and routes offered – embarkation point, cruise area and ports of call, excursions and sights, duration, days at sea, climate and any special events or themes on board.

- Type of ship – large/small, passenger crew ratio, passenger space ratio, name of operator.

- Range of onboard facilities – accommodation, food, entertainment, other facilities.

- Social aspects – for example etiquette, formality, tipping, dress code, payment methods.

- Nationality of passengers.

Who do you think would go on a fly-cruise and on a river cruise. What clues are there in the extract from the brochures or websites?

Share your findings with your group.

Luxury cruise

Ultra-luxury cruise lines are defined as ships with fewer than 1000 passengers, a passenger to crew ratio of no more than two to one and a space to passenger ratio of more than 40 square metres. One example of a luxury cruise is Silversea (you can find out more at www.silversea.com).

Special interest cruises

Sometimes cruises cater for a particular interest group or theme. This might relate to activities provided on board ship, for example cookery lessons or jazz music. When the whole cruise is billed as special interest, then passengers can expect experts to be on board to help them develop their interest. Providing these types of cruises helps cruise operators target particular groups of people who might be new to cruising and tempted by the possibility of pursuing a hobby whilst on holiday. You can find out about some particular special interest cruises at http://www.cruiseinstyle.co.uk/special-interest-cruises.phtml.

Sometimes special interest cruises cater for a younger clientele who are looking for more activity on their cruise and a little bit of adventure. Some Alaskan cruises offer excursions such as dog sledging, whale-watching and rock-climbing.

Celebrity Cruises offer a trip to the Galapagos Islands with lots of exploration for adventurous types, including going ashore in inflatable landing crafts.

Transatlantic cruises

A transatlantic crossing is a legendary travel experience. It copies the journeys of early cruisers like those on the great liners including the *Titanic* mentioned at the beginning of this unit. It is still a fantastic way of travelling to America. The *Queen Mary 2* in the Cunard fleet is one of the more famous ships making this crossing.

Did you know?

The *Queen Mary 2* allows pets on her transatlantic runs; she has a kennel on board with a full-time keeper. Travelling dogs and cats receive a complimentary gift pack and other animal amenities.

Sailships

An exciting way to cruise the Caribbean is to take a tall sailship cruise. This very informal type of cruising on a 'Windjammer' ship is described below.

Lazy days at sea – I spend hours reading the latest bestsellers and watching the sails in the breeze. Luckily no seasickness for me, though some of my friends are not so lucky. It's great to get away from city life – we don't have to dress up; in fact I only packed shorts, sandals and swimsuits. Some days I haven't even bothered to put shoes on. I'm slapping moisturiser on every five minutes but haven't used make-up.

The food on board is simple but tasty and we all sit round one huge table sipping rum punch along with our meal. You can have wine if you want it – but it costs extra. Soft drinks flow freely for the kids and iced water is always available.

When we reach the shore life is equally laid back. We transfer to a launch boat and go to the beach. There we can swim, sunbathe or snorkel to our heart's content.

An alternative to 'lazy days' is to sail the ship yourself. Such holidays are very adventurous and are offered on tall ships. A small crew sails the ship under the expertise of a permanent skipper and mate. The holiday is hard work but fun. Accommodation is hardly luxurious but very informal.

All-inclusive cruises

On all-inclusive cruises everything apart from excursions and tips is included: accommodation, food and drink, and entertainment. The term is used throughout the holiday industry but is particularly applicable in the cruise sector.

Formal and informal

The level of formality on a cruise depends on the ship and the clientele targeted. By formal cruise, we usually mean that customers wish to dress up every day for dinner and have a meal in a dining room with a high level of waiter service and attention to every need. Offshore activities will be visits to attractions and museums rather than more sporty or adventurous trips. At the other end of the scale, casual cruises mean no need to dress up, eating in a more relaxed environment and usually more choice of different styles of restaurant.

2.3 Ships
Size, tonnage and types of vessels

The largest ships are 70,000 tonnes and more. As we saw earlier, there is a trend towards larger ships as they can offer more amenities and different types of restaurant. They are also able to offer many theatres and bars with varying entertainment. A high passenger:space ratio means more space per passenger. Many of the new ships arriving up to 2012 were ordered before the recession and are just arriving now due to the time taken to build them.

Smaller ships may hold a few hundred passengers rather than thousands. Lounges are more intimate and the entertainment is likely to be less spectacular. However, because smaller ships have the advantage of reaching ports that large ships cannot enter, they may have more exciting itineraries. An example of a company offering small ships, more like yachts, is SeaDream, whose ships only hold about 100 passengers – and almost as many crew.

Another type of ship is a sailship which offers a completely different type of cruise. Windstar offers luxury cruises on sailships with between 100 and 400 passengers. Star Clippers offer informal cruises on sailships. Those who wish can even lend a hand sailing the ship.

Owners and operators

The largest ships are owned by the major companies that you have already met (page 8). Sailships and river cruises are sometimes owned by independent companies, such as Star Clippers.

Crew

A ship is a multi-national environment. Pay is generally poor and attracts people who cannot always find work in their native land. Carnival say that they have 50 different nationalities of crew on their ships.

What roles might crew on a cruise ship undertake?

2.4 Design features
Recent developments in ship design

As already mentioned a major trend is an increase in vessel size with ships able to carry more than 3000 passengers. Remember that there is a high ratio of crew to staff so a typical ship is almost a small town with more than 5000 people on board. The Royal Caribbean's *Oasis of the Seas* holds 5400 passengers and nearly half as many crew. This ship has more than 20 restaurants and has its own open air park and amphitheatre.

Newer cruise ships are more likely to be designed with an environmental agenda. This means they are more energy efficient with key cards being used to switch off electricity when cabins are vacated and sensors used to control lighting. Measures can be taken to reduce water consumption. For example, increasing the size of swimming pool surge tanks reduces water consumption.

Deck plans

Most decks on a ship are for accommodation. The top decks are used for entertainment, dining, sports and daily activities. All cruise brochures have pictures and deck plans included. Take a look at some and compare them.

Accommodation range

Choose some cruise brochures to study the range of accommodation available. You will find that the range is from inner cabins with little space and no view to suites with balconies where passengers can sit and admire the ocean. On some less luxurious ships, the smaller cabins have berths which may be positioned one on top of the other. The larger cabins have double or king-size beds. It is no surprise that the more luxurious the cabin the more expensive it is. Some newer ships only provide cabins with balconies, such is the demand. Of course, the crew do not get similar cabins.

Public areas

Entertainment

When cruising, part of the holiday experience is the entertainment. Cinema and theatre are on offer with some of the crew being employed as part of the entertainment team. This team will consist of singers and dancers who put on a number of different shows. In addition, celebrity entertainers may be brought on to a ship for a short time to perform. Celebrity chefs are often invited to do cookery demonstrations on themed cruises.

Restaurants

Traditionally on cruise ships two sittings were provided for dining, one early evening and one later. Guests would choose their sitting and dress formally for dinner. They would expect to be seated at the captain's table at some point during their cruise. Most ships are much less formal now and offer a range of dining options. Passengers may choose an Italian or Asian restaurant one night and a classic option another. They will also have self-service and snack restaurants available. For families flexible times are usually on offer so that children can eat earlier. Yachts of Seabourn ships even have barbecues on deck.

Bars

A range of bars is available on ships; some may be very informal and may offer entertainment. On the *Oasis of the Seas* there is a bar that moves. Called 'The Rising Tide' it rises very slowly up and down three decks.

Sports facilities

The large ships offer a full range of sports from line dancing, gym and keep fit classes to water sports and a rock-climbing wall. Smaller ships are unable to offer such a wide range but passengers will always expect a gym and free deck space where they can walk up and down.

Children's areas

Some cruise lines actively pursue the family market and provide facilities for children. These include recreation areas as you would find in any large hotel. Teenagers are often catered for too. Holland America have teenager spaces on board where no adults are allowed.

Spas

Spas have become very popular in the UK as a means of relaxation. Many spa hotels exist and the trend has been picked up by cruise lines who often provide them on ships. Princess Cruises, for example, have introduced spas on their ships. Holland America has spa staterooms, which are balcony cabins near the spa. They have Burmese mats and slippers and a concierge is available to make priority bookings for spa treatments.

Shops

Retail space is important on ships as it provides an extra source of revenue from a captive market. Passengers may need toiletries and books but they are also able to buy jewellery and clothes.

2.5 Products developed to expand the market

Freestyle cruising

We have mentioned the informal cruises that are now popular. These are sometimes referred to as 'freestyle' cruises where customers have lots of facilities and excursions to choose from so that once on board they can determine the kind of holiday that suits them. NCL is an operator that promotes this type of cruising. They claim that there are no restrictions, for example, customers choose when and where they want to eat and from a range of accommodation to suit their needs.

Fun ships

Disney cruises are growing in popularity in the UK. According to the PSA Annual Cruise Review in 2010 less than 5 per cent of Disney Line Cruise customers were from the UK, but Disney has plans to base the ship *Disney Magic* in Dover and operate Mediterranean and Baltic cruises from there.

Children's clubs

These are very common so that parents can have some time to themselves. Ocean Village (which was a P&O brand) provided a 'Girls Night In' in their spa

for teenage girls. Also available was a 'How to be a TV presenter' course. The Ocean Village brand was discontinued in 2010 but these ideas will no doubt be introduced on other P&O branded ships.

Activity: Family friendly cruising

Choose and research an informal sailing ship cruise and a more formal all-inclusive cruise from different operators.

1 Make a comparison of the two cruises' suitability for a family with two children aged 7 and 12 who are looking for a two-week sunny holiday with plenty of relaxation for the parents and activities for the children.

2 Analyse the appeal of the cruises in terms of itinerary, type of ship, onboard facilities and social aspects.

Assessment activity 11.2

P4 **P5** **P6** **BTEC**

Remember that you are on work placement with a specialist cruise agency. Following the success of your display at the cruise exhibition, you have been asked to produce a further display of informative leaflets for your retail agency. Make sure that you cover the full range, referring to the content and assessment guidance in the unit specification for detail required.

1 Identify major cruise areas available to UK customers. **P4**

2 Choose three different types of cruises and describe them. Describe the types of ships and their design features and link these to the types of cruises on offer. **P5**

3 Explain how cruise lines have developed products for a growing market. You need to identify a range of products, select a minimum of two and explain how and why the products have been developed. **P6**

Grading tips

P4 You could use a large world map or a variety of smaller maps

P5 Think about a type of cruise, for example, a river cruise on the Nile, and then think about the different types of ships, facilities, etc. that this type of cruise offers and how they differ.

P6 An example of a product could be a particular special interest cruise which has been developed to attract new customers to cruising.

PLTS

Planning and carrying out your research to meet the brief given will help you develop your skills as an **independent enquirer**.

Functional skills

Selecting and using different texts to obtain relevant information will help to develop **English** skills in reading.

3   Select cruises that appeal to cruise customers and meet specific needs

You need to be able to select the most suitable type of cruise for specific customers, recognising their needs and how particular cruises might appeal to them and meet their needs.

3.1 Types of customer

There are cruises to suit all ages, tastes and budgets. Some cruise lines aim their product squarely at a traditional market while others aim at younger and more adventurous customers.

While customers can always be categorised as families, couples, groups or individuals, it is more helpful to think about their needs in relation to age, lifestyle, income and special interest.

Age

The common perception of cruise customers is that they are old. In fact, as we saw earlier, the average age is now 53, but the age profile is continuing to change and more young people and families are taking cruises. Some companies, such as Royal Caribbean, target families with lots of facilities for them.

Saga cruises are exclusively for the over-50s. There are two ships to choose from, the *Saga Pearl II* and the *Saga Ruby*. It is possible to go on a round the world trip on one of these ships but there are also Baltic, Mediterranean and Caribbean cruises.

Lifestyle

Cruising has changed a lot and, on many ships, is much less formal than it used to be. This means that the dress code is more relaxed and restaurants are open almost 24 hours a day.

Some ships boast about not allowing children at all, catering for an adults-only lifestyle. An example is the *Arcadia* in the P&O fleet.

Cruise companies analyse their bookings so they know who their customers are. For example, Royal Caribbean appeals to couples and singles in their 30s to 50s as well as families. The average age is the low 40s. Royal

Caribbean say that their guests have 'an appetite for new experiences and an interest in activities that take them out of the ordinary, connect them with other people and enable them to explore new places and learn about other cultures'. From their bookings they can tell that more than a quarter are repeats. Most of them are North American customers.

What needs might different customers have?

Income

There are several budget cruises available. Thomson, for example, aims its cruises at its traditional package holiday customers. This means that people who previously thought cruising was too expensive for them are able to try it.

For those who want to take a budget cruise with fewer facilities there is the option of travelling on a working vessel such as the *St Helena*. This Royal Mail Ship provides a year-round service to the tropical South Atlantic island of St Helena. The ship holds only 128 passengers and the route takes in the South African coastline.

At the other end of the scale the cruise ship company Windstar provides luxurious cruises where the aim is to give cruisers the impression that they are on their own private yacht.

Special interest

Special interests can also be catered for by themed cruises. If you are a *Strictly Come Dancing* fan you can take a cruise with Island Cruises where celebrities from the show will dance with passengers. Cruise lines offer themed cruises on topics such as cookery, wine, photography, gardens, music and antiques. They hope to attract people who want to pursue their favourite hobbies on their holiday.

Whatever the type of customer, their choice of cruise will be affected by different appeal factors.

> **Think about it**
>
> What do you think influences a customer to take one cruise rather than another?

3.2 Appeal in relation to itinerary

The customer will consider whether embarkation is in the UK or whether they have to fly and then cruise. Fly-cruise saves time in getting to the cruise area but many people prefer to avoid the stress of airports and limitations on baggage, and board their ship in the UK. The itinerary is obviously important and passengers will have considered which destinations they would like to visit, how many ports of call are included on the cruise, what excursions and sights are included on the cruise, how many days are spent at sea or whether the cruise has a special theme. Some cruises pack as many ports as possible into the itinerary, others are more leisurely.

Passengers often consider climate when taking a cruise. Itineraries are planned with this in mind.

For example, P&O position many of their ships in the Caribbean during our winter months and then reposition them to the Mediterranean for the summer. This caters for passengers who are looking for sunny weather on their cruise. The popularity of Arctic cruises is enhanced in the summer when passengers can see the midnight sun along the Norwegian coast. Some areas like Antarctica are always cold but people still choose to go to see the spectacular scenery and will be advised to bring appropriate clothing.

3.3 Appeal in relation to the type of ship and operator

Customers must consider whether they want to travel on one of the huge new liners or have a more intimate cruising experience.

They can choose anything from the Royal Caribbean's *Oasis of the Seas* – the world's biggest cruise ship – to P&O's *Adonia*, one of the smallest ships available, holding just over 700 passengers.

Passenger crew ratios (PCR) and **passenger space ratios (PSR)** indicate to customers what type of experience to expect. These ratios will be given in cruise brochures.

> **Key terms**
>
> **Passenger crew ratio (PCR)** – gives the number of crew in relation to passengers; the higher the crew number in relation to passengers, the more likely the customer is to get superior service.
>
> **Passenger space ratio (PSR)** – compares the total public space to the passenger capacity; the more space there is in relation to the number of customers, the more spacious the ship is likely to feel.

The cruise operator may also be an important choice as different operators offer different types of cruise. For further information see page 17–20.

3.4 Appeal in relation to onboard facilities

The customer will consider the type of accommodation on offer in relation to the cost. As we have seen accommodation can vary from quite cramped berths with no view (although this is less common today), to luxurious cabins with balconies and a sea view. Facilities on board larger ships are more extensive with theatres, several restaurants, a wide range of entertainment, children's clubs and sports and leisure facilities (see page 21).

3.5 Appeal in relation to social aspects

The social aspects customers will consider include etiquette in terms of formality on the cruise, tipping and dress code. Cruises are mostly all-inclusive in terms of board, although easyCruise offers a model where meal plans can be bought as extras. Many cruise ships have specific restaurants included in the cruise price but others available at a supplement for those prepared to spend a bit more.

All meals are included on a cruise but not usually drinks. However, some cruise lines offer an amount of money towards drinks as an incentive to buy a cruise. This is not given in cash but held as credit behind the bar. The passenger can ask for drinks without paying until the credit is used up. Customers want to know what the policy on tipping is and what extras there are to pay for on board. Tipping is important for low-paid cruise ship employees and is usually expected, with an amount suggested to passengers. UK cruise passengers are not as keen on tipping as American cruise passengers and so some cruise ships which cater for British travellers include tips in the price of the cruise.

All purchases on a ship can be charged to a cabin and the bill paid at the end of the holiday, just the same as in a hotel. Traditionally, cruises were very formal and some ships still reflect that old-fashioned ambience with dining at set times, and dressing for dinner in evening dress and dinner suits. Younger people and families tend to prefer a less formal environment and a more relaxed atmosphere. Some cruise lines offer this with relaxed dining, less formal dress and plenty of fun activities to appeal to these markets.

Taking a cruise provides an opportunity to meet fellow passengers and these are most likely to be American or British as these nations provide the most cruise passengers. The nationality on board the ship will depend on which countries the cruise line company chooses to target for its marketing. For example, if someone chooses a P&O cruise they will find mostly British passengers as this is a UK brand. To grow their markets cruise lines are targeting customers from outside the traditional North American market. Princess report that a third of their passengers come from outside North America, and about a quarter of these are British.

3.6 Needs

When selecting a cruise it is important to consider the different needs of the customer in relation to itinerary, the ship, onboard facilities, and the social aspects of cruising. The different appeal that these can offer is outlined on the previous pages.

Assessment activity 11.3 P7 P8 D1 M2 •BTEC

You are still on your work placement at the cruise agency. You are thought to be sufficiently competent to deal with some real customers.

1 Study the customer profiles given below and then find a suitable cruise for two of the profiles using brochure information.

Provide written details of each cruise selected and identify the elements that meet the needs of the customer within the customer brief. **P7**

Profiles

- Graham Cutter is 75 years old and he is an experienced cruiser. He has been on 16 cruises. He always travels with his friend, Gordon. All the cruises they have been on have been luxury cruises and now they would like a world cruise – money is no object.

- Sanjit is a first-time cruiser and is choosing a cruise for his honeymoon. He wants to try scuba diving so he thinks the Caribbean is a good idea. He wants a romantic cruise and he doesn't want to be on a ship with hundreds or even thousands of people. He thinks a sailship might be a good plan. He wants a personal ambience.

- James and Jessie Stavros want a family cruise with their four-year-old son. They have never been on a cruise before. They don't want a long flight with a child. They hope that there will be other children so that their child will make friends and that there will be children's clubs and activities.

- A group of friends in their early 30s who have never cruised before don't want to spend more than £1000 each on a 7–10-night cruise. They can go anytime in the summer. They want to visit a lot of different places and they want plenty of activities on board. They are not interested in 'dressing up'.

2 Explain how the cruises you have selected meet the specific needs of these customers. **P8**

Your boss asks you to help write a newsletter that is going out to customers.

3. Research and write an article which:

- analyses the range of cruises and ships operating in **one** popular cruise area. Make sure you describe the cruises and the ships and how they appeal to different types of customer. **M2**

- evaluates how operator, product and ship developments have increased the appeal and growth of cruising over the last ten years and increased cruise operator employment. Include evaluations of how the following aspects have increased the appeal of cruising:

  - how operators have developed either through merger and takeover **or** by remaining independent

  - how products have been developed to meet specific trends and demands

  - how ships have been developed to accommodate trends and demands

  - how cruise employment has increased

Provide examples and statistics to support your explanation. **M2 D1**

Make sure that you cover the full range, referring to the content and assessment in the unit specification for the detail required.

Grading tips

P7 Identify the elements that meet the specific customer needs.

P8 Support your evidence with details of the cruise from brochures or a website.

M2 Make sure you cover all aspects of appeal as listed on pages 24–25.

D1 Make sure you show that you have an in-depth understanding of how the cruise industry has developed, how cruising appeals to a range of customer types and how this has led to a growth in employment opportunities.

PLTS

By connecting your own and others' ideas and experiences in inventive ways when you find suitable cruises for your customers, you will be developing your **creative thinker** skills.

Functional skills

By reading and summarising information from different sources, you will be practising your **English** reading skills.

4   Understand the effects of an expanding cruise industry

4.1 Potential future developments and impacts on cruise areas

Cruising impacts on the economy, the environment and society, like any form of tourism. As a ship is moving, not fixed, it and its passengers have impacts at every point of the itinerary from the home port to ports of call and on the sea. There is a particular impact on **gateway ports** as these have most traffic as they are heavily used for trade to access countries and by passengers arriving by ship to then visit a destination by other means. Any future developments will add to the impact on ports and destinations. Cruising now competes with the traditional package holiday as it has now become mainstream and appeals to those people who previously only considered land-based packages. The prices are comparable and cruising is considered good value for money.

> ### Key term
>
> **Gateway ports** – ports that provide a major link to other countries or access to destinations within a country for trade or passengers.

Both impacts and likely developments in the future will be looked at. You will examine the impacts in general terms and then look at how they apply to specific cruise areas.

Economic impact

The positive economic benefits of cruise activity and development are as follows:

- jobs in servicing the port and the ship
- jobs in construction – particularly in ship-building and in ports and shopping areas
- increased spending by visitors, boosting the economy
- increased prosperity for residents.

According to the the Annual Cruise Review (2009) in 2008, a record number of cruise ships – over 100 – called at UK ports. This meant 396,000 passengers visited, all with money to spend. More people are starting their cruises in the UK and these are not only UK residents but also passengers from overseas who join their cruise in the UK and spend money in the port before they board. People's desire to start their cruise here has led to UK port development with larger passenger ports needed with a range of facilities.

However, new development inevitably takes up land or sea and may result in the loss of historic landscapes. For example, all nature groups in and around Southampton are protesting about the potential port development at Dibden Bay which impinges on the New Forest National Park. This is a container port, not a passenger port, but would free up space for a fifth passenger terminal which would provide 3000 jobs. It would, however, destroy salt meadows and the habitat of rare birds and plants. Residents would experience an increase in heavy traffic to the port. The regional authorities argue that developing sea trade is vital to the region's economy.

According to VisitBritain – Foresight 2010 March, in 2008 the European cruise line industry had a direct economic impact of €14.2bn, underpinning more than 300,000 jobs across the continent. The UK is estimated to represent one-eighth of the direct value, or €2.3bn and 49,000 jobs.

The main economic benefits of cruising are achieved by ports. Building, decking out and furnishing the liners is a business in itself. Cruise ships generate local employment in the ports where they berth and their passengers and crews are potential spenders.

In addition, ships pay charges to visit ports which again benefits the local economy. However, not all port revenue comes from cruise ships – in fact about 90 per cent comes from cargo ships.

Environmental impact

The following extract from responsibletravel.com summarises the adverse environmental impacts of cruise ships.

According to Climate Care, a cruise liner such as *Queen Mary 2* emits 0.43 kg of CO_2 per passenger mile, compared with 0.257 kg for a long-haul flight (even allowing for the further damage of emissions being produced in the upper atmosphere). That means it is far greener to fly than cruise.

According to a report by The International Council on Clean Transportation (ICCT), worldwide, oceangoing vessels produced at least 17% of total emissions of nitrogen oxide and contributed more than a quarter of total emissions of nitrogen oxide in port cities and coastal areas. The report also points out that carbon-dioxide emissions from the international shipping sector as a whole exceed annual total greenhouse gas emissions from most of the developed nations listed in the Kyoto Protocol.

'International ships are one of the world's largest, virtually uncontrolled sources of air pollution … air pollution from international ships is rising virtually unchecked,' said ICCT president Alan Lloyd.

On a typical one-week voyage a cruise ship generates more than 50 tonnes of garbage and a million tonnes of grey (waste) water, 210,000 gallons of sewage and 35,000 gallons of oil-contaminated water. On average, passengers on a cruise ship each account for 3.5 kilograms of rubbish daily – compared with the 0.8 kilograms each generated by local people on shore.

(Source: www.responsibletravel.com)

Growing awareness of these issues has led to cruise companies being subject to basic environmental standards imposed by the International Maritime Organization. Also the International Convention for the Prevention of Pollution from Ships gives guidelines on how to dispose of rubbish, waste water and sewage.

Developments in environmental issues

Some ships are trying to reduce the waste produced by cutting down the use of disposable items. Recycling is one possibility, as is the use of advanced water purification systems. Royal Caribbean has installed systems on board all its ships at a cost of more than £50 million. The company also uses smokeless gas-turbine engines and burns bio-diesel when it is available.

US passengers who are concerned about the impact of their cruise on the environment can use Friends of the Earth's assessment of the environmental and human health footprint of cruise lines and ships operating in the United States. Entitled the *Cruise Ship Environmental Report Card*, Friends of the Earth ranked ten major lines according to three factors: treatment of sewage, air pollution reduction and water quality compliance.

Fuel efficient ships

New ships are designed to be more fuel efficient. Examples include the *Azura* from P&O Cruises and the *Queen Elizabeth* from Cunard Line.

Activity: Greener cruising

Find out more about the Friends of the Earth report system at www.foe.org/cruisereportcard.

How do you think such a system could be implemented in the UK? Discuss with your group.

Social/cultural impact

Where new facilities, such as shops and restaurants, are provided, they can bring a social benefit to local people – if they can afford to use them. However, many cruise shopping centres are closed to local residents and are built purely for the use of cruise passengers. With some types of tourism, local residents benefit from interaction with different cultures and from the provision of goods and services. Although we have noted that cruise passengers do increase spending in the ports of call, this type of tourism has severe drawbacks for locals: passengers get all their meals on board so they do not need to eat in port; they do not stay in hotels so they spend less than those tourists who stay for one or two weeks; they are unlikely to interact with local people on a fleeting day visit.

Think about it

What could passengers do to try to bring positive social impacts to a destination port?

Here are some examples of specific impacts on cruise areas and ports.

An important environmental problem in the Caribbean is that affecting coral reefs. Coral reefs are an essential part of marine ecosystems. They are home to many marine fish species and thousands of other species, are a source of income for fishermen, and a source for pharmaceutical compounds. They are also an attraction to cruise passengers. Cruise ships have to take responsibility for protecting the reefs and they can do this by careful anchoring so that they do not damage the reef, and by not discharging waste water near the reef. Cruise ships have been banned from anchoring at George Town in the Cayman Islands because of the damage caused to coral reefs and marine life.

What problems can cruises in the Mediterranean cause?

How is the Caribbean impacted by tourists?

The majority of ports in the Caribbean are ports of call. Many of them are isolated and have little infrastructure and few facilities. When ships call at ports without terminal facilities, they anchor out to sea and take passengers in by tender (a small boat). Local people are aware of cruise ship arrival times and will flock to the port to sell local produce or offer taxi services to the passengers. This brings economic benefit to the community.

Concerns about the environmental impacts of long-haul flying have contributed to growth in cruising in the Mediterranean, and yet ports are congested with ships, car parks with buses, and sights with tourists causing anxiety about their effect on historic sites.

Some ports have taken active measures to be environmentally friendly. An example is Oslo where policy includes reducing air pollution from berthed ships and shore-based activities, maximising efforts to limit noise, and reducing discharge into the water from ships and port activities. You can find out more at www.oslocruisenetwork.no.

Another problem for the area is that small communities of only a few hundred may be visited by more than one ship at time and be completely overwhelmed.

In the Arctic the shores are very delicate and vulnerable and subject to environmental danger.

The economic impact of cruising is estimated to be that over $1.07 billion is spent in Alaska – 66 per cent is retained in the state.

In 2006 a 'head tax' was imposed on cruise passengers taking cruises to Alaska. This increased the cost of cruising and reduced the numbers of visitors by about 140,000 according to the Alaska Cruise Association. The Alaskan governor proposed a reduction of $12 in 2010, which would reduce the head tax to $34.50

Antarctic cruises have to operate under high environmental safety standards to ensure the protection of the wildlife. The International Association of Antarctic Tour Operators sets guidelines on protection. There is a limit on the size of ships that can cruise Antarctic waters and also on how many people can be landed at sites around Antarctica. Cruise operators should abide by the Association's guidelines and can do this by issuing pre-departure information that includes a 'Guidelines for Low Impact Travel' booklet. Ships can offer an educational programme that informs passengers about environmental issues affecting Antarctica, such as how to approach wildlife and how to minimise their personal impact on fragile landscapes.

The river Nile is very busy with cruise ships – some might find it overcrowded – and when boats are moored for the night all the passengers can see is the next boat.

Activity: Responsible tourism on the Nile

You are a tour operator setting up in business with two ships which cruise the Nile. Produce a responsible tourism policy addressing the issues of economic, environmental and social impacts on the area.

A problem in the Black Sea is that of pollution. Surrounding countries have formed a commission to implement environmental safeguards. Overfishing is also a significant problem and has altered the sea's ecosystem.

Activity: Future development

Choose a cruise line and find out what its plans are for future development. A good place to start is the PSA Annual Cruise Review.

Consider
- how cruises are sold
- what types of ships are ordered
- how ships are made to be more environmentally friendly
- any new cruise areas to be visited
- new departure ports.

Assessment activity 11.4

Due to the success of the last newsletter sent out to customers of your cruise agency, your boss has asked you to prepare another one before you finish your placement. This one will be about future developments and the impact of cruising.

Prepare detailed notes in preparation for writing the article. Make sure that you cover the full range, referring to the content and assessment guidance in the unit specification for the detail required.

1 Outline at least two potential future developments in the cruise industry based on current trends. **P9**

2 Explain how one cruise itinerary impacts on one cruise area, its gateway ports and ports of call. **P10**

3 Compare the negative and positive impacts of cruising on two different ports within your one selected cruise area. **M3**

4 Evaluate how potential future developments could increase or decrease the negative and positive impacts of cruising. **D2**

Grading tips

P9 Make sure you support your article with evidence from newspapers, research and reports.

P10 You should try to include economic, social and environmental impacts and include both positive and negative factors.

M3 Use the same cruise area as you used for **M2**. Support your notes with statistics and information researched from newspapers and websites.

D2 Ensure that you evaluate both positive and negative factors of cruising.

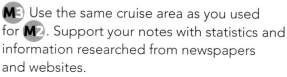

PLTS

In exploring the issue of impacts from different perspectives, you will be developing your **independent enquirer** skills.

Functional skills

By presenting information on a complex subject, concisely and clearly, you will be practising your **English** writing skills.

Malcolm Thorne
Port Presenter, Mediterranean Cruises

What does a port presenter do?

My job is to give talks on all the ports we are going to visit during a two-week cruise. The talks take place in the ship's theatre, usually the day before we visit a port. We might visit eight ports in two weeks so that's quite a lot of preparation as each talk is about an hour.

How do you have time to prepare all that information?

My contract is for five months but the first month is home based and that's when I do the preparation.

What do you do when you are not giving talks?

When we visit the ports I go on excursions with the passengers. This helps me to get to know the ports even better.

I go to all the cocktail parties in the evenings and chat to passengers. My role there is to provide a service to passengers in terms of information about the places we visit, but it's also to sell our excursions.

What is life like on board for you?

I hold officer rank so I have my own cabin and my own steward. The cabin has a bathroom, a fridge and television. I wear a uniform – a suit – on board and I also have a more informal quayside uniform which is a T-shirt and chinos or shorts.

I can use all the facilities on board the ship, although not all crew are allowed to do that. It depends on rank.

It sounds great, are there any disadvantages?

I am away from home for about four months so my friends are my workmates. The pay isn't very good but food and accommodation are covered. We don't have any days off while on board, so it is tiring.

What skills do you need?

It's quite daunting giving talks to hundreds of people in a theatre so you have to be really confident and very well prepared. I have to know a lot about the ports, their geography and what there is to do. I also need to know all the history. I need good presentation skills – the talks have to be interesting or the passengers will go to sleep!

Personal presentation and grooming are also important as I am representing the cruise line.

Think about it!

1 What kind of person would have the knowledge and skills to be a port presenter?
2 How could you prepare for such a role?

Just checking

1 Describe the 'golden age' of cruising.
2 What is a fly-cruise?
3 What are the benefits of integration?
4 What does the Passenger Shipping Association do?
5 What is the appeal of the Mediterranean as a cruise area?
6 Describe the different kinds of ports.
7 What is the environmental impact of port development?
8 Why is there an increase in cruising among UK tourists?
9 What are the pluses and minuses of working on a cruise ship?
10 Why are languages useful if you're working on a ship?

edexcel :::

Assignment tips

- www.pocruises.com/legalenvironment gives information about P&O's environmental policy.
- www.royalcareersatsea.com and www.dcljobs.com/crew-jobs-central.aspx are starting points for job opportunities.
- *Travel Trade Gazette* and *Travel Weekly* have regular cruise sections in their publications.
- Download the Annual Cruise report from the Carnival website – this has useful updates on all the Carnival branded cruiselines.
- Visit the Passenger Shipping Association website to find their Annual Cruise Review, which is a good source of statistics and trends in the industry.

13 Tour operations

Tour operators have been very important in the development of the travel and tourism sector, from the first Thomas Cook package to today's vast tour operating industry.

In this unit you will find out what tour operators do and how they link with other organisations in the travel and tourism sector.

You will learn about different types of tour operator and find out about the range of products they offer, from traditional beach holidays to special interest tailor-made holidays. Holidaymakers' demands change rapidly and tour operators have to respond to changes with new products and services, while remaining profitable. We will examine the particular challenges and responses tour operators face.

You will look at the business of tour operating, finding out about the stages of planning, developing and selling and about the operation of package holiday programmes. You will learn how to plan and cost a package holiday and carry out some exercises to help you practise.

Learning outcomes

After completing this unit you should:

1 understand the tour operations environment

2 know the range of products and services offered by tour operators for different target markets

3 know how tour operators plan, sell, administer and operate a package holiday programme

4 be able to plan and cost a package holiday.

Assessment and grading criteria

This table shows you what you must do in order to achieve a **pass**, **merit** or **distinction** grade and where you can find activities in this book to help you.

To achieve a **pass** grade the evidence must show that you are able to:	To achieve a **merit** grade the evidence must show that, in addition to the pass criteria, you are able to:	To achieve a **distinction** grade the evidence must show that, in addition to the pass and merit criteria, you are able to:
P1 explain the tour operations environment and the challenges it faces **See assessment activity 13.1, page 45**	**M1** discuss the impact of challenges facing tour operators **See assessment activity 13.1, page 45**	**D1** evaluate the effectiveness of tour operators in responding to challenges facing the sector **See assessment activity 13.1, page 45**
P2 describe the products and services provided by different categories of tour operator for different target markets **See assessment activity 13.2, page 49**	**M2** analyse how a selected tour operator's portfolio of products and services meets the needs of its target market(s) **See assessment activity 13.2, page 49**	**D2** recommend, with justification, how a selected tour operator could expand its range of products and services for its current target market or adapt its range of products and services to appeal to a new market **See assessment activity 13.2, page 49**
P3 outline how tour operators plan, sell, administer and operate a package holiday programme, identifying commercial considerations **See assessment activity 13.3, page 58**	**M3** explain ways of maximising profitability during the different stages of planning, selling, administering and operating a package holiday **See assessment activity 13.3, page 58**	
P4 plan and cost a package holiday for inclusion in a tour operator's programme **See assessment activity 13.4, page 60**		

How you will be assessed

This unit will be assessed by one or more internal assignments that will be designed and marked by your tutor. Your assignments will be subject to sampling internally and externally as part of Edexcel's quality assurance procedures. The assignments are designed to allow you to show your knowledge and understanding related to the unit. The unit outcomes indicate what you should know, understand or be able to do after completing the unit.

James, 24-year-old BTEC National learner

I worked for a tour operator before I started my course. I spent a year as a rep. When I decided to go back to college I thought that the knowledge I'd gained would help me. This is one of the units where it has, as I have been able to refer to my training manuals and company information. This material was useful to others in my group as well. I had to be careful though that I didn't only use one company for my research. I used www.aito.co.uk – the website of the Association of Independent Tour Operators (AITO) – to help me. There is a list of members there and I could link to their websites. Luckily, many tour operators give a lot of information on their websites, which is useful because, unlike travel agencies, it's not always easy to find tour operators in your local area.

Over to you!

1 Think of someone you know who has worked for a tour operator. What information can they provide you with?

2 Are there any tour operators in your local area? Would they be prepared to talk to your group?

3 How can the AITO website help you?

1 Understand the tour operations environment

A tour operator designs and puts together package holidays and tours for sale to customers. These products and services are sold through travel agencies or directly to the customer through call centres, websites and television channels. To put the package together, the tour operator must contract the services of airlines, hotels and transport organisations.

Reports from market researchers Key Note and Mintel in 2009 and 2008 stated that:

By 2013, the number of holidays taken will fall by 2.5% from 121 million in 2009, to 118 million while the overall value of all trips taken will increase by 7.6% from £39.5 billion, to £42.5 billion. This includes all types of holidays.

The traditional package holiday remains a huge market, with volume levels still 3.5 million trips higher than a decade ago, despite its market share falling.

The future of high-quality package holidays remains secure despite a rejection by many holidaymakers of the traditional package holiday because of a mass market image of 'crowded beaches and shoddy, noisy resorts with tower-block accommodation'.

Discuss the following:

- Why would the number of trips fall and yet the spend increase?
- What is meant by high-quality packages?
- What do you think are the reasons for package holidays holding on to their market share?
- What kinds of holiday are easier to book independently?

1.1 Links with other component industries

Travel agents

Tour operators traditionally sell their products through travel agents. They pay agents commission – this is variable, but can be in the region of ten per cent. They also provide travel agents with a range of support services to help them sell. These include training packages, special incentives and educational trips. They provide promotional material including brochures and posters.

The current situation is complex, as tour operators try to balance their relationship with travel agents alongside offering customers direct booking and internet services. Even where operations are vertically integrated, tour operators are looking closely at the role of the travel agent and deciding whether to maintain a number of branches or switch to other types of distribution.

Transport providers

Airlines

Tour operators use **charter flights** to provide transport to holiday destinations as part of the package. Some tour operators have their own airlines but still have to charter them within the group as they are run as separate companies.

If the own-brand airline cannot provide enough capacity, the tour operator will charter outside the group. Similarly, if the own-brand airline has excess capacity, planes can be offered for charter to another tour operator.

Charter airlines supply planes and staff to tour operators according to their specified needs. For example, a tour operator may ask for a plane and crew for a once-a-week service from Luton to Ibiza, from May until September. The tour operator orders planes for the routes and the length of time it needs. It has a contract with the charter airline and then sells the holidays itself. Many tour operators sell seat-only flights to fill spare capacity.

Tour operators also offer seats on **scheduled flights** on more 'upmarket' or long-haul packages. They may buy a block of seats and then incorporate them into a package, or they may request seats from the airline when customers book the package. Such seats often involve a supplement to the passenger as they are more complicated to arrange and are perceived as being part of a higher quality service.

Key terms

Charter flights – flights rented by a tour operator to fly for short seasons to holiday destinations. Small operators can group together to charter a flight.

Scheduled flights – flights which run to a set timetable throughout the year. Timetables are adjusted for winter and summer seasons.

Rail and bus companies

Tour operators often provide transport other than flights as part of a package holiday. For example, they may be organising a coach tour, in which case a coach must be chartered. Similarly trains must be booked for rail tours. The tour operator will get favourable rates for tickets depending on the quantity booked.

Tour operators need fleets of coaches to transfer holidaymakers from airports to their destination in the resort and to run their programmes of excursions.

Ferries and cruise ships

Camping tour operators in particular have traditionally arranged ferry crossings for customers who prefer to drive to their holiday destination. Some tour operators specialise in cruises and may book a number of places on ships or even own their own cruise ship.

Why might campers prefer to travel on a ferry?

Accommodation providers

Tour operators' links with hotels can be very complex. Large tour operators may have global deals organised centrally. There may be multi-property relationships when dealing with a chain of hotels, or there may be an individual relationship between a tour operator and one hotel. The tour operator has to contract accommodation – beds, rooms or tents – before the season. The number of units booked is known as the allocation.

Accommodation is central to a package. Both parties must agree on what is to be included and what the terms are. The allocation period must also be agreed. When bookings are taken, they are reserved from the allocation of accommodation units; any further capacity required is 'on request' from the accommodation provider.

Providers of ancillary products and services

Selling extra services brings more revenue to the tour operator just as it does to a travel agent or airline. A customer may find deciding whether to buy car hire, insurance or add-on products from the travel agent, tour operator or airline confusing as they are all in competition for the same business. Tour operators make deals with car-hire companies and finance companies to sell their products.

Case study: Jet2holidays

Yorkshire-based tour operator, Jet2holidays, has launched its brand new Winter into Summer brochure which is available to all agents now. The new additions to the Jet2holidays range bring the number of holiday destinations offered to 25, with a further selection of non-brochured holidays available online.

To cater for today's market, where price is key to every consumer, agents can offer customers the benefit of the lowest deposit in the market – just £30 per person – when booking a holiday with Jet2holidays as well as the financial security that comes with ATOL protection. Jet2holidays has also recently announced its seventh

UK base at East Midlands Airport. The new base means holidaymakers can fly to Turkey, Lanzarote, Tenerife, Crete, Cyprus, Corfu and Egypt from the East Midlands. Our specialist trade team at Jet2holidays is here to support agents building product and brand awareness;"To show our appreciation for the support we receive from agents, we also intend to announce new agent incentives in January 2010. Rewarding agents is key to developing the relationship we have with the trade and reinforces our commitment as the agent friendly tour operator."

Source: Extracted from www.easier.com/55870-jet2holidays-launches-new-brochure.html

Jet2holidays is a sister company of Jet2, the airline.

1 Explain how Jet2holidays links with its sister airline, travel agents and the Civil Aviation Authority.

2 How does the Jet2 operation differ from other tour operators?

Horizontal and vertical integration

Two major integrated travel and tourism companies dominate the UK market. In 2007, First Choice Holidays plc merged with TUI UK, and MyTravel Group plc merged with Thomas Cook UK Ltd. These companies are not only tour operators but own different brands of retail travel agents and airline operators.

The concepts of **vertical integration** and **horizontal integration** have been discussed in Unit 11 page 9 and the TUI example on page 39 clearly illustrates the extent of integration in one of the largest UK tour-operating groups. The example shows how it is possible for the company to vertically control the chain of distribution, from creating the package to selling it via their own travel agents. Horizontal distribution is also apparent, especially in tour operating, where the groups have several subsidiaries.

Key terms

Vertical integration – where companies at different levels in the chain of distribution merge or one takes over the other.

Horizontal integration – where two companies offering competing products merge or one takes over the other.

Subsidiaries – companies which are more than 50% owned by another company, known as the parent company.

There are benefits to integration:

- economies of scale as the company grows
- control over the supply of accommodation and flights
- control over distribution
- larger market share
- less competition
- established reputations.

A few years ago the large tour operators were in control of the holiday market and made many acquisitions from hotels to cruise ships. Although these companies are still vast, they are now consolidating their operations, merging similar **subsidiaries** and concentrating more on specialist operations in the face of a changing market, where customers are no longer seeking mass-market products and are happy to travel independently.

You can expect to see further changes in these large groups over the next few years. To remain competitive, they are getting rid of companies which are outside their core business of holidays, and they are changing the nature of their products, concentrating on more specialist holidays. In addition, distribution is changing and all the major tour operators have direct selling and online booking, although they have not abandoned the traditional travel agency route.

Here is an example of one of the major companies and its divisions.

TUI Travel plc is a global company with over 200 brands. In the UK its best known brand is Thomson.

It is structured in divisions:

Mainstream – this is the largest sector in TUI with a number of vertically integrated tour operators across Europe. It has about 150 aircraft and 3500 retail travel shops. You will have heard of Thomson, First Choice and Portland as examples of brands.

Specialist and emerging markets – in the UK, brands include Sovereign, Hayes & Jarvis and Thomson Worldwide. These are brands which offer luxury products. This division also includes Thomson Tailormade.

Activity – there are about 40 businesses in this division across eight countries. Their products relate to adventure, skiing, other sports and the student market. Brands in the UK include Crystal Ski and Headwater.

Accommodation and destinations – this division includes online and offline distribution channels offering accommodation, for example Hotelbeds. It also includes brands such as LateRooms.com.

Find out more about Tui Travel at www. tuitravelplc.com/tui/pages/aboutus/ companystructure

Think about it

Why do large tour operating groups have so many different brands? Do you think their customers will find this confusing? Should the brands make it obvious to the customer that they all belong to a particular group?

1.2 Links with trade and regulatory bodies

There are several associations and regulatory bodies which impact on tour operation. These include:

- ABTA – The Travel Association/Federation of Tour Operators (FTO)
- Association of Independent Tour Operators (AITO)
- European Tour Operators Association (ETOA)
- UKinbound
- Civil Aviation Authority (CAA).

ABTA – The Travel Association and Federation of Tour Operators

You were introduced to ABTA –The Travel Association in Unit 1 (page 10). Many tour operators join ABTA for the same reasons as travel agents. There are about 900 tour operator members and most of the UK's package holidays are sold through ABTA members. The **bonding** requirements apply to tour operators as well as to travel agents and to ABTA. The Federation of Tour Operators (FTO) merged with ABTA in 2008. Its role was similar to that of ABTA: to act as a point of contact between outbound tour operators and government bodies in the UK, the EU and in destinations served, on matters relating to tour operation.

Key term

Bonding – an amount of money to cover the cost of reimbursing/repatriating tourists in the event of tour operator failure.

Association of Independent Tour Operators

The Association of Independent Tour Operators (AITO) represents about 140 of the UK's specialist tour operators. All the members are independent companies and they are often owner managed. The companies which join AITO agree to adhere to its Quality Charter, which has three key principles – choice, quality and service. Full details of the charter and a list of members can be found on the AITO website, www.aito.co.uk. Like the other associations, AITO insists that its members are bonded and expects to see details of bonding arrangements before membership.

UKinbound

UKinbound is the official trade body representing UK inbound tourism. The association represents about 250 major companies and organisations in all sectors of the industry, operating over 4000 outlets in the UK.

Civil Aviation Authority

The Civil Aviation Authority (CAA) is the organisation responsible for regulating airlines. For tour operators it has a role to play in providing them with their Air Travel Organisers' Licence (ATOL).

1.3 Legal framework

Tour operators must adhere to relevant consumer legislation. Consumer protection laws affecting tour operators include the following.

EU Package Travel Regulations 1992

As a result of a European Directive, since 1993 all UK tour operators offering package holidays have been subject to the EU Package Travel Regulations. The regulations set out the tour operators' responsibilities to their customers and what customers can do if the regulations are breached. If there is a breach, the customer has a case against the tour operator, not each individual supplier.

The two principal sections of the regulations provide financial protection for prepayments and require tour operators to provide what is promised.

The main provisions are:

- Tour operators are responsible for the safety of their customers in the accommodation, on the flight and so on, and must provide assistance in the resort.
- Tour operators must not give inaccurate brochure descriptions.
- Last-minute surcharges cannot be imposed.
- If the operator is declared bankrupt, there must be a guaranteed refund.

There are also regulations covering the information that should be provided to the customer and what will happen if the contract is altered in any way.

There are requirements for the customer too. If customers have complaints they should report them in the resort so that the representative has an opportunity to resolve them. If they need to write to the tour operator to complain, this should be done within a reasonable period (usually 28 days).

Compensation and legal redress are available for customers through the UK courts when there is a breach of regulations. Booking conditions are issued by tour operators and explain all the requirements for both parties.

Did you know?

The Department for Business, Innovation and Skills provides information to explain the Package Travel Regulations. You can link to it from www.bis.gov.uk/policies/consumer-issues/buying-and-selling.

Consumer protection

Trade Descriptions Act 1968

This Act states that descriptions given must be truthful and accurate. It primarily affects tour operators, as they have to be careful that brochure descriptions adhere to the rules.

Supply of Goods and Services Act 1982 and Sale and Supply of Goods Act 1994

This Act states that the tour operator and the travel agent should ensure that the booking is carried out correctly and that the contract for the holiday is also carried out using 'reasonable skill and care'. The holiday should comply with any descriptions and be of a satisfactory standard.

Consumer Protection Act 1987

It is Part III of this Act that is of interest to tour operators as it states that 'All compulsory charges should be included in the headline price and accurate. Any additional charges should be clearly displayed and quantified when advertised.' This means that tour operators have to be very clear about what is included in their prices, as well as what is not included.

Disability Discrimination Act 1995

The Disability Discrimination Act makes discrimination against people with disabilities unlawful in respect of employment, education and access to goods, facilities, services and premises.

Disability can be described as a problem that occurs when a person's ability and the environment do not match. A disability can be a long-term, permanent impairment of mobility, vision, understanding, hearing or mental capacity that may not be compensated for by the environment in which an individual lives or works.

Tour operators, like many other organisations, are required to make reasonable adjustments to accommodate people with disabilities. Examples include facilitating wheelchair access and relocating people with limited mobility to the ground floor. This applies both to employees and to customers.

Contract law

If consumers think that the contract with a tour operator is unfair, they may have a case under the Unfair Terms in Consumer Contracts Regulations of 1999. The Office of Fair Trading gives examples of the kinds of terms which might be unfair. These include **contracts** where customers are not allowed to change holiday arrangements when they are unable to travel, even when they give reasonable notice, and where tour operators seek to put false limits on compensation for problems.

> ### Key terms
>
> **Contract** – a legally binding exchange of promises or agreement between parties that the law will enforce.
>
> **Bond** – a financial guarantee to refund travellers if the travel company collapses, provided by a bank or insurance company.

Responsible companies lay out conditions in a Fair Trading Charter, together with their booking conditions. These form the basis of a legally binding contract between the two parties.

There are many sources of help for customers wanting to make a complaint: they can approach their local Trading Standards Office; ABTA has an arbitration scheme; and there are consumer groups who will help holidaymakers register a complaint. Unfortunately, there are many people who complain not because contract conditions have been breached but because they have not enjoyed the holiday and not read the conditions properly. In this case the regulations help both parties.

Licensing

Air Travel Organisers' Licensing

All tour operators selling packages must be bonded or protect the prepayments they hold. That means if they become bankrupt before travel, customers are more likely to get a refund, or, if they are already abroad, they will be able to return home without any extra payment.

Package holidays that include flights must be protected by Air Travel Organisers' Licensing (ATOL). ATOL is a statutory scheme managed by the CAA to protect the public from losing money or being stranded abroad because of the failure of air travel firms.

All tour operators selling flights and air holidays are required to hold a licence from the CAA. In order to obtain a licence the company must provide proof of a **bond**. If the company fails, the CAA calls in the bond and uses the money to pay for people abroad to continue their holidays and to make refunds to those who have paid but not travelled.

ATOL is the largest travel protection scheme in the UK and the only one for flights and air holidays sold by tour operators. Unfortunately, companies frequently collapse and the scheme is much needed.

There has been much debate, and there are ongoing court cases from the noughties, about whether ATOL bonds are needed for tailor-made holidays. Without ATOL, or other bonding, travellers are at risk if their tour operator or travel agent goes bust before they have taken their holiday. They may lose their money or find that they are unable to get home.

> ### Activity: Looking at complaints
>
> Find a holiday complaint in a newspaper or on a website (search for 'holiday complaints'). Decide whether you think the complaint is valid and, if so, which legislation would apply. Swap your holiday complaint story with those of other group members.

> ### PLTS
>
> When you do your research you will be practising your **independent enquirer** skills.

1.4 External influences

Environmental

Environmental factors can adversely affect the whole travel market. Examples include hurricanes which are common in season in the Caribbean and Florida and the outbreak of diseases, such as swine flu. Other possible problems include floods, avalanches and oil spillages.

Obviously it is difficult to plan for natural disasters, but companies should have contingency plans in place to cover all eventualities.

Political

Sometimes, tour operators have to pull out of destinations completely because of political factors such as war or terrorism. The Foreign and Commonwealth Office (FCO) gives up-to-date information on its website at www.fco.gov.uk about the safety of destinations. Strikes commonly affect operations. British Airways has been hit by strikes from its employees for a few consecutive years. Each strike results in disruption to service on the day, but also puts passengers off booking with British Airways when a strike is threatened.

It is important for tour operators to conduct risk assessments and have contingency plans in place for when things go wrong. Staff should be trained in crisis response. They should also have a plan for dealing with media enquiries if a disaster occurs.

Activity: Hurricane to hit Florida

Tour operators and airlines are currently working on contingency plans for Florida as a force 4–5 hurricane is expected to hit the east coast of Florida and Orlando on Saturday. This will have a dramatic impact as airports will have to close and many flights leaving for the UK will be cancelled.

Both tour operators and airlines will be affected. They must primarily consider the safety of their customers. They must keep in touch with what is happening in resort and take necessary actions including evacuation if necessary.

What do you think tour operators should do in this situation to ensure the safety of their customers and carry on their business?

Present your ideas to your group, and discuss the implications of these measures for the tour operators.

Economic

Currency fluctuations

Many of the costs paid by tour operators are in foreign currencies, usually euros or dollars. Such costs include accommodation, airport charges and transport. When the exchange rate varies, tour operators may have to pay more, or less, than they had originally calculated. This could cause problems if the exchange rate is not in their favour.

What do tour operators need to do to ensure the safety of their customers?

Operators are legally prevented from passing on the first two per cent of an increase in costs to customers. Of course, tour operators are aware of this and 'hedge' funds. This means sufficient funds are exchanged in advance of need, or contracted to be exchanged at a fixed rate. The bank charges for this service, but it is invaluable to the tour operator.

Price of oil

The cost of air travel is dependent on fuel prices and tour operators often charge a supplement for fuel to cover price rises. There is controversy, however, when fuel prices fall and tour operators continue to charge supplements. There is no doubt that air fares are particularly dependent on the price of oil and tour operators are indirectly affected as they have to buy flights.

Social

UK demographics

Tour operators need to be aware of the demographics of the UK to determine what products are needed for which demographic groups. For example, research has shown that younger travellers are more likely than any other age group to book a package holiday. In spite of their familiarity with internet use they lack experience of travel and desire the reassurance of having everything organised for them.

The largest demographic group in the UK in terms of age is the 45–54 group. Being experienced travellers and quite affluent, they are most likely to use tour operators to book long-haul destinations which are less familiar to them.

Exploitation in host country

Tour operators must also recognise the social and economic situation at the destination and how tourism can impact on issues such as unemployment and poverty.

A group of tour operators from different parts of the world have joined together to create the Tour Operators' Initiative for Sustainable Tourism Development. It is open to all tour operators regardless of their size and geographical location. The aim is to encourage tour operators to accept their ethical responsibilities and adopt practices that promote local economic development and reduce the adverse environmental impacts of tourism.

Technological

Tour operators use reservation systems to communicate with travel agents to allow them to make bookings for their programmes. Many sophisticated Global Distribution Systems (GDS) are available; one example is Galileo. Tour operators have to negotiate fees with the GDS company to use their system. Some tour operators prefer to use their own systems. Travel agents are also able to log into these systems.

Websites are an essential feature of the tour operator's service and require the professional services of website designers. The sites must be easy to navigate and present clear information. There may be areas dedicated to travel agents. A good website provides a permanent advertisement for a company's services worldwide.

1.5 Challenges

The holiday market is very competitive. A number of the challenges which tour operators face are listed below.

Dynamic packaging

There has been a trend towards the introduction of niche or specialist packages from tour operators. Such packages can be tailor-made or 'dynamically packaged' to meet customers' personal needs. They can be marketed through call centres or through the internet. Tour operators are less likely to use travel agents for **dynamic packaging** services as this would reduce the ability to personalise the package and travel agents may be in competition with tour operators in these markets.

Key term

Dynamic packaging – accommodation, travel and other services are separately researched and put together in a package for the customer.

Distribution channels

The challenge for distribution is to ensure that products and services are available where customers expect to find them. This often means making sure that your tour operation is using the same channels as the competition.

Integration

The industry is constantly changing, as one company takes over another or sells part of its operation. Tour operators may find themselves subject to takeover bids themselves or face increased competition from merged companies. Two important examples occurred in 2007 with the merger of First Choice Holidays plc and TUI UK and the merger of MyTravel Group plc and Thomas Cook UK Ltd. The result was two huge international companies dominating the market (TUI Travel plc and Thomas Cook Group plc).

Budget (low-cost) airlines

Budget airlines are another factor leading to the increasing trend of passengers booking independently, as the low-cost airlines rarely link with tour operators and encourage direct internet bookings.

Maintaining market share

Tour operators have to try to maintain their market share in the face of a changing market. There are many e-commerce companies exploiting online booking, for example Expedia. In addition, profit margins are low and there is a great deal of price competition. There are a number of strategies that can be followed to increase competitive advantage and maintain, or even increase, market share. Examples include:

- introducing new products and services
- improved distribution
- marketing
- discounted pricing
- using new technology.

Trend towards independent travel

Independent booking, especially on the internet, has intensified. Even though packages are often cheaper than independently booked holidays, there is still a change in customer behaviour in favour of independent booking as access to the internet increases and people have more experience and confidence in using it.

Travellers may think that they can save money by booking the different components themselves. However, tour operators are often able to command favourable rates with airlines and hotels.

Even where there are cost savings to be made by independent booking, there are advantages to using a tour operator:

- good ones have specialist knowledge
- they do all the administration for the customer
- they make all the reservations
- they should be bonded – protecting the booking
- there is only one invoice to pay.

Responsible tourism

The travel and tourism sector is often criticised for not taking responsibility for its impact on the environment. For example, hotels use water and other scarce resources where native populations find them difficult to access or they are rationed. It is now customary for tour operators to have policies on responsible tourism and most offer advice to tourists. Criticism arises as the policies do not go far enough to mitigate the effects of tourism on the environment.

Activity: Improving responsible tourism

Find an example of a tour operator's policy on responsible tourism. Propose ways in which the policy could be improved to better protect the environment or the native population in tourist destinations. Present your case to the tour operator (or your group.)

Case study: Sustainable commitments

In 2010, Thomson and First Choice introduced a new brochure, Holidays Forever, which pledged 20 sustainable commitments. These include reducing carbon emissions on TUI Travel flights by 69 per cent by 2014, and recycling 30 per cent of cans on board which equates to 13 tonnes of aluminium in a year. TUI also aims to have all of its suppliers Travellife awarded by 2014.

1 Find out what the government target for reduction of aircraft carbon emissions is.

2 What is meant by 'Travellife awarded'?

3 Why do you think TUI does not aim to recycle all cans on board a flight?

Assessment activity 13.1

P1 M1 D1 **BTEC**

After finishing your BTEC course you have found a job with a medium-sized, independent tour operator specialising in packaged ski holidays, called Especially Ski. You work in the reservations department. You really enjoy your work, but you are keen to learn about other departments and make career progression.

At your appraisal, you discuss this with your line manager, who asks you if you would like to be involved in a project that the press office team has suggested. The press office is constantly receiving requests for information from students who want to know about tour operating and about how the company operates. The press team acknowledges that it is important to help students, but they find they are spending a lot of time answering questions and sending out information.

Your job is to compile a student pack that can be posted on the internet. It will be a series of downloadable fact sheets so that students can choose the ones they need. The press team has put together a list of the most frequently asked questions that they receive and they want each sheet to be a response to one of the questions.

Carry out the necessary research to allow you to produce a detailed response to the two frequently asked questions listed below. Put together an information page for each question. The pages must be suitable for inclusion on a website.

Make sure that you cover the full range, referring to the content and assessment guidance in the unit specification for the detail required.

Frequently asked question 1

In what kind of environment does Especially Ski work and what challenges does it present?

To fully answer this question:

- Explain the tour operations environment. You will need to explain links with travel agents, providers of transport, accommodation and ancillary products and services, as well as the relationship tour operators have with trade and regulatory bodies. You will also need to describe the relevance of key regulations, laws and licensing and demonstrate an understanding of horizontal and vertical integration with tour operation examples. Finally, you will need to demonstrate an awareness of how environmental, political, economic, social and technological factors can provide challenges for tour operators. **P1**

- Discuss the impact of challenges facing Especially Ski and other tour operators. You should include reference to a minimum of four challenges and ensure you include relevant examples. **M1**

Frequently asked question 2

How effective are Especially Ski and other tour operators in responding to challenges?

To fully answer this question, evaluate the effectiveness of tour operators in responding to challenges. Ensure you address at least two challenges and support your arguments with recent examples. **D1**

Grading tips

P1 You can include diagrams to support the explanation of the links.

M1 Ensure you examine and analyse the impact of at least four challenges and give relevant examples which show how the challenges you have selected impact on tour operators.

D1 You might consider supporting your examples with evidence of how tour operators have responded to the credit crunch or how specific tour operators have responded to challenges created by the internet.

PLTS

You will practise **independent enquirer** skills when you support conclusions, using reasoned arguments and evidence, to make recommendations for adaptations to products and services.

Functional skills

Selecting and using different texts to find relevant information will help you develop your **English** reading skills.

2 Products and services offered by tour operators for different target markets

2.1 Tour operator categories

Outbound

Outbound tour operators are the ones you will be most familiar with. As we have already seen, the major companies are TUI Travel and Thomas Cook with their many brands. They package holidays for tourists who are travelling from the UK to European and worldwide destinations. They may offer mass-market or specialist products.

Mass market

Mass-market products are designed for high volumes of passengers and operate on low margins and low prices. They offer a product that in theory appeals to most people. Mass-market packages are typified by beach holidays on Spain's Costa Blanca, with high-rise hotels in resorts offering British food and pubs. Such mass-market products are becoming less common as the population becomes more sophisticated about travel and more discerning. Operators order accommodation and flight seats from suppliers in bulk and command cheaper prices because of the size of their operations.

Specialist

Outbound operators also have specialist divisions to cater for the public's desire for personal service and a specialist, tailor-made product.

Specialists are also often independent operators who have chosen to operate in a niche market such as diving or a particular destination. These specialist independents are vulnerable to takeover by the large groups.

Inbound

Inbound tour operators direct their marketing towards tourists overseas who want to visit the UK. You may not be familiar with these as their advertising and their promotional material are targeted at other countries.

Domestic

Domestic tour operators operate within the UK, persuading us to take holidays in our own country. These are the most difficult packages to sell, as it is relatively easy for us to book and travel independently within the UK.

Case study: Kirker Holidays

Upmarket short-break specialist Kirker Holidays was established in 1986. It features more than 50 European cities in its programmes as well as many rural hotels.

Why Kirker?

Over the last five years the world of travel has changed dramatically, yet, in spite of the influence of the internet, our clients continue to rely on our service and advice to ensure that they get the best out of their holiday. If you delight in spending time surfing the worldwide web to secure the cheapest 'no frills' flights, and if you are confident in booking hotels on the strength of a tempting website photograph, then Kirker is perhaps not (yet!) for you. However, if you need flexibility, and would like the reassurance of speaking to a human being, then please do call us! Within our team we have over 150 years of experience and we willingly take responsibility for every aspect of your trip to ensure that we turn your short break into a really exceptional holiday.

(Source: www.kirkerholidays.com/about-us.aspx)

1 What type of tour operator is Kirker?

2 Find out about the products and services Kirker offers.

3 Can you find out whether Kirker belongs to a group and who it is?

4 Identify Kirker's target markets.

Activity: Categorising tour operators

Carry out some research and find an example of a brand of tour operator for each category in the following list:

- inbound
- outbound
- domestic
- mass market
- specialist.

Note that a tour operator may be in more than one category – for example, outbound and specialist.

Describe each tour operator and say what its products and services are and what target markets they serve.

State which associations each tour operator belongs to and why. You could present your work as a table, as in the example below. Add explanatory notes as needed.

Category	Tour operator	Products and services	Associations	Benefits
Inbound	British Tours	Personalised day tours in the UK for overseas customers, particularly from the USA	American Society of Travel Agents (ASTA)	ASTA: To gain representation in the US market
			UKinbound	UKinbound: To get support and representation in the UK
			London Tourist Board	London Tourist Board: To gain referrals
Outbound				
Domestic				
Mass-market				
Specialist				

2.2 Products and services

Components of a standard package

This is the definition of a **package holiday** under the Package Travel Regulations. It must:

- be sold or offered for sale
- be sold at an inclusive price
- be pre-arranged
- include a minimum of two of the three elements of transport, accommodation and other tourist services.

Most package holidays are presented in brochures by the tour operators. Customers get the brochures on destinations of interest to them either by visiting a travel agent or by ordering them directly from the tour operator.

Key term

Package holiday – a holiday including at least two elements of transport, accommodation and other services, for example the services of an overseas representative.

The brochure is an important sales tool for the package holiday. Because of the intense competition in the holiday industry, tour operators constantly review their products and introduce new packages.

Tailor-made package

A tailor-made package is dynamically packaged. That is, as we learnt earlier, the different elements of the package are specifically selected to meet the needs of a particular customer. Tour operators are offering tailor-made services much more frequently, as holidaymakers are often experienced travellers and do not appreciate the mass-marketing approach any longer. People have higher expectations in terms of product and customer service.

Range of destinations

Finding new destinations is part of product development for a tour operator. As people take more frequent holidays and become experienced travellers there is an increasing interest in visiting new places. These may be far flung and exotic or may be countries that are developing tourism, like those in Eastern Europe.

Accommodation choices

Offering different types of accommodation is another means of offering a differentiated product to customers. Tourists expect to choose between different types of accommodation, such as villas, hotels and camping. They are also used to choose board packages, such as bed and breakfast or all-inclusive. Tour operators also offer unprecedented luxury, such as beach bungalows in Thailand or holidays in deluxe resorts.

Activity: Explanations

Give an explanation for the following:

- full-board
- half-board
- bed and breakfast
- accommodation only
- all-inclusive.

Transport options

Once again, this is a means of offering options that suit whatever the customer desires. Examples include adventurous train journeys and first-class travel. On their own airlines, the major tour operators have introduced a whole range of optional extras, such as meals which are chargeable.

Ancillary products and services

The marketing activities of tour operators have become very sophisticated in that they offer a vast range of extras that the tourist can add to a holiday – again at an extra charge of course!

The advantage for customers is that all their needs are catered for through one contact. The disadvantage is that all these extras cost money and in some cases they are services that used to be included in a package, for example a meal on a flight. Here is a list of extras available on a typical package:

- holiday insurance
- foreign exchange
- airport car parking
- airport hotel
- airport lounge
- taxis
- car hire
- late check-out from the hotel
- upgrades to rooms
- kids' clubs
- tickets for attractions/events.

And on the flight:

- champagne
- chocolates
- in-flight meal
- extra leg-room
- seats together.

Think about it

If you were going on holiday, which of these extras would you be prepared to pay for? You could get these extras from the tour operator, the travel agent or arrange them yourself. Which is best?

2.3 Target market

Tour operators plan their products with specific target markets in mind. Specialist operators aim for a niche market, while other companies offer a range of products, each aimed at a different group or, as we have seen, at a mass market.

Products may be aimed at families, couples, solo travellers, specific age groups, special interests or people with specific needs.

Activity: Target marketing

Match up the products with the target markets.

Families	We specialise in holidays that take account of local culture and the environment
Couples	If you are passionate about diving we have over a hundred dive sites to choose from
Solo travellers	An operator that has been arranging painting holidays for over 50 years and has wide experience in matching destinations and themes to the expectations of amateur artists
Over fifties	We offer free child places, interconnecting rooms, kids' club, early meals and babysitting
People interested in the environment	Relaxing spa holidays in luxury resorts for adults only
People wanting an activity holiday	An Amazon cruise – chattering, brightly coloured birds, dense jungle and shrub reaching down the banks to the edge of the river
Special interest travellers	This resort is offered without single supplements at certain times of the season

Assessment activity 13.2

P2 M2 D2 BTEC

This assessment builds on assessment activity 13.1 where you can find a full explanation of the scenario and tasks. Make sure that you cover the full range, referring to the content and assessment guidance in the unit specification for the detail required.

Frequently asked question 3

What products and services are provided by Especially Ski? Are they same as other types of tour operator? How do they meet the needs of its target market?

To fully answer this question:

- Describe the products and services provided by different categories of tour operator for different target markets. Describe different categories of tour operators with examples (four in total). Select an example from each category, identify its target market and review its products and services. **P2**

- Analyse how Especially Ski's products and services meet the needs of its target customers. **M2**

Frequently asked question 4

How does Especially Ski ensure it increases sales or attracts new customers?

To fully answer this question:

- Recommend how Especially Ski could expand its range of products and services for its current target market or adapt its range of products and services to appeal to a new market. **D2**

NB In this assessment activity, use any ski operator to represent Especially Ski.

Grading tips

P2 Refer to Unit 5, page 145 in Book 1 for more information about target markets.

M2 You must show that you know what the needs of the target market are and analyse how they are met by a range of products and services.

D2 Ensure you support your recommendations with a clear rationale.

PLTS

In supporting conclusions, using reasoned arguments and evidence when you make recommendations for adaptation to products and services, you will be developing your **independent enquirer** skills.

Functional skills

You will develop your **English** reading skills by selecting and using different texts to find relevant information.

3 How tour operators plan, sell, administer and operate a package holiday programme

Imagine you are going on holiday and you have booked directly with a tour operator. Note all the things that a tour operator is responsible for in order to provide you with your holiday.

Responsibility	When?
Example: Contracting hotels, contracting flights, putting a brochure together	Pre-booking
	During booking
	After booking and pre-holiday
	During holiday
	Post-holiday

Discuss your ideas with your group and your tutor.

3.1 Planning

Planning includes the stages of:

- research
- forecasting
- product development
- methods of contracting
- costing the package
- data input
- working to a timescale.

Research, forecasting and product development

Research has to take place on a continuous basis. Research informs product development. Tour operators are constantly monitoring their sales, the competition and the market. This enables them to forecast what capacity should be offered in existing destinations, new destinations to adopt and old destinations to drop.

They use many sources of data and trends to inform this process:

- Sales figures – when figures go down, perhaps it is time to leave the destination; when figures go up, it may be worth investing in more capacity.
- Reports on consumer demand from salespeople in reservations and travel agents.
- Research findings, for example *Travel Trends*, Mintel reports and VisitBritain reports.
- Travel and tourism conferences.
- PEST analysis – analysing political, economic, social and technological factors.

An organisation that is aware of and using all this information will make informed decisions about which destinations to include in a package-holiday programme. In spite of this, there will be occasions when an operator has to pull out of a destination because of factors which could not be foreseen, for example a terrorist attack. Product development does not just include destinations. It may mean changing the range of excursions offered in resorts, the services offered during the flight or holiday, or the means of booking the holiday.

Think about it

Think of at least three destinations tour operators cannot offer at present. Why is this?

Methods of contracting

Contracts are typically fixed about 18 months ahead of the holiday season. This means that the tour operator needs to make an estimation of capacity in order to agree contracts with hotels and airlines. There will be some adjustments later, but it is difficult to make major changes as prices will have been agreed and brochures gone to print.

It is difficult to contract too far in advance, as tour operators have to make decisions, based on sales and other research, about what to include in their programme.

Different types of contract that might be organised for accommodation include:

- a fixed contract
- an allocation contract
- an ad-hoc contract.

The **fixed contract** is more advantageous to the supplier as it means that if the accommodation is not sold they will still be paid. Obviously this is not so practical for the tour operator.

Allocation contracts are also popular with hoteliers. To ensure that all their beds are sold, they contract with tour operators for more beds than they have available. The tour operator has to confirm, by an agreed date, how many beds it will actually take. This gives the hotel time to sell remaining beds at a competitive price.

Allocation contracts also apply to flights. A smaller tour operator cannot fill a whole charter aircraft, so it buys an allocation of seats on a flight. Once the allocation is sold, it requests seats for any extra bookings or looks for seats on an alternative flight. The customer may have to pay a supplement for these seats as they will not be acquired at the preferential rate of the original allocation. If the allocation is not sold, unsold seats can be returned to the airline, but the deadline for this is six to eight weeks before departure date.

An **ad-hoc contract** means that the tour operator agrees a rate with hoteliers but do not commit to a specific allocation. When the tour operator receives a booking, they take up the room at the previously agreed rate.

Key terms

Fixed contract – if the accommodation (or flights) are not sold, the owner is still paid.

Allocation contracts – the tour operator buys an agreed number of rooms (or flights).

Ad-hoc contract – the tour operator pays only for the rooms that they have taken.

Fixed contracts are less common than they used to be as tour operators look for greater flexibility and control over costs. However, the type of contract often depends on which company is the more powerful negotiator.

Activity: Getting the contract

Bella Vista is a glamorous new hotel overlooking a bay in Lanzarote. All the major tour operators want to feature it in their winter programmes. Damson, an independent tour operator, is in competition with the big four to secure 50 rooms for the season. Who has more power in this relationship? What kind of contract do you think will be issued? Check with your tutor to see whether you are right.

Flights are often contracted more than a season in advance and again the tour operators have to predict how many people will be prepared to book a particular holiday from a particular airport. If predictions are wrong they will have to make adjustments – but sometimes this is not possible. They may be able to contract extra aircraft if there are any available, but it is difficult to cancel one without incurring costs.

Where there is no possibility of achieving the required load factor on a flight, a tour operator may decide to consolidate two flights. This simply means that one will be cancelled and the passengers will be transferred to the other flight – or even another airport. This action often causes customer dissatisfaction as departure times will change. However, sometimes this can work in a customer's favour, as they may be given an extra couple of days' holiday to fit in with the new flight.

Costing the package

Margins on package holidays are extremely low at around 4 per cent. This means that costings have to be done extremely carefully with accurate forecasting. This is difficult as they are carried out about 18 months in advance of sales and many of the costs are subject to fluctuation. Fuel costs may rise and exchange rates may adversely affect costs. Another complication is that under the Package Travel Regulations late surcharges are not allowed to be added to the holiday price.

Data input

Once contracts are agreed, an assistant will load the supplier information onto the company database. They will ensure contract information is correctly entered and maintained.

Timescales

Planning a package holiday takes up to two years. The following case study explains why a company has an even longer-term plan and what stages are gone through before the holiday is ready for sale.

3.2 Selling

Brochure production

Holiday brochures are printed a long time in advance of the holiday season. The brochures include prices and obviously it is difficult to determine prices a long time in advance.

Tour operators produce several versions of a brochure in order to update prices. This practice is confusing for customers and travel agents and also wasteful. A solution would be to print brochures without prices and

Case study: Zodiac Homes

Zodiac Homes is a villa holiday specialist tour operator. One of its key areas is Croatia. Its operations director explains how the programme in Croatia was set up.

Planning is very important to our business and we have a five-year plan so that we know the direction we are heading in. We can be reasonably accurate with our three-year planning and definite plans are put into place about 18 months before the season. When we decided to go into Croatia, the perceptions of the country were poor. It was associated with the war and prior to that it had been an area of mass tourism.

We made four or five familiarisation visits seeking out suitable properties to rent. All the villas we let have pools so we had to persuade owners and developers to build pools in order to let their houses. Houses come to us in several ways:

- Existing owners tell others about us
- Tourist boards are a source of villa owners
- We look for villas ourselves.

Once we have found the villas we negotiate contracts with the owners. A fully guaranteed contract means we guarantee an amount for the whole season. This involves

us in financial risk as we have to pay the owner whether the villa is let or not. However, for a particularly good property it may be worth the risk. A minimum guarantee contract means we guarantee to pay for a fixed number of weeks within the season. This gives us less commitment and outside of our weeks the owner is free to take direct bookings, or we may book it if there is demand and it is still free. An ad hoc contract means we pay the owner only if we let the villa.

Our brochure is priced for accommodation only, although extras can be added. This keeps pricing relatively simple and means customers can take advantage of low-cost flights or drive to Croatia. When we set the prices, we use past experience to guide us, particularly comparing with Catalonia or France.

We employ representatives – they are people who live in the area so they have local knowledge. We sell via our website or by telephone. We give a personal service and have excellent product knowledge.

1 Draw up a flow chart explaining the stages in planning, selling and administering a villa rental programme. As the holidays are to be sold as packages you should include contracting of flights and transfers. Your chart should indicate which activities are sequential and which have to be done at the same time. Give an indication of timescales.

Make sure the chart is suitable for display. Add explanatory notes as appropriate.

2 Describe how the villa holiday programme is operated. You may need to do some further research on other villa holiday programmes to help you.

to confirm the price at the time of booking, but this is illegal in the UK – a price must be set for the package.

It has been suggested by Trading Standards officers that a maximum brochure price is set which cannot be exceeded, but which can be discounted. This suggestion has not yet been adopted.

The brochure is an important sales tool and traditionally the main source of information for the customer. Unless the business is new, or a new venture for an existing operator, the brochure will be largely based on the previous year's version. This means it is unnecessary to photograph every hotel every year and rewrite all the copy (text). In spite of this, it still takes a lot of time to produce. Time is needed to:

- design the brochure
- write copy
- determine prices.

The brochure must appear in good time to allow sales to take place. A brochure for the summer season will be published in the spring of the previous year.

Think about it

Since travel agents have to throw away so many brochures, why don't you ask an agent if you can have some copies for your school or college? They will help you with your research.

There is a solution to the brochure problem. Technology allows for printed brochures to be abandoned in favour of **e-brochures**.

Key term

E-brochures – electronic versions of tour operator information of the type that traditionally appears in print.

There are advantages to these – e-brochures do not waste paper, ink, space or money. They can also be more precisely targeted, as a travel agent or other intermediary can download information that is of interest to a specific customer.

However, an e-brochures system is not as simple as transferring the brochure to the internet. It requires investment in a content management system by the tour operator in order to be done properly.

The main question for tour operators is whether their customers prefer e-brochures in place of print brochures they can browse through at home.

Activity: Brochures

1   Find a tour operator's e-brochure online. You could look at www.kuoni.com. Compare the experience of using the e-brochure with a traditional brochure. Make a comparative table.

2   Gather a selection of summer sun brochures. Choose a mainstream summer sun holiday in Spain. Find the same holiday (same resort, same hotel, same dates) in three package-holiday brochures. Compare the prices charged by the different operators for a one-week holiday, for half-board, for a couple. Put your results in a table and comment on your findings.

Pricing strategies

A number of pricing strategies are commonly used by tour operators. These include the following.

Discount pricing

Prices may be discounted if holidays remain unsold. By fixing contracts, and therefore prices a long time ahead of the season, tour operators purchase their supplies (flights and rooms) at the cheapest prices. In order to ensure that holidays are not left unsold and that cash flow is good, tour operators must encourage early bookings. When early bookings are high, the tour operator knows whether there will be any excess capacity in holidays – hopefully none – and takes a substantial deposit per person. Tour operators are able to use or invest this money as they do not need to pay their suppliers until the holidays are taken.

When there is excess capacity, tour operators are forced to discount holidays at the last minute. Tour operators aim to sell 95 per cent of holidays available in order to maintain profitability. This means it is important to try to match supply and demand very closely.

Large tour operators achieve very small margins of profit. They may make only 4 per cent of the price of the holiday as profit. In fact, the CAA states that some margins are as low as 3 per cent If the holiday is discounted, they may not make any profit. In that case the aim is to cover the costs.

You can see why the selling of ancillary products is so vital – this is where the profits are to be made. Tactics employed by tour operators with discounted holidays include charging for the transfer, charging a late booking fee and charging for a meal on the plane.

Seasonal pricing

Tour operators divide the year into different seasons. First, there is a broad division into winter and summer season. In summer there are more beach holidays and in winter ski programmes are running. A summer brochure will typically cover the period May to November and a winter one will run from November to April. Within these periods there are **peak seasons**, **shoulder seasons** and **off-peak seasons**.

Key terms

Peak seasons – the busiest times, coinciding with school holidays.

Shoulder seasons – the slightly less busy times either side of the peak season.

Off-peak seasons – the least busy times.

Tour operators vary their capacity during the season, but must fill the planes they have contracted. This can result in discounted prices at shoulder season. At peak season – the school holiday period of July and August in summer and the Christmas holidays in winter – demand, and therefore prices, are at their highest. Tour operators have been heavily criticised for charging their highest prices in school holiday times, but they have to make their profit when they can.

Activity: Distribution

Choose a well-known tour operator. Find out how its products are distributed. To do this you will need to visit a travel agent, look on the internet, and also see if its products are listed on teletext or available by telephone.

Distribution

Tour operators must determine how best to distribute their products and services in order to maximise sales. Traditionally, distribution is via travel agents who stock tour operators' brochures and sell on their behalf on commission. Although this method is still common, it is now used in conjunction with internet distribution where customers can find information and even book via the tour operators' own websites or via a travel agent's website. When products and services are sold via the tour operator's website or by telephone, this is known as direct sell. Some tour operators, for example Portland, only use direct methods. Most tour operators use a combination of distribution methods.

Functional skills

You will demonstrate skills in **Maths** when costing for package holidays.

Case study: Pricing

1. Give reasons for the variations in price shown in the table.

2. When are the peak seasons and the shoulder seasons?

3. What else do you think a couple would have to pay for on this holiday?

4. Make notes for discussion with your group.

5. Calculate the price of a 7-night holiday leaving on 16th July. Our couple wants a return taxi transfer and a room with a mountain view.

Departures on or between Prices are in £s per person	Nights	01 May 12 May	13 May 19 May	20 May 26 May	27 May 31 May	01 Jun 09 Jun	10 Jun 23 Jun	24 Jun 07 Jul	08 Jul 14 Jul	15 Jul 21 Jul	22 Jul 16 Aug	17 Aug 20 Aug	21 Aug 24 Aug	25 Aug 30 Aug	31 Aug 14 Sep	15 Sep 21 Sep	22 Sep 28 Sep	29 Sep 13 Oct	14 Oct 20 Oct	21 Oct 25 Oct	26 Oct 31 Oct	Room & Board Upgrades per person per night from
Savoy Gardens	7	625	635	655	665	645	629	655	675	695	715	699	699	649	749	719	695	695	705	765	705	Mountain view £7
Half-board	10	755	765	785	809	785	785	799	815	865	889	889	875	829	905	875	849	859	855	885	855	
Code *SAV*	11	785	825	845	869	855	855	865	879	939	959	959	945	905	979	945	919	929	925	939	925	Suite £17
Standard, sea view / 2 adults	14	895	885	915	975	969	969	975	995	1065	1099	1095	1055	1035	1115	1069	1045	1055	1035	1015	1035	Junior suite £11
Holiday upgrades from		Coach transfer **INCLUDED**					Return taxi transfer from **£19** per person														

These prices are a guide and apply to selected flight departures between each date range. All prices can go up and down; please check at the time of booking for the most up-to-date price. Under-occupancy charges and flight supplements may apply. Age restrictions may apply. See our A–Z at the back of the brochure for any additional charges (e.g. flight and/or fuel) and important holiday information.

Want flexibility? A wider range of durations are available – check out our website.

Promotion

Promotion is the work of marketing personnel, as you saw in Unit 10, pages 291, 309–16. The nature of promotion depends on the budget available and ranges from television advertising campaigns to press releases about new products and destinations. You can find examples of the use of press releases in travel trade magazines. Promotion may be aimed at the final consumer or at the trade. Trade promotion can be just as important as consumer promotion as travel professionals can bring preferred products to the attention of their customers. Examples of trade promotions include educational trips for agents to resorts, competitions and sales incentives.

Reservations

Most tour operators use computerised reservation systems. Reservations staff are salespeople so they have to be well informed about the products they sell. This is easier for tour operators than for travel agencies, as the salesperson needs to know about only one company's products and will have received intensive training.

Reservations staff may be at a call centre, in which case they have targets to meet in terms of calls answered and sales made. Others take bookings over the computerised reservation system from travel agents or over the internet. They will need to contact customers only if there is a query about a booking or availability. Once a booking is made, a reference code is assigned to it alongside the customer details, so that the booking can always be traced through the system.

Commission

The tour operator pays commission to travel agents but can negotiate this. They also receive commission from third parties whose products and services they sell, for example car-hire and insurance.

Late sales

Holidays are perishable – once the flight has departed the opportunity to sell that holiday is gone. Late sales mean that at least some contribution to costs is made even if no profit is made. Tour operators prefer to avoid late sales. They deplete an already very tight margin. If forecasting of demand is accurate, then late sales can be avoided. There are websites dedicated to making late sales, e.g. www.lastminute.com.

3.3 Administration
Confirmations, itineraries and tickets

Once reservations are made, further administration is dealt with by another team. They issue booking confirmations and invoices after booking and send out reminders for payment. They issue any tickets, itineraries and other documentation; this can be quite complex. Camping operators send out guides to the campsite, a guide to the local area, car stickers and maps, as well as the booking details.

Passenger manifests and rooming lists

The administration department has to make sure that suppliers are informed of bookings. **Passenger manifests** and details of forthcoming bookings are sent to airlines and hotels. Rooming lists show which passengers are acommodated in which rooms. If cancellations are made these too must be dealt with by the administrative team and suppliers notified.

Key term
Passenger manifest – a list or record of passengers.

Errata

This is a term used in publishing and refers to corrections made after a publication, in this case a brochure, has gone to press. Rather than republish the whole brochure at great cost, a list of corrections is sent out to be read alongside the brochure.

Cancellations and amendments

Any cancellations or amendments made by the tour operator must adhere to the EU Package Travel Regulations. A customer will be able to read policies on cancellation or amendment in the tour operator's terms and conditions when they book their holiday. If the tour operator has to cancel a holiday they will offer a full refund or an alternative holiday.

3.4 Operations
Consolidations

Consolidations occur when insufficient bookings mean there is spare capacity of air seats or hotel rooms. Rather than leave these flight seats or rooms empty and yet paid for, capacity is cut and flights and rooms cancelled (where contracts allow). People with bookings for these cancelled flights or rooms are transferred to other flights which have seats available or different accommodation.

Load factors

The load factor refers to the ratio of paid passengers to the total capacity, that is seats, available on a flight. Ideally tour operators would like a 100 per cent load factor and aim for this.

Overbookings

These are unusual but problematic when they occur. If holidays are overbooked in peak season, customers may arrive at the airport or even resort and find no seats or accommodation are available for them. It will be the tour operator's task to solve the problem.

Transport operations

This refers to the organisation of charter flights and in-resort transfers. Transfers are usually included in the package. The transfer from the airport to the hotel is usually by coach. On many late bookings, tour operators now charge extra for the transfer to compensate for discounting the holiday. Representatives take it in turns to be on airport duty – normally one day a week. These representatives meet the plane and accompany the coach loads of passengers to their accommodation.

The tour operator may use other forms of transport and will have a close working relationship with whichever suppliers it uses.

Duty office

Smaller tour operators may not have a dedicated duty office, but they always have a designated member of staff on call outside office hours. The duty office provides an essential link between the UK and the resorts. The office deals with any non-routine occurrences, for example medical problems where an insurance company has to be contacted. If delays occur at airports, they will make sure that passengers receive the information, meals or even accommodation that they require.

UK and overseas resort liaison

Package holidays include the services of a representative. The representatives are employed directly by the tour operator in areas where the operator has a large programme with many holidaymakers. In other circumstances, representatives

are hired from local companies and will take care of people on holiday with several different tour operators. This latter group is more likely to be made up of local people.

The staff are in communication with the UK and receive daily information updates, for example passenger manifests and special requests. Sometimes the resort staff have to allocate accommodation where customers have booked late at a discount for 'allocation on arrival'.

Health and safety

The representatives will have a degree of responsibility for health and safety. Under the EU Package Travel Regulations, the tour operator, not the hotel, is responsible for the customer's health and safety. If the representative notices any breach of health and safety, or is informed of one by a customer, they must ensure it is put right.

Emergency situations

In addition, the representatives must deal with emergency situations. A good tour operator lays down procedures to be followed in such cases. Most emergencies are health-related or involve crimes. The worst scenario involves someone's death. This is a terrible situation for all concerned, but it is not unusual for representatives to have to deal with it and there will be procedures to follow.

Crisis management

The most demanding situation for a representative is dealing with a crisis that affects a lot of customers. Examples include mass food poisoning, a bus crash or a hurricane. In such situations there should be a crisis management procedure that can be put into operation, but representatives would also expect senior management to oversee these procedures. An incident control centre would be set up at head office and would liaise with staff in the resort. The head of incident control would issue a carefully considered company policy statement on any incident to try to minimise concern or even panic and to maintain good public relations.

The representative would be expected to adhere to company policy and to remain contactable at all times.

Quality control

Quality control is ensured by different methods. Surveys are often undertaken asking for customers' views on their holiday. You might have noticed these on the return flight from a package holiday. If customers come to them with problems, representatives in the resort complete a series of reports. The reports are monitored in resort by senior staff. They need to know what has happened and that any incidents or complaints have been dealt with correctly.

Customer service

Tour operators provide routine customer service departments. They may be divided into pre-departure customer service and post-holiday customer service.

Before departure, the customer service agents deal with enquiries and provide information. They may give information about passports, visas and vaccination requirements. They will also deal with any booking amendments and pass on details to reservations.

After the holiday, it is mostly the customer service department that deals with any complaints. The agents answer telephone, email and postal complaints. The large tour operators computerise the systems for dealing with complaints and scan all correspondence into an individual customer file saved on the system.

Targets are set for responding to complaints and letters are automatically generated as far as possible, although obviously some complaints require a unique response. The aim is always to solve the complaint as quickly and as cheaply as possible. The customer service department's workload is much reduced where overseas representatives are empowered to resolve complaints in the resort if they can. The tour operator will try to resolve any further complaint to the customer's satisfaction and to avoid possible legal action. However, many people complain after their holiday simply because they had expectations that were too high, or experienced poor weather. The tour operator has to respond to such complaints, although there is no obligation to provide any form of compensation.

Excursion sales

Excursions are a very valuable source of income and an important part of the representative's job is to sell them. They can often be bought prior to departure.

3.5 Commercial considerations

Maximising profitability

The tour operator has to maximise the profitability of the planned package holiday programme. Profitability has to be considered throughout all stages of planning, selling, administration and operation. There are various means of achieving this.

Links to different planning

Negotiating a more flexible contract with a supplier means that if insufficient bookings are made they can be cancelled without penalty. Remember: a fixed contract means that rooms or plane seats have to be paid for whether they are filled or not.

Forecasting numbers of customers and peak periods as accurately as possible means that the correct number of rooms and flight seats will be booked. Accurate costing of the package with adequate margins aids profitability.

Rates of exchange should be monitored and currency should be bought when the rate is favourable and banked until invoices have to be paid.

Selling

Using appropriate pricing strategies maximizes profitability. For example, discounting before absolutely necessary would damage profits.

Customers pay deposits on their holidays and pay the balance about six weeks before departure. Paying for holidays upfront helps the operator's cash flow and allows them to earn interest on sales before they have to pay suppliers. Some tour operators requested full payment 12 weeks before departure in the recession of 2009. This had a positive impact on the businesses' cash flow.

Administration

Having effective systems saves on costs. Where two companies merge economies of scale can be achieved by merging administration and operational systems.

Tour operators' terms and conditions include details of cancellation charges. If a customer decides to cancel their holiday they will lose a percentage of the cost of their holiday. This increases on a sliding scale the nearer to the departure time the cancellation is made. The tour operator is free to resell the holiday.

You can find details of these charges in the terms and conditions of the holiday brochure.

Operations

If load factors on flights cannot be achieved, money can be saved by consolidating flights. Where small numbers of passengers are to be transferred from airports to hotels, the transfer options should be studied. It can be cheaper to hire taxis as needed rather than half-fill coaches. Transfer costs are sometime passed on to customers.

Costs of customer service can be reduced if resort staff are empowered to deal with problems and complaints in resort rather than incur costs of lengthy discussions post-holiday.

Assessment activity 13.3

P4 M3 **BTEC**

This assessment builds on assessment activities 13.1 and 13.2. You can find a full explanation of the scenario and tasks in assessment activity 13.1. Make sure that you cover the full range, referring to the content and assessment guidance in the unit specification for the detail required.

Frequently asked question 5

How do tour operators plan, sell, administer and operate their package-holiday programmes?

To fully answer this question, describe the different aspects of planning, selling administering and operating the package-holiday programme, identifying commercial considerations. To achieve a pass, make sure you describe the functions of:

- planning
- selling
- administration
- operations.

Give examples of how these functions are carried out and refer to timescales and commercial considerations. **P4**

Frequently asked question 6

How would Especially Ski maximise the profitability of their package holiday programme?

Explain ways of maximising profitability during the different stages of planning, selling, administering and operating a package holiday. Explain how aspects such as methods of contracting, consolidations, currency exchange, cancellation charge and commission could contribute to profitability. **M3**

Grading tips

P4, **M3** Give specific examples where you can.

PLTS

You will be practising your **creative thinker** skills when you generate ideas for maximising profitability.

Functional skills

You will be developing your **English** writing skills by using a style of writing appropriate for the tour operator's website.

4   Planning and costing a package holiday

In this section you will be given the opportunity to work on an example which will allow you to practise planning and costing a package holiday. You must bear in mind that you are unable to access the negotiated rates that large tour operators can achieve. Nor will you be able to find out the costs of chartering an aircraft. These figures are negotiated for each deal and are not in the public domain. However, you will be able to carry out research and go through a process which is similar to that of a small operator.

Activity: Planning and costing

The example is a specialist tour operator which is bringing out a new product and brochure called 'Spa Bliss'. The product is to be based in hotels all over the world, each one very special, exclusive and offering a full range of spa therapies. Most of them have been sourced and contracted, but the owner wants one more to finish off the programme. Your role is to find an extra special spa hotel in an exotic location and then create a package around that hotel.

How do you do this?

4.1 Plan

Destination and accommodation

Decide on the destination and the spa hotel. The easiest way for you to do this is to search on the internet for spa hotels. You cannot get the information from another package holiday brochure as you need to access the hotel's rates, so you need to visit the hotel's own website. Search for 'spa hotels' and find one that is suitably exclusive and luxurious for the 'Spa Bliss' programme. Make sure that no prohibitive factors apply to the destination – that is, no political or environmental factors would prevent people from travelling there. Select some photos that you could use in your brochure. Check rates, particularly of a twin room per night.

What type of board will you offer your customers? Check what the hotel offers, from bed and breakfast to all-inclusive. Check the rates again.

Transport

Decide how customers will get there. Find out what scheduled flights serve the destination – make sure there is a direct flight. Start by searching British Airways. Check prices and try to find an average price.

Additional services

Decide which treatments and activities will be included and which will cost extra. List everything. Check prices. Think about excursions in the area – will any be included or will they be optional?

Contract

What kind of contract will you arrange with the hotel? This is a new venture and you don't know how many bookings you will get, so perhaps the first season should be on an ad-hoc contract.

Transfer

Decide how you will transfer your customers from the airport to the hotel. If they are paying a lot of money, they will expect a taxi. How much will that cost? Try www.holidaytaxis.com for quotes.

Fixed costs

You have an office with three staff in the UK. Allow fixed costs of £8000 per month for running the office.

You are ready to start costing this project – as you are buying rooms, and seats on scheduled aircraft, you do not need to worry about load factors at this stage.

4.2 Cost a package holiday
Load factor and mark up

For our spa holiday example, you are not using load factors but for your assessment you can calculate using a load factor of 80 per cent. This would apply if you were chartering a whole plane. When you are buying seats on an existing flight you just add your mark up to the price of the seats. The mark up on luxury holidays is higher than on mass-market holidays and you need to get a speedy return on investment, so go for a relatively high mark up. Start with 20 per cent – this will be in off-peak and you can price up from that for shoulder and peak times.

Fixed and variable costs

Fixed costs are those which do not alter and will have to be paid no matter how many bookings you take, for example the price of a charter flight. Variable costs are those which change according to number of bookings, for example catering costs and hotel rooms.

Note in a table the costs of everything you want to include in your package. Do this for a 7-night and a 14-night period. Remember you will get commission from the suppliers on everything you book. Assume this is 10 per cent and take this off. Add on your mark up. The figure you have left is the basic price.

At this stage you should look at some other spa packages and see how your basic price compares. Is it realistic?

Currency conversion

Decide on the season, perhaps November to April. Divide the season into peak, shoulder and off-peak periods and adjust the prices. You also need to convert prices into sterling if they are quoted in another currency.

Collate a list of supplements, activities and excursions with the prices you will charge for them.

Keep all your notes from each stage so that you are able to explain how you arrived at your package. Put your information together as a brochure page. Present your proposal to your tutor.

Assessment activity 13.4   (P4) **BTEC**

In this activity you are a small tour operator in the Midlands specialising in holidays to France. You are planning to add the Côte d'Azur next autumn and you need to plan and cost the holidays for inclusion in your programme.

You are using the services of a local agent on the Côte d'Azur and he has been able to offer contract rates for 3-star hotels in different resorts. You must choose one hotel and resort for your programme and decide on the board basis and method of contract.

B & B rate per person per night inclusive of taxes	St Raphael	Cannes	Antibes
3 star hotel – fixed (guaranteed) contract	€25	€30	€33
3 star hotel – allocation contract	€30	€35	€38
Supplement for half board per person per night (optional)	€15	€15	€15

Assume that the passengers will travel by air from Birmingham each Saturday and stay for 7 nights. You have a fixed contract for 50 seats on a flight chartered by another company. You have agreed a rate of £120 per person return, including all taxes. You will pay in advance for the 50 seats on each flight, even if you do not have passengers booked.

The agent has quoted a rate of €10 per person for the return transfer by coach between Nice airport and any

resort on the Côte d'Azur or €25 per person return trip by taxi. He will also charge a flat sum of €100 for each group to cover the cost of a local representative making a daily visit to the hotel.

1 Use the internet to help you choose which resort to offer and find a 3-star hotel suitable for a group of up to 50 (don't worry about the price – your agent has sorted that out!)

2 Calculate a selling price in £ per person for a 7-night package, identifying both fixed and variable costs. Apply a load factor, make any necessary currency calculations (using the current bank rate) and add a suitable mark up.

3 Produce a short description of the planned package, including suggestions for a range of activities and optional excursions that could be offered to holidaymakers.

Make sure that you cover the full range, referring to the content and assessment guidance in the unit specification for the detail required.

Grading tips

(P4) Prepare an accurate breakdown of your costing.

(P4) Provide a rationale for the decisions made on load factor and mark-up.

PLTS

You will be practising **independent enquirer** skills as you carry out research to find suitable accommodation.

Functional skills

You will be demonstrating **Maths** skills in this assessment when you produce a costing for the package including mark up and load factor.

Simon Allan
Managing Director, Canvas Holidays

Canvas Holidays is a tour operator specialising in family camping and mobile home holidays. The company has been in business for over 40 years and is now part of Wyndham Worldwide, a leading hospitality company. Simon was appointed Managing Director at the end of 2009.

I have been with Canvas Holidays for 20 years and I am delighted to have become MD.

I started as a representative on a campsite. I intended to do it for a season while I thought about what 'proper' job I would get. However, I loved it so I stayed and very soon I became an Area Manager then Head of Purchasing. I was responsible for buying everything from tents to phone systems and even mobile homes.

From that job, I moved to be Operations Manager and was responsible for everything that happened abroad to deliver our products and services on campsites.

In 2000, I joined the Board as Operations Director. This gave me increased responsibility, not only for operations but also for contracting campsites and pricing.

What does your job as MD involve? Is it very different to being Operations Director?

As I am new to the post I have to learn quickly about all the functional areas of the business, not just my own area of Operations. I spend time with all our managers – Finance, Marketing, Overseas Operations, IT, the Contact Centre Manager and HR. I find out what they are doing each day. This gives me the overview I need of the business.

It is my responsibility to put in place the strategies to steer the business in the right direction. I have to think where we intend to be in three years time or five years time. This means thinking about what challenges the business faces. Where is the growth in terms of new markets or customers? What new products are needed? It is also my job to make sure we meet our financial targets day-to-day.

Do you travel a lot, Simon?

In my previous roles, I travelled a lot to France and Spain where most of our campsites operate. Now, I am more likely to be travelling to Amsterdam or Copenhagen for business meetings with our partners.

Did you study Travel and Tourism?

I did a Geography degree with a Travel and Tourism module included.

Do you enjoy your work?

It isn't just a job, it's a passion. I love the business. I love France and travel.

What advice would you give to Travel and Tourism students?

Succeeding is about working hard and seizing opportunities.

Think about it!

1 How would you cope with the responsibility of running the whole company?

2 Find out more about Canvas Holidays and Wyndham Worldwide on their websites:

- www.wyndhamworldwide.com – look in Corporate Information
- www.canvasholidays.co.uk – look in About Us.

Just checking

1 What are the benefits of integration?
2 Identify the associations that support tour operators.
3 Give examples of environmental influences which might affect tour operation.
4 Explain how tour operators charter aircraft.
5 Define a package holiday.
6 Explain why ancillary products are important to tour operators.
7 What are the different kinds of contracts between tour operators and suppliers?
8 Describe the different pricing strategies used by tour operators.
9 What is an e-brochure?
10 What are the functions of a duty office?
11 Describe the main provisions of the EU Package Travel Regulations.

Assignment tips

- Contact local travel agents and ask if you can have any brochures that they no longer need.
- www.careerintravel.co.uk/tour-operators.htm has links to lots of tour operator websites.
- www.localtouroperator.co.uk will help you find out about smaller tour operators.
- www.ukinbound.org has information about inbound tour operators.
- www.caa.co.uk/default.aspx?catid=27 gives information about the ATOL scheme.
- www.aito.co.uk, the website for the Association of Independent Tour Operators, has information and links.
- Make sure you are reading the travel trade press regularly to find out about new products and services from tour operators.
- Remember that ABTA – The Travel Association represents tour operators as well as travel agents. It is now merged with the Federation of Tour Operators – found at www.abta.com.

15 Working as a holiday representative

Most learners look forward to finding out about working as a holiday representative. You have probably seen representatives when you have been on holiday and thought that it looked like an exciting life. It can be a very interesting and fulfilling job, but you should realise that it is often very hard work too. It is a job that gives you great experience of customer care and organisational skills and allows you to live abroad if you choose. It can be a fun temporary job in a gap year or after leaving education, or it can be a serious career path leading to other positions within a tour-operating company.

The role of holiday representatives is to look after holidaymakers while they are on holiday either in the UK or abroad. In this unit you will find out about the different types of holiday representative and their roles and responsibilities.

You will find out how a holiday representative deals with customers and will carry out some practical activities to deal with customers in a range of situations. We will look at the legal responsibilities of holiday representatives and their role in ensuring holidaymakers have a safe and healthy environment.

Learning outcomes

After completing this unit you should:

1 know the roles, duties and responsibilities of different categories of holiday representatives

2 know the legal responsibilities of a holiday representative

3 understand the role of the holiday representative in creating a safe and healthy holiday environment

4 be able to apply social, customer service and selling skills when dealing with transfers, welcome meetings and other situations.

Assessment and grading criteria

This table shows you what you must do in order to achieve a **pass**, **merit** or **distinction** grade and where you can find activities in this book to help you.

To achieve a **pass** grade the evidence must show that you are able to:	To achieve a **merit** grade the evidence must show that, in addition to the pass criteria, you are able to:	To achieve a **distinction** grade the evidence must show that, in addition to the pass and merit criteria, you are able to:
P1 describe the roles, duties and responsibilities for different categories of holiday representative, highlighting changing roles and working practices	**M1** compare the roles, duties and responsibilities for one category of representative with two different tour operators **See assessment activity 15.1, page 80**	**D1** analyse how the current and changing roles, duties and responsibilities of holiday representatives can contribute to the overall holiday experience **See assessment activity 15.1, page 80**
P2 outline the legal responsibilities of holiday representatives in different holiday situations		
P3 explain the role played by holiday representatives in creating a safe and healthy holiday environment **See assessment activity 15.1, page 80**		
P4 use social, customer service and selling skills to deliver an arrival transfer speech and a welcome meeting and make a sale **See assessment activity 15.2, page 90**	**M2** demonstrate effective social, customer service and selling skills when delivering a transfer speech and welcome meeting, and making a sale **See assessment activity 15.2, page 90**	**D2** consistently project a confident, professional image when carrying out resort activities and dealing with customers in different situations **See assessment activity 15.2, page 90**
P5 use social and customer service skills to deal with customers in different situations, completing appropriate documentation **See assessment activity 15.2, page 90**	**M3** deal effectively with customers in different situations and accurately complete all relevant documentation **See assessment activity 15.2, page 90**	

How you will be assessed

This unit will be assessed by one or more internal assignments that will be designed and marked by your tutor. Your assignments will be subject to sampling internally and externally as part of Edexcel's quality assurance procedures. The assignments are designed to allow you to show your knowledge and understanding related to the unit. The unit outcomes indicate what you should know, understand or be able to do after completing the unit.

Shazia, 18-year-old BTEC National learner

My sister was a holiday rep for two weeks last summer. Yes, only two weeks and then she came home. She was really homesick – I think she is too shy and quiet to be a holiday rep. I was disappointed because I was planning to visit her in my holidays.

When she told me about it I knew I would like it. She lived by herself but in a hotel where she had a room. All her meals were provided in the hotel restaurant. She could use all the facilities but she said she didn't have time as she was always working. She did get one day off a week and she spent it on the beach with some of the other reps.

Well, she hasn't put me off. I know it's hard work but I am going to do it. I love this unit. We are having a lot of fun practising welcome meetings and handling complaints. I spent a lot of time looking at the types of jobs available and I know which ones I am going to apply for. Some of my friends are doing a ski season but I want to go somewhere warm.

When I was doing my assignment I found a lot of information on the internet but I also borrowed all the training documents from my sister's job. I am good at ICT and I like design so I liked designing the forms that we used. The best part of the assignment was the role-plays.

Over to you!

1   What kind of person makes a good holiday rep? Think about the qualities needed.

2   As you see, the job of a holiday rep is not for everyone. You have to be away from home, work long hours and like dealing with people. You might live with the holidaymakers so it is hard to be off duty. Do you think you could do it?

3   Find out more in the WorkSpace at the end of this unit.

1 Roles, duties and responsibilities of different categories of holiday representative

Set off

Many young people take jobs as holiday representatives as it is an exciting way of learning about different places while working in a holiday environment. It is an opportunity to develop customer service skills that can be useful in any future job. Many people see it as a temporary career but in fact there are lots of opportunities in travel and tourism for progression for representatives. Remember that holiday representatives are employed by tour operators so there are opportunities to apply for other tour operation jobs. Some people like being in resort so much that they look for a career there, becoming resort managers with substantial responsibility.

Have a discussion about the types of job that working as a holiday representative might lead to. Think about the career structure in resort and in a head office.

1.1 Categories

There are many different types of holiday representative. The most common example is the overseas resort representative, in uniform and working for one of the large tour operators.

There are many others. Camping and holiday home operators employ a lot of seasonal representatives who spend their summers under canvas. Some overseas representatives look after customers from several tour operators at once and are employed by local companies and, of course, there are holiday representatives working in holiday parks and hotels in the UK looking after domestic and inbound tourists. Some representatives have specific responsibilities, for example, looking after children.

In this first section of the unit we will find out about the roles and responsibilities of the different types of representative and consider where they might be located. Their responsibilities are not just to the customers, but to the organisations they work for and the suppliers, such as the hotels, they work with.

Resort representatives

The most common of these is a property representative. A property representative is responsible for customers in a number of different hotels, apartments or villas in a resort. Their role typifies that of a holiday representative and is the

role that most people employed by the major tour operators have. Property representatives live in the resort, usually in separate accommodation from the guests but with other representatives.

Roles, responsibilities and duties

Representatives have the following general responsibilities:

- Represent the tour operator – the representative may be the only person from the tour-operating company that the holidaymaker meets. Therefore, the impression presented by the representative is of vital importance. A poor representative can lose many customers and do great harm to the company's image.

- Give customer service – the representative is there to make sure that the customer has an enjoyable holiday and any problems are swiftly solved.

- Maximise profitability by selling excursions and car hire – in this role the representative also has a responsibility to suppliers.

The duties of a representative include:

- conducting welcome meetings for new arrivals

- preparing an information file about the resort for guests' use

- keeping the notice board in the hotel or apartment block updated

- visiting properties every day to answer guests' queries
- selling and booking excursions
- handling payments
- keeping paperwork up to date
- booking hire cars etc. for guests
- guiding tours
- doing airport transfers according to a rota
- participating in entertainment for guests
- checking properties for health and safety
- liaising with hotel management
- dealing with problems and emergencies.

The representative will receive training on their role, responsibilities and duties and be given a uniform. They are also provided with accommodation and a basic salary. Commission is earned on excursions sold.

You can see that there is a lot to the job and, of course, the representative has to be on call in case of emergency, although when there are several representatives in a resort they have a rota for this. Problems may range from overbookings to serious illness or even death. You will have an opportunity later in this unit to consider some of the problems that you might face as a representative and see how you would deal with them.

Think about it

Take a look at www.firstchoice4jobs.co.uk and make some brief notes on the types of representative jobs available.

The duties of the representative vary according to the type of property and holiday brand the representative is working with. We are going to look now at some of the variations on the property representative role.

Holidays for 18–30s

Representative work for companies such as 18–30s, 2wentys and Escapades is often very appealing to young people, as there is a great deal of partying! These representatives have to party almost every night – even when they don't feel like it.

In addition to the usual duties of a representative, they are expected to take their guests out and to arrange games and drinking competitions so that the guests go home having had a wonderful time.

Representatives need to have lots of energy and stamina, as there isn't much time for sleep, and they need to be able to keep sober and sensible when all around are not. They must have initiative because with the kind of nightlife that is going on there may be problems of sickness, injury or theft to sort out.

These positions are seasonal and the representatives can expect to be employed from May to September or October. There is a lot more demand for 18–30-type holidays in the peak summer season so there are more jobs for representatives in that period which means this job can fit in with studying. These representatives work in major summer holiday resorts all over western Europe.

Would you like to work as a holiday representative for 18–30s?

Over-50s representatives

Most tour operators have brands that are aimed at older or more discerning customers. You can imagine that these customers are expecting a different kind of holiday from the 18–30s customer and so a different personality of representative is needed. Tour operators look for representatives with more maturity, good communication skills and a second language, as shown in the extract below from a tour operator's website.

Halo Holiday Executives

Halo Holidays is celebrated for delivering world-class customer service. Their excellent reps give vital information on the local area, advise on excursions and take great care of their customers.

To work for us you should be at least 21 years old, with a mature outlook. It would be ideal if you can speak French or Spanish and you must have superb interpersonal skills. We will provide a car so you need a current, clean driving licence.

Some tour operators deliberately target more mature people in their recruitment as they think their older clients will be more comfortable with a more mature representative. They do have to abide by laws on age discrimination, of course. Note how Halo gives these representatives a special title to give them enhanced status.

Holiday village

Some companies own and run hotel complexes called holiday villages. They are designed so that holidaymakers never have to leave the village; everything is provided for them including lots of activities for children. If you are working as a representative in a holiday village you will have the same responsibilities as any other property representative but you will always be situated in the holiday village.

Villa holiday representative

Working for a villa holiday company means that the representative will usually be provided with transport as the villas are likely to be located over a large area. A variation to the normal duties is that the representative must ensure that the holidaymakers arrive at their

villa. The holidaymakers may arrive at an office first and then be guided to their villa from there by the representative. The representative will be available daily in a central location in case customers need their services and will, like other representatives, be contactable by phone.

Do you think there would be any disadvantages to working in a holiday village?

Ski-resort representatives

Ski resorts offer lots of seasonal jobs and if you work successfully as a ski-resort representative you should not have any problem getting a transfer to warmer climes in the summer. Tour operators prefer to retain and use trained and proven staff. Ski-resort representatives do the same job as other property representatives. They are allocated a number of hotels or chalets and visit their guests, solve problems and sell excursions in the same way. They are likely to be keen skiers or snowboarders as that is all there is to do in their free time.

Activity: Chalet host

The following extract outlines a typical day in the life of a chalet host.

Daily
7.30 Arrive in chalet.
8.30 Serve a full cooked breakfast with choice of bacon, eggs and sausage.

Prepare evening dinner as far as possible.

Bake cake for afternoon tea.

9.30 Clean all main rooms (not bedrooms).Pay particular attention to bathrooms.

Order any provisions needed.

Set up afternoon tea.

Approx 10.15/10.30 Finish.
Free for skiing or boarding.

17.00/17.30 Return to chalet.
Do any further cleaning and clearing away from the morning and afternoon tea.

Prepare table for dinner.

Finish preparing dinner.

19.30 Serve dinner.

Approx 21.00/21.30 Finish.

Produce a flyer for recruitment purposes that describes in detail the role and responsibilities of the chalet host job illustrated above. Don't forget that the chalet host has extra duties on departure days. Present the information in a way which is appealing for potential applicants.

In addition to the property representative you will find chalet hosts and assistants in the ski resort. A chalet for 12 people will typically be run by two chalet hosts. They are expected to clean daily, order food and cook for the guests. If they become very efficient they can get their morning breakfast and cleaning routine finished by late morning. Then they are free until it is time to cook the dinner at about 5p.m. This gives a good few hours skiing a day and is definitely the perk of the job. The chalet hosts are expected to give excellent customer service but don't book excursions or do airport duty. They can call on the property representative if they have any problems.

Transfer representatives

Role

Transfer representatives meet and greet holidaymakers at the airport and take them by coach to their hotel. If passengers are travelling by taxi, or hire car, they are welcomed and sent on their way.

The job of the transfer representative is possibly the least appealing of the representative jobs as the hours are long and there is little variation in the work. You might be interested in this work if you really like a challenge, because transfer representatives face all the problems caused by delayed aircraft, including having to deal with angry customers. Property representatives often take turns to do airport duty to share the load.

Duties

The duties of a transfer representative include:

- meeting and greeting guests arriving at the airport
- checking arrivals against the manifest (list of passengers)
- directing guests to coaches or taxis
- accompanying guests on the coach
- giving a welcome speech and a commentary
- checking guests into their hotel
- collecting guests from their hotel at the end of their stay
- accompanying guests to the airport
- directing guests to check-in
- staying at check-in until all guests are checked in.

Some ski operators such as Crystal and Thomson offer a more unusual form of transfer representative job. This is the job of ski-train representative. The job involves working weekends and accompanying customers on the ski-train from the UK to France. The representatives have to welcome customers as they check in for the train and show them to their seats or beds. If necessary, they issue tickets and deal with any paperwork. They sort out any problems and maintain a high level of customer service. They also have to speak French.

Children's representatives

A children's representative usually needs to hold a Level 3 qualification in Childcare and a First Aid certificate and have some experience of working with children. A Criminal Records Bureau (CRB) check will be required, as it is whenever someone works with children.

Duties involve looking after groups of children for several hours a day and organising activities for them. There is usually different provision made for different age groups. The screenshot from Canvas Holidays' website (Figure 15.1) shows that they have four different levels of free club activity, a good selling point for families. At Canvas the children's couriers are expected to help with other duties if needed. Canvas do not ask for a specific childcare qualification, but do require formal experience of working with children.

Figure 15.1: Good provision for families

(*Source: www.canvasholidays.co.uk/Canvas-for-Families.aspx*)

Activity: Canvas Holidays

The following extract has been taken from Canvas Holidays' children's courier job description.

Job title: Children's Courier

Reports to: Area Manager, Site Manager, Site Supervisor, Senior Courier

Liaises with: Camp Proprietors, Operations Department, Warehouse Personnel

General function: To ensure that every aspect of our customers' holidays is of as high a standard as possible by participating in montage and demontage and, in the role of Children's Courier, by being fully committed to providing excellent Customer Service through the regular organisation and supervision of safe and fun children's activities on site.

This will be measured through feedback from Customer Questionnaires and Area Managers.

Duties and responsibilities

- Participate in montage and demontage as and when required, ensuring compliance with Health and Safety guidelines and in accordance with laid down procedures and standards.

- Assist the Campsite Courier, as per duties and responsibilities laid out in Campsite Courier job description as and when required.

- Organise and supervise a regular programme of events for children, aged 4–11 years, 5 hours per day, 6 days per week, ensuring that the programme is advertised in a way that Canvas customers are kept aware of the programme of events and timings.

- Ensure the safety of all children whilst attending Hoopi Club.

- Encourage participation of all Canvas Holidays' customers' children, regardless of nationality, to be achieved by the use of all available resources such as noticeboards, flyers, Welcome Sheets and daily customer visits.

- Maintain staff accommodation unit and the unit/equipment supplied specifically for the children's Hoopi Club, ensuring hygienic and safe living and play conditions for themselves and their clients.

(*Source: www.canvasholidays.co.uk*)

Produce a flyer for Canvas Holidays for recruitment purposes, describing in detail the roles and responsibilities of children's couriers. Present the information in a way that is appealing to potential applicants. Analyse the contribution that the children's representative can make to the customer's overall holiday experience. Present this as an information sheet to give to Canvas's recruitment manager.

Campsite representative

These representatives are often students who want to work abroad for the summer and are also known as campsite couriers. Besides all the usual tasks described above, couriers are responsible for cleaning the tents and holiday homes in between clients. This can be quite a task – depending on how customers leave their accommodation. The couriers are provided with tents in a staff area of the campsite. The downside of this kind of work is that the guests know where you live and will find you!

1.2 Changing working practices

In-resort customer service centres

These are special centres that some operators set up to provide a central point for customer service, e.g. through the service centre you can register complaints or book excursions.

The resort team will be responsible for:

- managing sales, operations and customer service
- providing an office that customers can visit and where they can buy excursions or ask for advice
- delivering excellent customer service.

Pre-holiday excursion sales

Holiday brochures usually contain details of excursions. Tour operators and travel agents prefer to sell these excursions before their customers leave the UK for their holiday. This has advantages for the company:

- sales agents get commission on the sales
- staff in the resorts are better able to plan transport and staffing for excursions if they know in advance how many people are likely to attend a tour.

Duty representatives in the UK

Large tour operators have a fully staffed (24/7, 365 days a year), always available Duty Office so that someone is always on call in the UK in case an incident occurs in a resort. A rota will be planned so that a senior person can also always be contacted. This is a measure of how important it is to be prepared for any incident or crisis. A senior manager can guide resort staff on their actions, making sure they comply with legal requirements and can also manage any media response needed following an incident.

Did you know?

If you want to find out about holiday representative jobs there are careers sections and links to jobs on all the major tour operators' websites. Just search for the name of the tour operator that interests you.

2 The legal responsibilities of a holiday representative

2.1 Legal responsibilities and situations

Early in 2004, holiday firms were told by the **Office of Fair Trading (OFT)** to offer consumers a fairer deal. New guidance was issued on unfair terms in package holiday contracts.

Key term

Office of Fair Trading (OFT) – the government office set up to oversee trading practices of organisations and individuals in the UK.

Denying liability after a short period of time (i.e, the holidaymaker has to be allowed time to make their complaint) or unfairly limiting compensation when a holiday goes wrong are among the acts deemed unfair. The guidance came about because numerous tour operators were found to have contravened the Unfair Terms in Consumer Contracts Regulations 1999 and the EU Package Travel Regulations 1992.

Working within the legal framework

EU Package Travel Regulations 1992

As far as the holiday representative is concerned, their most important legal responsibilities are covered by the EU Package Travel Regulations.

Regulation 15 covers unsatisfactory holiday arrangements

Regulation 15 imposes a strict fault-based liability on the tour operator for the proper performance of the obligations under the contract by their third-party suppliers.

This means that the tour operator is responsible for anything that goes wrong in the hotel or other accommodation and during transfer and has to compensate the customer for any faults. These faults can occur at any point in the holiday, including at the airport or on an excursion. The holiday representative has responsibility for carrying out health and safety checks in properties and reporting any faults.

Regulation 14 covers alternative accommodation arrangements

Regulation 14 states that if after departure a significant proportion of services contracted for is not provided, the organiser will make suitable alternative arrangements, at no extra cost to the consumer, for the continuation of the package and will, where appropriate, compensate the consumer.

For the holiday representative this means that in the case of overbooking or accommodation being unavailable, they must offer the customer alternative accommodation of at least the same standard.

There are requirements under the EU Package Travel Regulations for the customer also. If a customer has a complaint they should report it in resort so that the representative has an opportunity to resolve it. If they need to write to the tour operator to complain, this should be done within a reasonable period (usually 28 days).

Supply of Goods and Services Act 1982

The Supply of Goods and Services Act 1982 (amended 1994) says that the tour operator must ensure that the contract for the holiday is carried out using 'reasonable skill and care'. Also, the holiday should comply with any descriptions and be of a satisfactory standard. Some holidaymakers take their holiday brochure with them. This means they can easily check whether the holiday has been described accurately. The operator may also have committed a criminal offence under the Trade Descriptions Act of 1968 if there is a misdescription.

Health and Safety at Work Act 1974

Safety and security factors must be considered in resort and legislation such as the Health and Safety at Work Act 1974 must be adhered to. Specific regulations also apply where food is served or where there are chemical hazards, for example in a swimming pool. All these requirements are important.

Trade Descriptions Act 1968 and 1972

The purpose of this Act is to control the accuracy of statements made by a business about its goods and services. It is an offence to apply a false trade description to goods, or to supply goods to which a false trade description is applied. The Act also applies to services like holidays, but its contravention here is difficult to prove as the false statement must have been made 'knowingly' or 'recklessly'.

Disability Discrimination Act 1995

The Disability Discrimination Act makes discrimination against people with disabilities unlawful in respect of employment, education and access to goods, facilities, services and premises. Disability can be described as a problem that occurs when a person's ability and the environment do not match. It can be a long-term, permanent impairment of mobility, vision, understanding, hearing or mental capacity that may not be compensated for by the environment in which an individual lives or works.

Contractual responsibilities

Each representative is issued with a contract that lays down their responsibilities and the terms and conditions of employment. These will include place of work, hours of work, holiday entitlement and notice periods to be served.

Booking conditions

Booking conditions are laid out in the brochure or provided to the customer before departure. They are based on the requirements of the EU Package Travel Regulations but written in plain English so that they are easily understood.

The booking conditions are fairly lengthy and will run to two or more pages. The extracts below, from the Thomson Summer Collection brochure, illustrate the refund and compensation arrangements if booked accommodation is unavailable.

The representative would ensure that conditions specified by the tour operator were met and set in motion the paperwork to arrange compensation.

The second extract illustrates how Thomson accepts its liability for the facilities and services of its suppliers being below acceptable local standards. Again this relates to its responsibility under the EU Package Travel Regulations.

Major changes to your holiday

Occasionally we have to make major changes to the flight or accommodation making up your holiday with us. If we tell you about any of these changes after we have confirmed your holiday booking you may either:

– accept the new arrangements offered by us; or

– accept a replacement holiday from us of equivalent or similar standard and price if one is available; or

– cancel your holiday with us and receive a full refund of all monies paid.

Either way we will pay you compensation … unless the change is for reasons beyond our control … and we will always refund the difference in price if the replacement holiday is of a lower standard and price.

(Source: Thomson Summer Collection brochure May 2010–October 2010)

Our responsibility for your holiday

We will arrange for you to receive the services that make up the holiday that you choose and that we confirm. These services will be provided either directly by us or through independent suppliers contracted by us. Except where we are a Booking Agent we are responsible for making sure that each part of the holiday you book with us is provided to a reasonable standard and as was advertised by us (or as changed and accepted by you). If any part of your holiday is not provided as described and this spoils your holiday, we will pay you appropriate compensation.

We have taken all reasonable care to make sure that all the services which make up the holidays advertised by us are provided by efficient and reputable businesses. These businesses should follow the local and national laws and regulations of the country where they are provided. However, overseas safety standards are generally lower than in the UK, for example few hotels yet meet EC fire safety recommendations even in Europe.

(Source: Thomson Summer Collection brochure May 2010–October 2010)

Documentation

Holiday representatives have to deal with quite a lot of paperwork to make sure they help the tour operator comply with the legal requirements. In addition to paperwork for excursions and sales, they have to complete reports and accounts. During their training, the representatives are shown how to complete all the forms, including those for sales of excursions and expenditure and standards are set for completing paperwork. These standards include:

- recording dates in full
- using a 24-hour clock for times
- writing names in full
- giving full resort details
- only reporting facts and not opinions
- meeting deadlines for completion.

Reporting and recording

The holiday representative will also have to complete forms if there are customer complaints and if any compensation is given. Customers and representatives will both sign these forms. An example of a customer complaint form is given later in this unit. Accident reports are another type of documentation that the representative is responsible for.

Liaising with the resort office and the UK

Resort representatives are usually part of a team managed by the resort office. They are able to contact their line managers at this office should any situation arise where they need help. If a problem cannot be resolved in resort then the customer service department in the UK will be notified and take over on receipt of full reports. The resort representative will also liaise every day with both the resort office and the UK office to keep up to date on passenger manifests and arrivals. In addition, as already discussed, there is always someone contactable in the UK duty office in case of emergency.

3 The role of the holiday representative in creating a safe and healthy holiday environment

3.1 Health and safety risks and hazards

Identification of health and safety risks and hazards

A direct responsibility is placed on tour operators for the safety of their customers under the EU Package Travel Regulations. Tour operators are legally responsible for the components of the package (transfers, hotels etc.) if negligence is proved. As the holiday representatives are in the resort, they are in a position to carry out regular health and safety checks on behalf of the tour operator. Before a property is contracted, the tour operator will carry out a full health and safety survey and make recommendations to the hotel management about any changes to be made. The tour operator must ensure that suppliers make adequate health and safety provision as the tour operator, not the supplier, is liable if something is wrong. This means it is of vital importance that any incidents are fully logged by the representative at the time. They should collect full details and photographs, diagrams and statements.

The following are some of the things the representatives might check.

Accommodation – including hotels, mobile homes, apartments and tents

- Quality standards should be met.
- Gas and electricity should be provided safely.
- Hygiene standards will be checked.

Facilities

- Swimming pools should have notices with depths marked.
- Children's playgrounds and clubs must be carefully checked as the potential for accidents when using equipment is great.
- Balconies can present a hazard particularly for small children. There have been occasions when holidaymakers have fallen over balconies. The representative should warn parents about low balconies and advise that children should not be left alone on balconies.
- Lifts must be checked by representatives to ensure that they are in full working order.

What other kinds of safety notice might you find on holiday?

Fire safety

- Fire exits must not be blocked.
- Notices must be displayed to aid exit.
- Particular restrictions are needed for tents, for example on candles and barbecues.

Resort safety

The representative must additionally check that health and safety standards are adhered to not just in the resort itself, but also on coaches and other transport, and on excursions. Representatives will also advise on crime (e.g. muggings) and how to stay safe, as well as sea currents or other possible issues.

3.2 Minimising risks

Providing information

Information about minimising risks is given to customers in brochures and leaflets before they go on holiday. This could include information on health and safety issues such as safe sunbathing, use of pools or even crime.

This is repeated during airport transfers and in resort on notice boards and in information books. The representative attempts to reach those who choose not to read about these issues by raising them again at the welcome meeting.

Did you know?

A national newspaper carried out a poll finding out about sunburn. As many as 1 in 10 Britons admitted to having to visit a doctor with sunburn. People coming back from Tenerife had the highest incidence of sunburn with 11 per cent of those polled saying they had been burnt.

(Source: Daily Mail)

Routine procedures

Representatives carry out regular health and safety checks and complete reports on their findings. In addition, they complete reports on any accidents and incidents and return them to head office.

Health and safety check forms are issued and if defects are found these must be reported. An example of a defect form is given in Figure 15.2.

Holiday representatives will sometimes have to carry out risk assessments. For example a children's representative often takes children on outings and they must make sure that the new environment is safe. Figure 15.3 on the next page shows an example of a form that can be used for wildlife activities.

Health and Safety Defect Report

Property _____ Company _____ Area _____

List other participating companies: _____ Date _____

The summary below should be completed at properties where any health and safety issues have been highlighted on the health and safety audit.

DEFECT DESCRIPTION	REPORTED TO	DATE	ACTION TO BE TAKEN	TARGET DATE	ACTION TAKEN	DATE
Management Effectiveness						

I confirm that a representative of Fabulous Holidays has reported the defects, detailed above, to me.

COMPLETED BY _____ SIGNED _____

Figure 15.2: Health and safety defect report

Activity: Risk assessment

Imagine you are taking a group of children on an outing in your locality. Design a form similar to the example in Figure 15.3 and carry out a risk assessment on the area to be visited. Discuss your findings with your group.

WILDLIFE ACTIVITY RISK ASSESSMENT

Activity name	Activity on/off site (delete as applicable)
Assessed by	Distance of walk
Date of Assessment	Recommended age group

For off-site walks please write a description of the intended route:

Please note:
- ✓ All supervised walks must use public and not private land/footpaths
- ✓ Children must be accompanied by parent/guardian on all off-site activities
- ✓ Activities just for children are always based on the property
- ✓ Before taking a group off site inform your fellow couriers of your route

Don't forget:
- ✓ Phone numbers of nearest emergency services
- ✓ Office phone number
- ✓ Your consent forms

For the activity you intend to carry out please consider and identify any hazards and what safety measures you will take. Prior to the activity check out the route/venue. Using the form, mark the hazards you see. Write down wether the risk is LOW, MEDIUM or HIGH and note what safety measures you will take. Fill in any additional hazards. Remember, these may relate to the environment, people, nature of activity and any tools or equipment you plan to use.

HAZARD Here are some hazards you may find/look for others	RISK Low, medium or high	SAFETY MEASURE What can I do to reduce the risk?
Mud and debris		
Uneven/holes in ground		
Steep slopes		
Fallen trees		
Litter		
Stinging/prickly plants		
Poisonous plants or fungi		
Water		
Wild animals		
Stinging/biting insects		
Adverse weather		
Possible diseases		
Medical conditions		
Clothing of participants		

Other risks:

Figure 15.3: Wildlife activity risk assessment

Reporting incidents

An incident is something that happens that is not presenting immediate danger but should still be dealt with. All incidents are logged by the representative and transferred on to a form which is handed into head office, usually monthly. The most important role of the representative in reporting an incident is to gather information and pass it on to the right people. It is also important for the representative to stay calm and in control of the situation as customers look to the representative for help. An emergency requires immediate assistance and must be dealt with straight away. In the case of serious illness or death the representative would call in a manager. However, the representative would have to liaise with the resort office and deal with family and friends. Medical report forms would be completed and sent to the resort office.

Accident reports

If an accident occurs the representative will fill in an accident report. Figure 15.4 provides an example. Note that it includes guidelines for completion.

Why is it important to report all incidents?

Activity: Dealing with legalities

Explain the legal responsibilities of representatives in each of the following situations. For each one, explain how you, as the representative, would deal with the situation.

1 You are a transfer representative. One of your customers is a wheelchair user. They have arrived safely at the arrival airport but they are upset because of an incident at the departure airport in the UK where they were told no one was available to help them board. Eventually a fellow passenger was able to help them. The airline is one of your sister companies.

2 A couple arrive in the hotel where you are the representative. They had booked a suite but one is not available and they have been allocated a standard room.

3 You carry out a routine safety check in the hotel where you are the representative and notice that a fire door is locked.

4 A family on holiday complain. They point out that the hotel, where you are the representative, is advertised in the holiday brochure as four-star. However, a sign on the front of the hotel and all its literature show that it is a three-star hotel.

Activity: Reporting an accident

It is very important to have records of accidents as there may be insurance claims later. Design your own form, or copy the one in Figure 15.3, and fill in a report for the following accident.

You are a representative in Fuengirola in Spain. You happen to be visiting a hotel when an accident occurs and you are called to the scene. A child has slipped while running near the pool and fallen into the water. The child was rescued from the water by Jo, the lifeguard, and seemed to have a slight concussion and a broken leg. The lifeguards called the ambulance and the child went to hospital escorted by her parents.

FABULOUS Holidays

REPORT OF AN ACCIDENT OR DANGEROUS OCCURRENCE

Notes on how to use this form are included at the end of this form

A. Person making the report   Property _____

Name _____

Your role on the property _____

B. Date, time and place at which the accident took place. It is important that you be as precise as possible in completing this section.

Date of accident _____ Time _____

Address where the accident took place: _____

Specific location where the accident took place: _____

Was a photograph of the location taken? **YES/NO**_____

Normal activity carried out at this place: _____

Why was the injured person there at the time? _____

C. The injured person

Name _____ Ref. No. _____ Pitch No. _____

Address _____

Nature of injury and condition and part of the body affected: _____

D. Witnesses

Name _____ Name _____

Address _____ Address _____

E. Describe the event and how it happened. Please refer to the note. Draw a sketch if appropriate.

_____

_____

_____

_____

_____

_____

NOTES ON HOW TO COMPLETE THIS FORM

1. Please be as clear and precise as possible when completing this form.
2. In section E, you are asked to state only the facts relating to the incident, not opinions as to who is at fault. Details you must include are: what happened; information relating to any police involvement in the matter; and action taken by yourself or any other person involved in this matter. You should also include a sketch of what happened, in the space provided in this form.
3. Fax one copy **immediately** to the Operations Department and one copy to your Area Manager.

Figure 15.4: Report of an accident or dangerous occurrence

Federation of Tour Operators and ABTA – The Travel Association guidelines

The Federation of Tour Operators (FTO) devised a code of practice which gives advice on health and safety matters including:

- fire safety
- food safety
- pool safety
- general safety
- beach safety
- Legionella management (Legionella is a bacterium that causes a form of pneumonia called Legionnaire's Disease)
- children's clubs
- incident management.

ABTA and the FTO merged in 2008 so the advice offered is now available from ABTA – The Travel Association. A resort checklist is available on their website. A new code of practice providing guidelines for the safe provision of land transport arrangements is available. Also, ABTA – The Travel Association has a leaflet aimed at holidaymakers entitled *How to have a safe and healthy holiday*. Visit www.fto.co.uk/health-and-safety/preferred-code-of-practice to find out more.

Activity: Ensuring health and safety

You are responsible for the well-being of guests with your company in five hotels near to Palma. Individually, produce a list of four health and safety issues that a representative might come across in the course of a day. Pass your list to colleagues. Discuss the issues together.

Think about how you would deal with each issue and what knowledge you would need to have in order to deal with it. Produce a fact sheet, as a group, which covers the health and safety issues raised and the actions that a representative could take to ensure health and safety.

Why is health and safety so important?

Assessment activity 15.1

P1 P2 P3 M1 D1 · BTEC

Task 1

> **No more reps?**
>
> Reps everywhere are wondering how safe their jobs are as tour operators search for more cost-cutting measures. Is the service of a rep really essential? Aren't customers confident enough to look after themselves on holiday? After all many of them are managing to book holidays over the internet without using a travel agent. Can't they book their own excursions and hire cars as well?
>
> At the moment it's just accommodation-on-arrival deals that seem to be targeted, with many tour operators suggesting they might do away with reps on these deals. But where will it end? Surely some customers choose well-known tour operators just because they offer excellent service through their reps. What about the legal aspects of the rep's job? Who is going to check health and safety in the resort? Some tour operators are arguing that late bookers tend to be less well off and have lower expectations than other customers – so they don't need reps – or they don't pay for them.
>
> *(Source: Travel News, 21 September 2007)*

You work as a holiday representative for a tour operator and your boss is horrified at the tone of the article. She has been asked to respond at a forthcoming travel market, a trade exhibition where she will be giving a presentation to members of the trade, including tour operators. She needs to present the case for holiday representative services and you are to help her by preparing her notes. The notes can be in the form of cue cards with supporting notes or in the form of information sheets from which she can then form cue cards.

You are to cover:

- a detailed description of the role, duties and responsibilities of a property representative, a children's representative and a ski representative. **P1**

Task 2

Outline the representative's legal responsibilities in the following situations. **P2**

1. A hotel is overbooked and alternative accommodation is needed for a family of four.

2. A flight is cancelled and the passengers have to wait 12 hours for another flight (the airline is part of your operation).

3. A guest points out that the beach is much further away than described in the brochure and demands a daily taxi from the company.

4. The tour guide booked for an excursion fails to arrive.

5. A safety rail is missing from the balcony of a second-floor apartment.

Explain the role played by holiday representatives in creating a safe and healthy holiday environment. Identify risks and hazards in the holiday environment and show how representatives can minimise risks. **P3**

Task 3

Compare the roles, duties and responsibilities for one category of representative, for example property representative, with two different tour operators. **M1**

Task 4

You need to put forward a case for retaining holiday representatives. Analyse how their current and changing roles, duties and responsibilities can contribute to the overall holiday experience. **D1**

Make sure that you cover the full range, referring to the content and assessment guidance in the unit specification for the detail required.

Grading tips

P1 Don't reproduce job descriptions from tour operators. Write everything in your own words.

P1 Don't forget to mention changes that have taken place in the working practice of representatives.

M1 Explain the similarities and differences in the roles with the two tour operators.

P2 For each scenario, explain what the responsibility is, what action should be taken and complete any necessary documents.

P3 Make sure you include safety in the accommodation, especially fire safety and hygiene, on transfer coaches, in excursions and organised activities, and in the resort.

D1 You need to think about how the role of a holiday representative has changed and how it is important to customers in terms of safety and information.

4 Social, customer service and selling skills for dealing with transfers, welcome meetings and other situations

4.1 Social skills

Here are some general rules to help you develop your social skills:

- Don't worry about what people think about you.
- Concentrate on making others feel comfortable.
- Smile at people.
- Ask people their names and remember them.
- Listen positively to others.
- Use appropriate language and adapt your approach according to the type of customer.
- Ask people questions about themselves.

Creating rapport and providing a welcome

All customers should be properly greeted. A smile and a handshake will give a warm impression. Representatives can ask questions to make their customers feel comfortable, for example 'Have you settled in?', 'Have you been here before?'. Customers can be asked what they are looking forward to on their holiday. These types of question demonstrate an interest in the customer.

Empathising

This is done by trying to put yourself in the customer's place and understanding how they feel.

Providing a helpful and friendly service

This is achieved by taking time to listen to the customer's needs and finding positive solutions while maintaining a calm and friendly manner.

Choice of language

More formal language should be used with customers. Don't call them by first names unless invited to do so. Don't use slang and never swear.

Informal and formal communications

Your style of communication will vary according to the situation. For example, when addressing a large group of customers in a welcome meeting or when dealing with a complaint, a representative should adopt a formal style. A less formal, more friendly style might be adopted when chatting with customers or meeting them out and about. Remember that you are still representing your company and must not be too informal.

Responding appropriately to different customers

Representatives should be aware of the appropriate manner to adopt with different customers. With older people, it is likely that more formal communication is required. For example, customers on an 18–30 holiday will accept a less formal approach than prestige customers. Children may be spoken to in a less formal way too.

4.2 Customer service skills

Identifying and meeting customer needs and dealing with queries

When you deal with queries you might be asked for non-routine information that you have to go and find out about or you may be given a request for something out of the ordinary.

Product knowledge and providing information

A representative routinely supplies knowledge by preparing an information file and a welcome meeting.

You have explored these skills in detail in Student Book 1, Unit 4. Now you can practise them with the following role-play.

Activity: Customer service in practice

You have just conducted a welcome meeting at Albufeira in the Algarve. Among the guests are the Jenkins, a couple who have arrived for a five-week winter holiday. This is their first trip abroad and they are very unsure about what to do and where to go. They ask you several questions.

- The couple want to hire a car but neither has brought their driving licence. Suggest other forms of transport.

- Mr Jenkins has some escudos that his daughter gave him. Explain that he cannot spend them and that euros are now needed in Portugal. Tell him how to get some.

- The couple have booked a half-board package. Explain what this means and where they can eat.

- The Jenkins are Roman Catholic and want to go to mass on Sunday. They have no idea where the Catholic church is. Explain that you will find out and let them know.

Find out also if there is anything else the Jenkins need.

You should divide into groups of four for this activity. Two students play Mr and Mrs Jenkins, one plays the representative and the other observes and evaluates the performance of the representative. You can change roles to repeat the role-play.

Activity: Dealing with situations

1 You are a holiday representative in Florida. A guest has a terrible accident, falling off the top of the water slide by the pool. They need to go straight to hospital. Explain what you would do, remembering to deal with insurance and documentation, as well as the customer.

2 A guest has been robbed. They left their bags on the beach while they were swimming and when they returned the bags were gone. What would you do for them? What information would they need?

3 A customer in Paris wants to go home early. They do not have a specific complaint – they just want to go home and will pay for a new flight. You are their representative. How will you help them?

Deal with these situations and complete any necessary documentation.

Handling complaints

Complaints are very challenging, but they provide an opportunity for representatives to find out how their service can be improved to ensure satisfied clients.

The process for handling complaints is as follows:

- Listen.
- Empathise – show you want to help and don't make excuses.
- Ask questions to get the facts.
- Agree a solution.
- Follow up.

Listening skills

When you are communicating with an individual you should make sure you are listening as well as talking. In order to listen properly you must be totally focused and maintain eye contact. Show that you are listening by using the **active listening** techniques you have learnt about. If you don't listen you will not understand what the customer needs.

Key term

Active listening – the process of demonstrating to another person both verbally and non-verbally that the information is being received. It is done by maintaining eye contact, nodding and agreeing in appropriate places.

Finding solutions

It is important that you look for realistic solutions which are within the power of the representative. You can ask the customer what they want and if you can't do it, tell them why. Always make sure that you do what you said you would.

Communicating with groups and individuals

Individuals the holiday representative deals with include holidaymakers, hotel employees, airport workers, drivers and tourist guides. They should be treated with courtesy and consideration at all times. Sometimes the representative will be communicating by telephone and should remember the individual might not speak English.

Image

Holiday representatives are the face of the company and the way they present themselves reflects the company image. The tour operator will provide a uniform for their representatives and this should be worn during working hours. It should be worn with appropriate accessories and should be clean and ironed. Even if the uniform is informal, for example shorts and a T-shirt, these guidelines still apply.

Image is not just about what is worn. It is also about grooming and bearing, and the attitude you have towards the customer. Being well groomed means always being clean and fresh smelling. This seems obvious but is more difficult to maintain in hot climates and in stressful situations. Nails should be clean and unbitten. If varnish is worn it should not be chipped. Hair should be neat and clean. Long hair should be tied back for work.

Bearing is about the way people hold themselves. It is about presenting positive body language and showing confidence (even when a situation is difficult). Holiday representatives have to learn to present a calm and controlled bearing even if things are going wrong.

The holiday representative should show respect for their customers, colleagues and their company and never speak in a denigrating way about any of them. It is also important that the holiday representative treats everyone equally regardless of their accent, race, religion, age or gender. The holiday representative can be a role model for young people on holiday who have ambitions to be a representative in the future.

Non-verbal communication

Using visual aids

Visual aids help to make a talk more interesting. They can make a point and help the representative remember what they have to say. They can be used in a welcome meeting and might include handouts, welcome packs, leaflets and videos.

Body language

It's not what you say, it's the way that you say it. Our body language gives a lot away. Holiday representatives have to assume that they are always on view. Even when they're on a day off at the beach there may be customers around so they have to think about the image that is being presented. On a property visit, even before they meet the customers, they should be walking tall and looking ready for business. In presentations on the coach, or at the welcome meeting, all eyes are on the representative so it is important to give the right signals. Remember the following body language points:

- head held high
- good posture
- no hands in pockets
- no fiddling with jewellery or hair
- make eye contact
- smile.

Think about it

Next time you are in class look around you and note the body language of the group. Can you tell what they are feeling? What about the tutor? What about you?

Are there any trips arranged for learners in your college or school? Why don't you ask if you can guide the trip? It's a great opportunity to practise communication skills and may provide you with some assessment evidence.

Communication skills using natural and amplified voice

If you are talking to a group of people you will need to use a microphone or project your voice. On a coach a representative would expect to use a microphone. At a welcome meeting it is likely that you would have to project your voice to be heard. Both need practice and a representative's training will include this. You should always begin by making sure everyone can hear you. It is important to speak clearly and consider the tone of voice, so that it is not a monotone, and also make sure that the pace is neither too slow nor too fast.

Children's representatives have to communicate with children and would not expect to use formal communication with them. They should be especially aware of the tone of their voice and ensure it is not too strident, which could be construed as anger and thus be frightening to small children. It is important to speak clearly and in plain English. A representative is likely to have children of different nationalities in their group. They might not understand English so the representative has to be quite innovative and imaginative to help them understand, using tone of voice and body language.

Written communication

Completing forms, writing reports and putting information together are all part of the holiday representative's job. One aspect of written communication with customers is the notice board.

FABULOUS Holidays

Departure details

Flight BL 2031

Please note for those people leaving on Monday 3rd February, the coach will be arriving at the hotel to pick you up at 9.20.

Please leave your cases at the reception desk ready for transfer by 9.00 that morning.

Figure 15.5: Example of a notice

Notice board

This is situated in a central location such as the reception area of the hotel or apartments. If a guest needs to find out how to contact the representative or remind themselves of the visiting times, they should find the information on the notice board. The representative can use the notice board to give details of excursions and to advertise special events. Guests will also use the notice board to check details of their return transfer and flight, even though these details should also be communicated individually to each customer.

The presentation of the information on the board gives an impression of the representative and the company. If it is poorly presented with spelling mistakes and scraps of paper then the company does not look professional.

The following are some points to remember when presenting a notice board:

- Word-process information.
- Use a clear font.
- Use colour.
- Use headings.
- Make sure spellings are correct – if you have any doubts, use a dictionary or check with someone reliable.
- Do the same with punctuation.
- Laminate posters and information sheets.
- Take down out-of-date information.

Activity: Notice board

You are a holiday representative working in San Antonio in Ibiza for the summer season. What kind of information would you expect to place on a notice board?

Information file

A file of local information is prepared by the holiday representative at the beginning of the season. It is time-consuming to produce but if it is done well it saves the representative work as the guests can find useful facts and information without having to contact their representative constantly. The file is kept in a reception area for easy reference.

A tour operator may have a set presentation style for the file and will probably state what information should be in it. The following are some general guidelines for contents:

- representative's details including contact numbers and visiting times
- any local regulations
- local transport
- beach distance and directions
- shopping information
- sunburn warnings
- medical contacts
- currency and exchange
- telephoning instructions
- excursion details
- health and safety information (lifts/pool/resort)

- brief history of the resort
- recommendations for restaurants
- departure details
- useful expressions in the local language.

A representative may not have to start from scratch to find this information. Previous representatives will have put together an information file. The internet can be used to find the local tourism website. Guidebooks and the local tourist office are also sources of information. Representatives should get to know the resort and investigate restaurants and local haunts. It is a good idea for a holiday representative to do research before they go to their resort so that they are well prepared.

The points made above about how to present information on a notice board also apply to information files.

Activity: Information file

As before, you are working as a holiday representative in San Antonio. Produce an information file suitable for guests aged 18–30 staying in the Hotel Florida. Make sure you include everything listed above. Limit the number of excursion details to four trips.

4.3 Selling skills and situations

Selling is difficult at first. The holiday representative has to sell the excursions in order to earn commission and fill up the tours. However, the guests do not want to sit all day listening to detailed talks about tours. A meeting which is too long is counterproductive and it should be limited to 30–45 minutes.

The best way to sell excursions is to present guests with a leaflet containing full details of the excursions, so that they can refer to it later. The representative should give a brief outline of the various excursions, in an enthusiastic and interested manner. They might point out those tours which sell out quickly and need to be booked early. This is a good closing technique. Having done this, the representative should allow

guests to leave the meeting and invite those who want to book excursions immediately or get more information to stay behind. At this point they might be able to use their **upselling** skills to persuade guests to go on more excursions. The representative must be able to work in the local currency and calculate exchanges as necessary. They must also complete the necessary paperwork for their sales.

Unit 4 covers selling skills in detail, but remind yourself of the different stages of a sale.

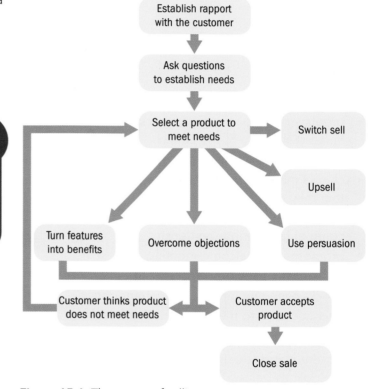

Figure 15.6: The stages of selling

Key term

Upselling – refers to selling a more expensive product or adding options to a product being sold. It is most likely to occur in the selling of excursions, perhaps by selling a full day rather than a half day, or by selling more than one excursion to a customer.

4.4 Transfers

Preparation

In preparing to organise transfers, the representative:

- ensures they have a copy of the departures and arrivals, as well as details of customers' accommodation
- checks the documentation and times of pick-ups at the hotel
- puts departure information on the notice board
- checks which transfers they are responsible for.

Arrivals

When holidaymakers arrive, the representative:

- goes to arrivals and checks the status of arriving aircraft
- checks coach numbers for return to resort
- greets arriving passengers, checks them off the list and directs them to the coach
- makes their way to the assigned coach
- checks that the right people are on the coach and that they are safe and comfortable
- gives a welcome speech and an information commentary during the transfer
- promotes the welcome meeting and excursions
- explains the accommodation check-in procedure
- checks everyone into their accommodation
- says goodbye to the driver and finishes.

The transfer commentary

The content and structure of the speech should follow the guidelines below. The representative:

- introduces themself and the driver
- extends a warm welcome from themself and from the company
- gives the local time, route and how long the journey will take
- explains safety features of the coach
- gives out welcome packs
- gives some local information

- provides information about weather conditions, changing money, drinking water, sunburn etc.
- gives information about checking in at the hotel.

Think about it

What information do guests want or need to know when they are on the coach after arrival?

Technique

Using a microphone takes practice. Some people have a tendency to raise their voices as they would when talking to a coachload of people without a microphone. It is important to talk in a normal tone so that you are not shouting at the customers.

Departures

When holidaymakers are going to leave, the representative:

- arrives at the first pick-up point in good time and in the correct uniform
- meets the driver and checks the coach is clean and tidy
- gets off at each pick-up and goes to reception to greet and check off departing guests
- introduces themself
- checks passengers have paid bills, returned keys, etc.
- at the last pick-up does a head count as an extra check
- gives information about how to check in and flight details
- at the airport thanks the passengers for holidaying with the company and goes to find out where the check-in desk is
- informs passengers of the location of the check-in desk and makes sure passengers take all their belongings
- stays at the check-in desk looking after any problems until everyone is through.

Case study: Sophie's transfer

Sophie has been working in Ibiza until very recently, but has just moved to Marbella to work as a transfer representative. This is the transfer commentary she gave on the way from Malaga airport to accompany guests on their way to Marbella. The guests are all staying in four- and five-star properties.

Hello everyone I'm Sophie and this is your driver (talks to driver to ask his name) and this is your driver Jiame.

Has anyone been to Marbella before? Come on shout out if you've been before!

Welcome to the Costa del Sol on behalf of The Luxury Holidays Company.

It's 5 a.m. here so set your watches. We'll be in Marbella in about 40 minutes so you've got time for a bit of shut-eye if you're tired after your journey.

There is an emergency exit at the back of the coach and one at the front and there are safety belts on the seats. Please use them.

I'm going to come around with your welcome packs now. (Sophie distributes the welcome packs which are personalised – she gets to a young couple half way down.) I don't seem to have one for you – are you on the right coach? (They reply that a representative directed them to this coach and Sophie soon realises they are on the wrong coach). I'm going to put you in a taxi to your hotel at the first stop. I am sorry – she was a silly woman wasn't she?

(Back at the front) OK everyone just a few bits of information about life in Marbella – great fun, loads of clubs, do put the sun lotion on, it gets very hot. Don't drink the water, stick to vodka (laughing).

What about a bit of a sing-song before we get there?'

1 Comment on Sophie's commentary and say how you would change it.

2 Role-play the scene and show the right way and the wrong way of doing the commentary.

4.5 Welcome meetings

The welcome meeting normally takes place the morning after the guests arrive. They will then have recovered from their journey and will be eager to learn about their new surroundings. The meeting will take place in a hotel lounge or bar and complimentary drinks are usually served, depending on the time of day.

It is important to be well prepared for the meeting. The representative should do the following:

- give out invitations on the transfer
- be there in good time in the correct uniform
- make sure the room has a suitable layout with enough chairs (see Figure 15.6)
- have promotional materials ready
- have resort and accommodation information ready
- ensure drinks are ready
- have cue cards and visual aids ready
- have any documentation ready, including booking forms and tickets
- know which guests to expect.

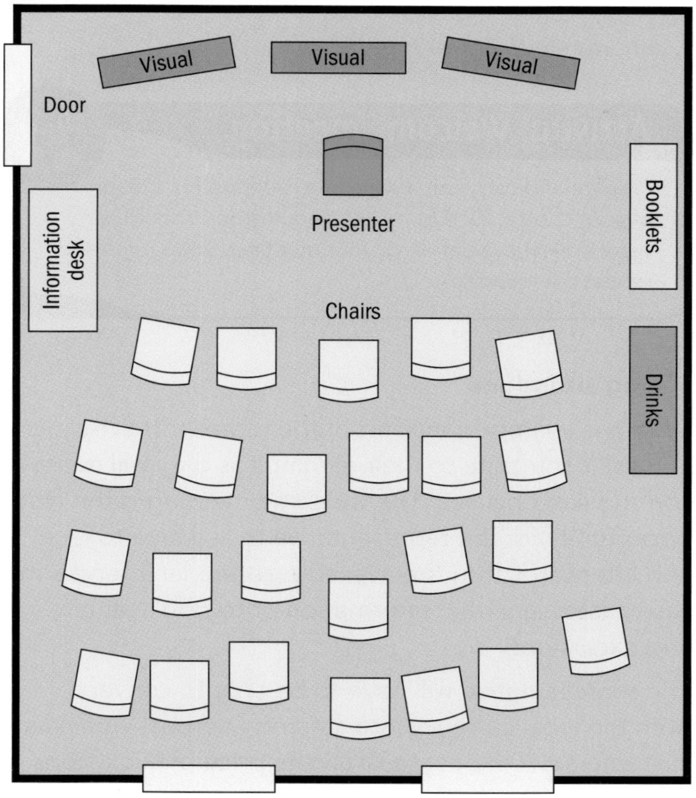

Figure 15.7: Floor plan of welcome meeting venue

Content and structure of presentation

The following points should be covered in the meeting. The representative:

- introduces themself, welcomes the guests and makes sure they know customers' names
- makes sure refreshments are served
- asks if everyone has settled in
- distributes information sheets on excursions
- provides information on hotel facilities, for example changing money, swimming pool, restaurant times and safes
- provides safety information
- provides local information, for example transport, beaches, restaurants, shopping, telephoning and medical information
- tells guests about the location of the notice board, information file and representative's visiting times and contact details
- explains the programme of excursions
- takes excursion bookings for interested parties
- extends thanks and says goodbye
- answers individual questions.

Activity: Welcome meeting

Prepare and carry out a welcome meeting for a resort of your choice. One or more of your group should carry out a critical evaluation of your meeting. Swap roles and repeat the exercise.

Selling situations

Selling is an important part of the representative's job and will contribute to their earnings as they will recieve commission on sales. The welcome meeting is the first opportunity for the representative to sell face to face and afterwards they are available at regular intervals in case customers want information or to book car hire and excursions.

The representative will have to be able to convert from the local currency into sterling and back again as customers will expect to know the price of excursions in their own familiar currency.

Selling leads to completion of associated paperwork, for example sales documentation and receipts. There is more paperwork in resort than in many sales

situations as the representative will often be working between sites without access to a PC.

Complaints

A complaint is always recorded so that it can be established how it was dealt with and whether further action is necessary. Some complaints might result in litigation, for example a serious accident. In these cases records are even more important and an accident form would be completed.

There could be a range of complaints about the hotel, for example the rooms, the pool or the restaurant food and service. All these complaints can be resolved by the hotel, so the representative needs to establish a good relationship with the duty management and with the respective heads of housekeeping, restaurants etc., and report problems to the appropriate department. Representatives should ensure that the customers are satisfied with the response to their complaint.

A problem that might occur in peak season is that of overbooking. This may mean finding alternative accommodation for the overbooked customers. As long as the new accommodation, or flight, is of superior quality, or class, the situation can still result in a satisfied customer.

If a customer thinks their holiday has been misrepresented, for example the hotel does not have the facilities advertised, the representative must find some means of placating and compensating the customer to remedy the situation. This is best done in the resort rather than on return to the UK.

Handling complaints

People on holiday are likely to complain if facilities do not match up to their expectations or if something goes wrong. Remember that representatives are expected to solve as many complaints as they can in the resort so that the customer is satisfied and does not pursue the complaint once they get home. Companies do work hard to minimise complaints but there is no doubt that every representative will be on the receiving end of many complaints whoever they work for, particularly if the weather is poor.

Customers are told in booking conditions that they should report complaints to their representative and then the representative has an opportunity to resolve the complaint. If the representative is unable to resolve the complaint, it will be referred to a manager. Agreed company prodedures must be followed when handling complaints.

The complaint, if handled well, is an opportunity to give excellent customer service and turn the complainant into a very happy, loyal customer.

- The representative should listen to the complaint, remembering active listening techniques.

- Complaints should not be taken personally; they are usually not about the representatives themselves but about situations.

- The complaint should be summarised and reiterated to the customer to make sure it is understood properly by the representative.

- The representative should empathise with the customer's situation without admitting any liability for the complaint.

- The customer should be told what the representative is going to do about their complaint and when.

- It is essential that the representative stays calm and professional.

- A solution should be agreed with the customer.

- Appropriate records should be made.

Other complaints might be about length of transfers. In this case, the representative should reassure passengers that the holiday will be worth the journey.

Case study: Dealing with complaints

I won't go into the exact details, all I will tell you is that the service was appalling and one of the restaurant 'specials' was spam in gravy … enough said! Anyway … after about four days of horrible food and service I complained to the rep in our resort. She was very helpful and said that she would sort things out with the restaurant manager. In spite of that, even though she tried, the restaurant situation still didn't improve. We then wrote out a customer complaints form (you have to do this in resort if you intend to complain when you get home – you need your rep's signature).

1 Could the representative have resolved this complaint, so that it was not pursued on return to the UK? If so, how?

2 What would the representative do if she thought the customer's complaint was not valid?

HOTEL FACILITIES COMPLAINT FORM

- Please complete this form AS SOON AS POSSIBLE following a customer complaint regarding the facilities.
- It is essential you bring the matter to the attention of the hotel management with a note of any action to be taken.
- The hotel management must sign this form in acknowledgement of the complaint.

Property _____ Date _____

Brief summary of complaint _____

_____

_____

_____

_____

_____

_____

Customer name: _____ Ref. No: _____

_____ - _____

Reported to member of hotel management: _____

Action to be taken with agreed timescale: _____

_____

_____

_____

_____

_____

_____

Signed on behalf of the hotel: _____

Signed staff member: _____ Date: _____

Figure 15.8: Hotel facilities complaint form

Activity: Getting satisfied customers

Role-play the following situations ensuring you use appropriate social and customer service skills. Take it in turns with members of your group to play representative and customers. Your aim is to deal effectively with the situation and end up with satisfied customers.

1 You are working as a holiday representative in a ski resort, La Plagne, which is located in the Alps in France. You are holding your welcome meeting and it is going very well, but you are aware of a couple whose body language indicates that they are unhappy about something. They are not smiling or showing any enthusiasm about anything you say. When you have finished talking about the excursions and invite questions, they begin to complain loudly about their chalet, in particular the standard of cleanliness and the attitude of the chalet hosts. They say that their pillowcases were used and they found sweet wrappers under the bed. The rest of the group is listening with interest. What will you do?

2 You visit one of your assigned chalets in La Plagne to find that a member of the party has a leg in plaster. It seems he broke his leg and was airlifted off the mountain. It was day one of a 7-day holiday. He does not want to go home, but he needs you to help him with his insurance and suggest things for him to do for the rest of the week. You must also complete an accident form. Deal with this situation.

3 Some of your guests stay in a hotel and you make a visit most days. You are unhappy to see Mrs Allan waiting for you on your arrival. She has already complained twice about the sauna in the hotel. She likes to have a sauna when she comes off the slopes and on three occasions in the last week it has not been working. You have reported it to hotel management twice, but nothing has been done. Your task is to appease Mrs Allan and to fill in a complaint form.

Assessment activity 15.2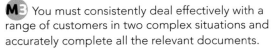

Your boss is so pleased with the work that you did to help her prepare her presentation that she agrees to post you to your chosen resort for the summer season – Palma, Majorca!

You are expecting a very busy season and these are some of the duties you are faced with. You should role-play each of these situations. Make sure that you cover the full range referring to the content and assessment guidance in the unit specification for the detail required.

1. Part of your role is to collect guests from the airport and transfer them to their hotel. Prepare and carry out the arrival transfer speech using a microphone you will give on the coach. **P4 M2 D2**

2. Prepare and carry out a welcome meeting for your guests. **P4 M2 D2**

3. A customer wishes to book an excursion by coach to the local market. It costs 10 euros per person and there are three people in the party. Try to sell her a full day excursion which also includes a visit to a leather factory and lunch as well as the market (40 euros per person). Complete the booking form. NB: Your tutor will provide the booking form. **P2 M2 D2**

4. A customer is unhappy with her accommodation. She says the room is not clean and is too small and she does not consider that it reaches the standard of a four-star hotel which it claims to be. The hotel is full. Decide what to say to this customer and deal with her. Complete a complaint form. **P5 M3 D2**

5. The lifeguard has pulled a child, one of your customers, from the pool. The child is fine, but has a deep cut on his toe and is frightened. His mother is hysterical. You have been called from the lounge where you were meeting some other guests. Deal with the situation and complete an incident form. **P5 M3 D2**

Grading tips

P4 P5 You must use social and customer service skills effectively and complete appropriate documentation in complex situations.

P4 Expect to receive questions to answer in your welcome meeting. Make sure you use visual aids and remember to think about your body language.

M2 You must demonstrate effective social, customer service and selling skills throughout the assessment.

M3 You must consistently deal effectively with a range of customers in two complex situations and accurately complete all the relevant documents.

D2 To reach distinction level, you must consistently project a confident, professional image when dealing with customers in different situations. You must demonstrate a smart, professional appearance.

Katie Smith
Holiday representative, Minorca

What is a typical day like for you?

I work for a major UK tour operator and every day is different when you are a holiday rep, as there is so much to do! The hours are mainly morning and late afternoon based around airport transfers and hotel welcome meetings!

Two days a week, the day starts with getting up early to do an airport transfer. I meet the coach and driver and then we collect the holidaymakers to take them back to the airport. With my checklist I know exactly who I am collecting and once everyone is on board, I will speak on the microphone for about 10 minutes just going through general things, such as 'have all your documents ready for when we get to the airport' and explaining what they will need to do once we arrive.

Then it's back to resort with a new group of holidaymakers on the coach with more information and entertaining to be done on the microphone.

What else do you do apart from transfers?

The rest of the time is spent doing welcome meetings and paperwork! You must be very independent and confident for this as you have to write your welcome meeting and present it to large groups, at the same time as trying to entertain and sell to them! Then there is question time afterwards.

The main aim is to sell excursions and then spend the week getting money in and tickets sorted! The drive behind this is a commission.

One night a week we do cabaret – we have to get our holidaymakers to and from the show and be in it!

Being a rep is not an easy job, you work long hours but it is exciting and certainly great experience in dealing with people.

How did you get your job?

I did have a Travel and Tourism Diploma but when I left college I worked in a retail travel agency for a year. I knew I wanted to be a rep but I waited until I was 21 and had a bit more work experience. Then I applied to three companies and got two interviews. I was offered this job first and I wanted to go to Spain as I had been studying Spanish.

Think about it!

1. What languages can you speak? If none other than your native language, how might you start learning?

2. How would you cope with speaking to a large group of people? How can you practise while doing your course?

3. How do you think you would cope with living away from home and working long hours?

Just checking

1 Describe three different kinds of representatives.

2 Why might a company prefer a more mature representative?

3 Which piece of legislation is most important for a representative to know about?

4 Name two other Acts which representatives should be aware of.

5 What kinds of things are checked in a health and safety check?

6 Who is liable for negligence, the tour operator or the supplier?

7 What points relating to body language should a representative consider at a welcome meeting?

8 What information should be included on a notice board prepared by a representative?

9 What is the purpose of a welcome meeting?

10 Why is image important for representatives?

11 What is meant by social skills?

12 What would happen if a representative gives poor customer service?

13 What forms of compensation might a representative give to a customer when they have made a valid complaint?

edexcel

Assignment tips

- Talk to as many 'real' holiday representatives about their jobs as you can.

- Practise delivering welcome meetings and giving transfer speeches lots of times before your assessment.

- Use the ABTA website to learn more about health and safety in resorts.

- Look for examples of holiday representative jobs on the internet. Sometimes there are videos to watch about the jobs.

- Much holiday representative work is seasonal. If you want to try it out, investigate doing a summer season during your holidays.

17 Events, conferences and exhibitions

In this unit you will examine the fast-growing event, conference and exhibition industry and how it relates to travel and tourism in terms of use of hospitality, accommodation and transport. You will also look at the trends and issues affecting the industry by researching travel and tourism exhibitions and, if possible, by visiting them.

You will learn about the different kinds of events, conferences and exhibitions, their venues, and the variety of organisations involved in setting them up. You will decide which venues are suitable for different types of event.

You will learn how to propose and cost an event, conference or exhibition in response to a given client brief. Planning an event, conference and exhibition will help you to develop your organisational, teamwork and problem-solving skills and to show your initiative.

Learning outcomes

After completing this unit you should:

1 understand the event, conference and exhibitions environment in the UK

2 understand types of venues utilised for events, conferences and exhibitions

3 be able to propose and cost events, conferences and exhibitions.

Assessment and grading criteria

This table shows you what you must do in order to achieve a **pass, merit** or **distinction** grade and where you can find activities in this book to help you.

To achieve a **pass** grade the evidence must show that you are able to:	To achieve a **merit** grade the evidence must show that, in addition to the pass criteria, you are able to:	To achieve a **distinction** grade the evidence must show that, in addition to the pass and merit criteria, you are able to:
P1 describe the event, conference and exhibitions environment in the UK	**M1** explain how trends affect the event, conference and exhibitions environment **See assessment activity 17.1, page 107**	**D1** assess growth potential of the event, conference and exhibitions environment **See assessment activity 17.1, page 107**
P2 explain the intrinsic links between the event, conference and exhibitions environment and the UK travel and tourism sector		
P3 explain the appropriateness of different types of venue for events, conferences and exhibitions **See assessment activity 17.1, page 107**		
P4 produce proposals for an event, conference or exhibition to meet a given brief	**M2** explain how the proposals and costings meet the brief **See assessment activity 17.2, page118**	
P5 prepare costings for an event, conference or exhibition for a given brief **See assessment activity 17.2, page 118**		

How you will be assessed

This unit will be assessed by one or more internal assignments that will be designed and marked by your tutor. Your assignments will be subject to sampling internally and externally as part of Edexcel's quality assurance procedures. The assignments are designed to allow you to show your knowledge and understanding related to the unit. The unit outcomes indicate what you should know, understand or be able to do after completing the unit.

Emma, 18-year-old BTEC National learner

Before we started this unit we visited the World Travel Market at ExCeL in London. This was the first exhibition that I had been to and it was great fun.

I visited lots of stands and really enjoyed the buzz of an environment that showcased different destinations and cultures. I collected a lot of material to help me with my European Destinations unit. I wasn't really thinking about the events unit at the time. I wish I had been as I could have collected more information about the organisation of the event and thought about the layout. However, we were able to discuss what we had seen and what we could remember and it helped the group get started on the unit.

We were keen to visit another exhibition so we organised a visit to Clothes Show Live as that was coming up. This time we looked at the marketing, types of stands and exhibitors and the target market. Then I went to a local wedding fair with my sister as she is getting married. That was a small event so I was able to talk to some suppliers and even find out how much it cost to exhibit.

When it came to the assessment, a lot of my research was done on the internet but I also visited two local venues where conferences are held and found out about costs and what equipment is available. This helped me with the assessment where I had to put a proposal together for an event.

Over to you!

1 What exhibitions could your group visit? Can you think of exhibition centres that you are able to reach, for example the National Exhibition Centre in Birmingham or the GMEX in Manchester?

2 Which conference venues are local to you? What information could you get from them?

1 The event, conference and exhibitions environment in the UK

The conference industry gives people the opportunity to communicate face to face. There were an estimated 67 million attendances at events in 2008 (at an estimated 1.31 million events with an average attendance of 51 people). The market is worth over £7 billion in the UK according to the UK Events Market Trends Survey (UKEMTS).

However, many people are very comfortable with remote communication such as emailing, text messaging and so on. Do you think that the rise in remote communication could lead to the demise of events, conferences and exhibitions?

1.1 Types of event

Corporate hospitality

Corporate hospitality refers to the provision of hospitality and entertainment to customers of a company. It is done to develop good relationships with customers and to encourage new business.

For example, a company might hire a marquee at Wimbledon and invite business guests to watch the tennis and have drinks and strawberries and cream in the marquee. Many sporting venues provide facilities for corporate hospitality and it is a lucrative market for them.

Case study: 'Corporate hospitality wins all'

At Wimbledon, fans can queue up and get tickets on the day – or can they? Some seats are reserved for those who queue. The rest of the seats are booked and many are bought by companies to entertain clients at a match as part of their corporate hospitality. A company will usually use a hospitality company, such as Keith Prowse or Wimbledon Hospitality, to organise their corporate event. Besides the tickets, a menu will be created and a suitable venue chosen, such as a table in a restaurant at the ground or even a dedicated marquee. Customers choosing a marquee use their own corporate branding in it.

In addition to a meal, guests can expect champagne, afternoon tea and lavish treatment,

all timed so that they enjoy the game. The events company will issue a contract for the company to sign so that they are clear about what they are booking for their corporate hospitality.

Choose a sporting venue in your area, for example a football club. Find out what corporate hospitality packages are on offer and what they cost. Make notes and comment on whether they represent value for money.

Team-building events

Team-building events are usually arranged as staff development exercises to bond teams and get them to work more effectively. When we think about team-building events, physically demanding courses come to mind, such as outward bound courses. These are fun but not suitable for everyone. Other types of team-building activity are available and there are companies which specialise in running them.

The following case study gives an example from a team-building events company, Sandstone.

Case study: Romanbar

Probably our most 'out and out fun' team building activity. Certainly a very popular one!

When you want a session with some real team building flavour, why not try a full-bodied business simulation? In a Romanbar session, product sampling isn't the only aspect that involves the participants! In the idyllic setting of Oldetown, Devashire, each team starts a wine bar within the franchised Romanbar family.

Collectively, they must be competitive enough to wrestle business away from the pre-existing competition. Individually, each team will want to be the best.

Teams make their first decisions and the venture begins! Their deliberations are computer analysed and the results fed back on a 'weekly' basis in the form of financial statements and general information on the state of the business.

But no business or service is only about facts and figures, of course. It's also about knowledge, skill and application. Our wide range of activities allow you to:

- Learn bar flair from our speciailist trainer. Watch those bottles fly!
- Mix 'traffic light' cocktails and learn about many more.
- Volunteer for your bar's cheese rolling team and take on the other bars.
- Have a fantastic time and take away real team improvements. Brilliant!

Your new-found expertise converts prospective customers into revenue.

Can you demonstrate an understanding of the marketplace as a whole? Can you collaborate with the other Romanbars? They are, after all, part of the same organisation ...

This is a popular team simulation that highlights issues and decisions that affect all organisations. It is ideal when you want to mix business with pleasure in a challenging and motivating activity that people will really enjoy. And if you want to spice the competition up a little, we recommend the use of prizes for the winning team.

Bottles of wine, of course.

(Source: www.sandstone.co.uk)

1 Determine the objectives of a Romanbar team-building activity for a team of staff who work for a reservations call centre.

2 What advantages does this kind of activity have over a physical team-building session?

Activity: Team-building in action

Organise a team-building event for your group. You can find out about activities in your local area. What about devising your own team-building course and running it for another group of students?

Incentives

Incentives can be used for employees or for customers. Offering incentives for employees is a way of rewarding staff for hard work or loyalty and of motivating them to improve performance. Similarly, customers can be rewarded for loyalty or encouraged to make future orders through incentive events. These may take the form of corporate hospitality or travel, or even gifts.

An incentive and promotional marketing show (Incentives and Promotional Marketing Live!) is held at the National Exhibition Centre (NEC) in Birmingham, organised by Waypoint Exhibition and Event Group. The following are some examples of what is exhibited:

- achievement awards
- business gifts
- competition and game prizes
- experiences
- incentive travel
- promotional merchandise and clothing
- fundraising.

Fundraising

Some organisations hold fundraising events and donate the funds to their chosen charity. Such events have several benefits:

- they raise money for charity
- they allow staff to work together for a common cause
- they get useful publicity for the company.

Some charities are proactive in using tourism to help them raise funds. The charity Mind organises, alongside travel professionals, a series of treks, for example in Cuba. Participants raise money from sponsors to pay for the trip and to donate money to the charity.

Product launches

Events are held to launch new products or new company names, or to raise awareness of existing products. These events are not always open to the public but are aimed at the press with the aim of generating press coverage and publicity.

Music events and festivals

There are different types of music events held around the UK. These include festivals, such as Reading and Leeds. The music magazine NME has a website which gives details of all upcoming festivals at www.nme.com. For opera enthusiasts, the Glyndebourne festival is a must. Performances are held at Glyndebourne from May to August. It has become popular for stately homes to stage outside concerts in the summer. These may range from popular music concerts to classical performances.

Did you know?

A great way of finding out how a festival is organised and seeing bands for free is to work as a volunteer. Volunteers help festival-goers find their pitches, collect litter or work in bar areas. They look out for any problems and report them. In return they get a crew pass and uniform. Volunteers camp in the crew area and can watch the bands when they are not working. You can volunteer as long as you are over 18. One way to apply is to go to www.hotboxevents.com – you will have to provide a refundable deposit which is usually the cost of a festival ticket.

Do you think music festivals have any similarities with other events?

Other events

Other types of events include wedding fairs and reunions. Wedding fairs are often organised at local hotels as a business opportunity to bring all wedding-related goods and services into one place for customers to access.

Reunions are popular events, especially since the growth of the website Friends Reunited which has facilitated people getting in touch with old school friends. Reunions require a venue and hospitality just like any other event.

Activity: Putting on an event

Put on a launch event as a means of raising awareness locally about new programmes or courses at your school or college. Hold a discussion about how you would do this. Draw a flow diagram with all the steps involved.

1.2 Types of conference

Political conferences

The most famous political conferences are the party political conferences held each year by the leading political parties. Popular venues for the main parties are Brighton, Blackpool and Bournemouth. It is not mere coincidence that they are held in these seaside towns. The seaside resorts heavily rely on conference business outside the summer holiday season so the party political conferences provide an important revenue stream which they carefully target.

Political conferences related to travel and tourism include those held by the World Tourism Organization.

A full list of its events can be found on its website at www.unwto.org. An example is the UNWTO International Conference on Tourism Statistics – Tourism: An Engine for Employment Creation which was held in Bali in 2009.

Business meetings

Many business meetings are held on work premises as part of the working day. However, there are occasions when this is unsuitable:

- When a group of staff need uninterrupted time to discuss policy or issues – they may hire a room in a local hotel.
- When a supplier needs to meet a customer – if only two or three people are involved in a meeting they can meet in the lounge of a hotel or airport without any charge.
- When everyone needs to come together for a full meeting such as an Annual General Meeting (AGM).

Annual conferences

Annual conferences may be held by a single company to bring their employees together or they may be organised to bring interested professionals together to discuss industry issues.

Medical conferences are often held and sponsored by drug manufacturers to promote discussion of good practice and new procedures and also to promote products.

Educational conferences may be organised by unions, such as the National Union of Teachers (NUT).

1.3 Types of exhibition
Trade fairs

The World Travel Market is held annually in London and is probably the best known travel-related **trade fair**. It attracts visitors from overseas as well as the UK. In recent years it has moved to the ExCeL venue in east London. Trade fairs provide an opportunity for industry members to meet up and conduct their business. They also give an opportunity to find out about latest developments in the industry.

Key term

Trade fair – an exhibition held for people working within a particular industry. It gives an opportunity for people to meet and do business together and see what new products and services are on offer.

The Best of Britain & Ireland Travel Trade Forum is held annually. In 2010, it took place at Olympia in London. The exhibition is dedicated to domestic tourism.

International Confex is a trade fair about trade fairs! It is billed as the UK's leading event exhibition, and brings together event organisers, venue providers and support services in the UK and abroad.

Did you know?

Restricted student attendance (in groups and with a tutor) is allowed at travel trade fairs on some of the days. These are useful events to attend to carry out research and learn how the industry networks.

Promotion

Most exhibitions have the aim of promoting new sales and attracting potential customers. Examples in travel and tourism include the Travel Technology Show. Such a show would not be of interest to the public but would attract trade customers who need to update technology in their business. This particular event boasts over 100 suppliers exhibiting.

Further examples of exhibitions are the holiday and travel shows held annually in Glasgow and Manchester. Visitors at these events are potential holidaymakers from the general public. These are known as consumer exhibitions rather than trade shows.

Many people attend shows on products or themes which interest them as a leisure activity. Examples are the London Model Engineering Exhibition and the Knitting and Stitching Show held in London. With this in mind, exhibitors provide entertainment, free samples, etc. to attract more visitors, but the ultimate aim of the exhibition is to sell.

Roadshow

An exhibition is a roadshow if it travels around different locations. This is costly as, of course, all the equipment and exhibits have to travel with it.

Think about it

The website www.exhibitions.co.uk lists all the trade fairs and exhibitions in the UK. Have a look and see if you can find travel and tourism exhibitions.

1.4 Specialist organisations

Venue-finding agencies

Most organisations involved in venue-finding offer the service as part of an extended range of services. Once the venue has been confirmed and booked for the client, they will offer a conference-organising service too. Venue-finding agencies build up databases of contacts and find suitable venues to match their clients' requirements. They do not charge clients for the venue-finding service as they earn their fees on commission from the venue. However, they need to offer more services than venue-finding, as it is easy for customers to trawl the internet themselves and find suitable premises.

Some Tourist Information Centres (TICs) offer venue-finding services. They have excellent knowledge of local venues and can advise on suitability. The service allows them to make some extra revenue in commissions and they can offer other services to organisers and delegates, for example souvenirs of the area, visits to attractions or walking tours.

Conference organisers

Around one-third of conferences are booked by a professional conference organiser or a venue-finding agency. Organising an event or conference is very time-consuming and within a company it may be that a busy member of staff has this task on top of their normal duties. Conference organisers take the stress away from companies, who merely tell the organiser what their requirements are and allow them to do all the work. The service they offer will include:

- offering a choice of suitable venues
- putting together a delegate package
- making all bookings
- liaising with the venue
- organising catering
- organising signage
- booking accommodation
- arranging speakers
- booking transport
- arranging audio-visual equipment.

Exhibition organisers

There are several large exhibition organisers in the UK. Reed Exhibitions, whose headquarters are in the UK, is the world's leading organiser of trade and consumer events.

Reed is a major player with over 470 events in its portfolio held all over the world. The events serve over 40 different industries. You can find out about their exhibitions at www.reedexpo.com.

Event-management companies

These companies are experts in organising and managing events to a given client brief. Everything they do is tailor-made to fit that client's needs. They will have a network of venue providers, caterers and entertainers to call on to provide services at competitive rates. They save the client a lot of time and anxiety in putting on an event. Event-management companies organise many different kinds of events rather than specialising in one type such as exhibitions. Events range from dinners to award ceremonies, from parties to conferences.

1.5 Customers

Corporate

Customers at exhibitions and events fall into two main categories. Firstly, there are the exhibitors. These are the buyers of space and stands and they are the main source of income for the exhibition organisers. These are corporate customers. Secondly, there are the people who attend the exhibition and usually pay an entrance fee. This is the second strand of income for the exhibition organisers. These customers may be corporate in that they represent their business or they may be private individuals.

The exhibitors may be companies, government organisations, such as VisitBritain, or trade associations, such as the Federation of Tour Operators (now part of ABTA – The Travel Association). Of course, the nature of exhibitor depends on the type of exhibition.

Those attending the exhibition may be corporate customers or members of the public or a mixture of both. Again this depends on the type of exhibition or event.

The customers for a conference are the delegates who attend – they are usually corporate customers as they represent their companies.

These customers may be domestic, that is UK-based, or international. The UK conference market's international customers are mainly from the USA, Germany and France. Emerging markets are China because of 'approved destination status' granted to the UK and other European countries. Central American countries such as Panama, Nicaragua and El Salvador have had rapid growth in their economies and are likely new customers for UK conferences.

Associations

Customers can be associations, for example ABTA – The Travel Association, who wish to put on a conference or event for their members. The Association of British Travel Organisers to France holds an annual conference for members – in France of course. The Institute of Travel & Tourism holds events for members of the sector. These include suppers at the House of Commons, with after-dinner speakers from travel and tourism businesses and an overseas conference.

Government

Government departments, agencies and local authorities are often customers of conferences and corporate events. Conferences may be held to discuss policy on tourism or other matters.

Private individuals

Many leisure exhibitions are open to the general public and attract individuals. Examples are the Ideal Home Show and the Boat Show.

Case study: The National Exhibition Centre – Birmingham

Figure 17.1: Clothes Show Live at The NEC, in Birmingham

Figure 17.1 illustrates the different companies involved in the annual Clothes Show Live at The NEC in Birmingham.

Produce a diagram similar to the one in Figure 17.1, showing the different companies involved in the annual World Travel Market. You will find the information you need on the website for the World Travel Market at www.wtmlondon.com.

1.6 Links with the travel and tourism sector

Accommodation and transport provision

Delegate rates for conferences at hotels are quoted with or without accommodation. Where an overnight stay is required it is sensible to book a conference venue that offers accommodation. This need not be a hotel – it could be university accommodation out of term or a purpose-built conference centre. If accommodation is booked separately it will be less convenient for delegates and will also be more complex to arrange.

Transport should be arranged to ferry delegates from railway stations or airports to venues, and for any inter-site travel needed. Where all delegates are travelling together to a destination a bus can be organised.

Popularising destinations

Some destinations invest heavily in the conference market, developing purpose-built facilities or hotels with conference facilities. Examples include Brighton, Blackpool and Bournemouth – the resorts that host the party political conferences.

Extended stays

When people attend an event or conference for business there is an opportunity to offer leisure facilities to partners, or to delegates, to enjoy an extended stay after business is completed.

Sometimes day trips are organised as part of a conference to give a break from work and entertain the delegates.

1.7 Trends

Popularity of unusual venues

The most popular venues for conferences are hotels, universities and other academic venues.

However, organisers of corporate events are looking for more unusual venues where an event can be organised around a particular theme and where customers or employees can enjoy a more unusual experience. Some of these more unusual venues are introduced in the next section.

Why do you think seaside towns are popular conference destinations?

Growth of venue-finding and event-management companies

An internet search will find hundreds of venue-finding and event-management companies. There is a trend to use them as they are experts and save time for busy managers. Although they usually charge a fee for their services, the overall cost of the event is not necessarily increased as they are able to get services at good rates.

Impact of web-conferencing, web seminars and e-meetings

The advent of **web-conferencing** did not have the expected impact on conferences and business meetings. It seems that people still prefer to meet and talk face to face. With web-conferencing, the camera focuses on the person who is speaking so it is impossible to gauge reactions of the rest of the participants and to get an instinctive feel for the meeting. It is least suitable for large meetings.

Key term

Web-conferencing – a system that allows two or more people in different locations to link up and communicate by video over the internet.

Growth of special interest trips and packages

As tour operators strive to offer specialist holidays catering for any interest, they may offer packages to events. Many of these are sporting events but there are other examples, such as champagne tasting in Reims or organised trips to the Chelsea Flower Show.

Growth of budget class meeting facilities

There is a trend for meetings to become smaller and shorter. This is so that companies can control spending, so that more frequent and flexible meetings can be held and because employees are reluctant to spend long periods of time in meetings they feel are not always relevant to them. This trend has led to companies choosing smaller and cheaper venues for meetings and often seeking out the more unusual venues.

Increasing security procedures

Some events have been cancelled because of terrorist fears in major cities. Organisers must have sufficient security procedures in place to reassure delegates and customers. People attending exhibitions may be subject to bag searches and other security procedures.

For an event, security personnel will be needed and there are specialist agencies who provide security. They can take charge of crowd management, car parking, entry control, front-of-house security and other safety issues. At a large event it is worth getting a specialist company to oversee security as they will also be able to advise on what is required for a particular event.

Sponsorship

Sponsorship can benefit events. It gives kudos to an event if a well-known brand provides sponsorship and it also relieves the budget. Drinks companies, such as Moët & Chandon, Evian or Kronenbourg, often sponsor events to promote their brands but this type of organisation will be very careful only to sponsor events that complement their brand values.

A sponsor may send a representative to make sure their logo, name and products are being represented properly. The representative should be given VIP treatment at the event. When setting up the event the organiser must consider the sponsor's needs and incorporate them into the room plan.

An example of sponsorship is the Chartered Institute of Marketing's Travel Industry Group (CIMTIG) sponsoring the Travel Marketing awards. These awards take place every year with the objective of recognising excellence in marketing and raising standards in the travel sector. Find out more at www.thetravelmarketingawards.com.

Activity: Facilities on your doorstep

Study a city or major town in your own area and describe the event, conference and exhibition environment. Give examples of provision in each category. Explain what trends and issues affect the provision of events, conferences and exhibitions in the area.

2 Types of venue utilised for events, conferences and exhibitions

2.1 Venues

Purpose-built centres

Purpose-built centres are the least popular venues for conferences. However, national exhibitions are held in purpose-built centres as they are so large and they need to be in venues that can accommodate large numbers of visitors, and that are accessible by all modes of transport.

There are several purpose-built exhibition and conference centres in the UK. We have already mentioned The NEC in Birmingham, the UK's biggest venue. You may have heard of Olympia and Earls Court in London and GMEX in Manchester. In Glasgow, there is the Scottish Exhibition and Conference Centre.

Did you know?

The NEC is part of The NEC Group, which includes The International Convention Centre and The National Indoor Arena in Birmingham city centre, as well as The NEC and the LG Arena in Solihull. The NEC Group also operates national ticketing agent The Ticket Factory.

Every year over 2.3 million people visit more than 140 exhibitions and conferences held at The NEC, including massive international trade events such as Spring Fair International – the largest trade event in Europe – and consumer exhibitions including Clothes Show Live and Crufts.

Hotels

Hotels are the most popular venues for conferences. The average number of conferences held each year in hotels is over 500 according to the BCVS Conference Survey 2006. All hotels want to cultivate the business market and will provide conference and meeting facilities. In addition, local sales exhibitions are held at hotels. Examples include wedding fairs and property exhibitions. Hotels are also suitable for many events as catering and entertainment facilities are readily available.

Academic venues

Academic venues are ideal for conferences and meetings as they have all the necessary facilities inbuilt. Student rooms can be used to accommodate delegates and catering facilities are readily available. Lecture theatres provide room for large numbers of people and there are audio-visual facilities for speakers. Universities and colleges are pleased to have the opportunity to hire out their premises and facilities outside term time.

Sporting venues

We have already mentioned sporting venues in terms of corporate hospitality. They also often provide conference and meeting facilities in order to make use of the facilities when sport is not taking place.

Activity: Kicking off business at Old Trafford

Manchester United is known as an organisation with great business acumen. Part of its business activity involves a complex of function rooms at its home of Old Trafford for social or business use.

Visit Manchester United's website at www.manutd.com and look in the conferences and events section to find out what kind of facilities are offered at Old Trafford and what they cost. Decide on an event you might hold there and write some notes on the products and services you would hire.

Unusual venues

Many venues, not traditionally used for conferences and events, are now vying for the lucrative conference trade. The advantage of holding a conference at a more unusual venue is that it adds an extra incentive for the delegates to attend and the conference can be combined with corporate hospitality. Examples include Xscape, a snow centre in Milton Keynes where conference rooms and facilities are available and delegates can go skiing as well, and London Zoo, where events or conferences can be hosted. Boats are popular on the River Thames and in York where Yorkboat offers tailor-made cruises on the River Ouse for conference organisers and delegates.

Civic venues

Civic buildings usually have boardrooms and meeting rooms where council meetings are held. When not in use for these purposes they may be hired out to local businesses for meetings.

2.2 Facilities

Room and space options

A conference will require a large room to hold all delegates comfortably and may also require breakout or seminar rooms. An organiser must know that the capacity of the room is adequate for the numbers expected and add extra rooms as required. The organiser will also determine the layout of the room.

Hospitality

Most venues, particularly hotels, have in-house catering supplies and will not allow organisers to use outside contractors. Where such services are not on offer the organiser will have to seek another contractor.

Large exhibition centres provide different kinds of catering, for example at the ExCeL Exhibition Centre in London a number of sandwich bars, cafés and restaurants are provided on-site for the benefit of visitors and exhibitors alike. In addition, stand catering is available, where exhibitors can order catering items for their stands from an on-site shop. The shop delivers the goods directly to the stands. The shop will also offer coffee machines, napkins, cups, etc.

Overnight accommodation

Accommodation is often required at conferences which is why hotels are a popular venue. Hotels open near exhibition centres to benefit from the visitors' custom. In hotels that are aimed at the business market, there may be more executive and single rooms available to cater for the needs of the business customer.

Licences

Venues must have licences to play live music, to provide entertainment and to serve alcohol. As these are the responsibility of the venue, the organiser need not worry about them.

As a result of the Licensing Act 2003, responsibility for licensing the provision of alcohol, entertainment and late-night refreshment has been passed from magistrates to local councils.

If a one-off event is held then a temporary event licence can be applied for. This applies if fewer than 500 people are attending and the event lasts for no more than 96 hours.

Entertainment

Whether entertainment is provided depends on the type of event. It could take the form of an after-dinner speaker, as we noted for the House of Commons suppers organised by the Institute of Travel & Tourism. If the event is a formal dinner, or ball, then a band could be provided.

Equipment

For meetings and conferences the venue usually supplies any audio-visual equipment or projection equipment required. Sometimes more sophisticated equipment and technicians are needed and then a specialist company may be hired. Venues or conference organisers have contacts with such companies or they can be found easily on the internet. The services they offer may include:

- web-conference production
- set design (where a themed event is desired)
- graphics
- multimedia presentations.

Exhibitions are arranged in an entirely different way with space requirements determined by the number of stands and therefore exhibitors that can be fitted into a venue. Exhibitors choose stand location and size according to their budget.

Activity: Looking at facilities

Choose two local venues, each one from a different category with different types of facilities, and arrange to visit them as a group. Compare the facilities provided at these venues.

Activity: Looking at layouts

Here are some examples of layouts.

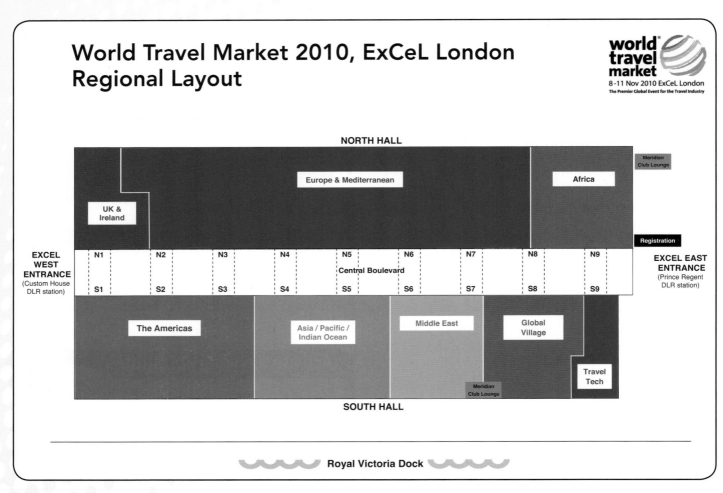

Figure 17.2: Example room layouts

Which configuration is:

- Theatre
- Classroom
- Boardroom
- Banquet
- Cabaret
- U-shaped?

World Travel Market 2010, ExCeL London Regional Layout

world travel market
8-11 Nov 2010 ExCeL London
The Premier Global Event for the Travel Industry

NORTH HALL

Europe & Mediterranean

Africa

Meridian Club Lounge

UK & Ireland

Registration

EXCEL WEST ENTRANCE (Custom House DLR station)

| N1 | N2 | N3 | N4 | N5 | N6 | N7 | N8 | N9 |

Central Boulevard

| S1 | S2 | S3 | S4 | S5 | S6 | S7 | S8 | S9 |

EXCEL EAST ENTRANCE (Prince Regent DLR station)

The Americas

Asia / Pacific / Indian Ocean

Middle East

Global Village

Meridian Club Lounge

Travel Tech

SOUTH HALL

Royal Victoria Dock

Figure 17.3: Floor plan for World Travel Market

(Source:www.wtmlondon.com/page.cfm/link=28)

Assessment activity 17.1

P1 P2 P3 M1 D1   BTEC

You recently gave advice to a company named Slovenia Tours who were hoping to set up an office in the UK promoting Slovenia as a destination to UK outbound tourists. They have been very successful in the holiday market and have returned to you for advice once again. They are now interested in the event, conference and exhibition market which is in its infancy in Slovenia. They see the development of their business in organising conferences in Slovenia for international businesses. They want to know how conferences and events are organised in the UK and what issues affect the market. They think that knowledge of the UK experience will help them build their business in Slovenia.

Produce a report in which you:

- Describe the events, conference and exhibition environment in the UK. **P1**
- Explain the intrinsic links between the event, conference and exhibitions environment and the UK travel and tourism sector. **P2**
- Explain the appropriateness of different types of venue for events, conferences and exhibitions. You must describe five venues, one of each type. **P3**
- Explain how trends affect the event, conference and exhibitions environment. **M1**

- Assess the growth potential of the event, conference and exhibition environment. **D1**

Your report does not have to be written. You may report orally if you prefer.

Make sure you cover the full range, referring to the content and assessment guidance in the unit specification for the detail required.

Grading tips

P1 Include examples of events, conferences and exhibitions. Consider who uses the services provided and how their needs differ.

P2 Show how event organisers use transport services, accommodation and catering. Make sure you describe at least three trends.

P3 Name the venues and give their location. Say what the venue offers and give examples of recent events.

M1 You must show that you understand the impact of the trends, for example the impact of web-conferencing on conferences.

D1 You need to think about where the areas of growth are in events, conferences and exhibitions. Find the UK Events Market Trends Survey (UKEMTS) on the internet published by Eventia to help you.

PLTS

By supporting your conclusions using reasoned arguments and evidence when you explain how trends affect the industry, and when you assess the growth potential of the event, conference and exhibition market, you will be developing your **independent enquirer** skills.

Functional skills

When you are researching venues and what they offer, you will be using ICT-based information and assessing its fitness-for-purpose, and so will be practising your **ICT** skills.

3 Proposing and costing events, conferences and exhibitions

3.1 Brief

If you are organising an event, conference or exhibition you will receive a brief from the customer. The brief is essential for you to produce a proposal that meets or exceeds the needs of the customer.

The brief will include the following information:

Objectives

It is for the customer to determine the objectives of their event but they must be clear from the outset. It is usual to communicate the objectives to the delegates or participators for the event beforehand. This could be achieved through the promotional material issued before the event.

Customer

The brief will include the customer details. These are essential so that the event organiser can easily communicate with the customer. It is useful also for the customer to provide some background information about their company and its products and services.

Target market

The brief must include information about the intended delegates or participants for the event, so that the organiser can suggest relevant means of reaching the target market.

Budget

The customer will state how much money is available for the event. It may be broken down into different areas, for example, venue hire, promotion, etc.

Facilities required

The brief will say what is needed in terms of exhibition space, layout of room/s and equipment.

Dates

The customer may be specific about dates or may be flexible in order to obtain a suitable venue.

Delegate numbers

Minimum numbers relate to costs and cost-effectiveness. If the event, conference or exhibition is meant to be profit-making, then a break-even point will be calculated for a minimum number. If that number is

not reached, it may be necessary to cancel the event. The organiser will need to know the minimum numbers for break-even, and the numbers anticipated by the customer, so that a suitable sized venue can be found.

Case study: Organising a day trip

A group of students organised a day trip to a go-kart track. They had all managed to find sponsors based on the number of laps they planned to achieve. They had to organise transport and the entrance to the track. They managed to have the track to themselves as they were a group. They took lots of photos and wrote a press release which they sent to the local newspapers. The funds raised were donated to charity.

1 What do you think were the objectives of this event?

3.2 Proposal

When preparing a proposal the organiser needs to read the customer's brief carefully to make sure they fully understand what is required.

Once they have a clear understanding of what is needed they can start putting their proposal together. The proposal will provide all the details of the event. It will demonstrate why the customer should choose that organiser to deliver the event, rather than someone else. The proposal should be a written document and remember that if you are the organiser, the customer will be judging you and your work so you should ensure that all your documents have been proof-read and spell-checked and that your personal appearance and presentation are suitably professional.

Format of event

The organiser will follow the brief to arrange the format or will suggest a format to the customer. A conference has a very different format to an exhibition. It will require a large space for delegates to sit and hear speakers and will also need rooms for breakout sessions. An exhibition is more likely to have people coming and going at different times and they will need space to look at exhibits.

Venue

The following venue factors must be considered when planning an event, conference or exhibition:

- capacity
- accommodation and quality
- facilities
- availability for specific dates
- access for visitors
- parking
- cost.

Facilities to be used

Once a venue has been chosen, the size of room needed must be determined and the organiser will also be given a choice of layouts for the room. Different layouts are suitable for different degrees of formality in meetings. Conferences for large numbers of delegates will need theatre-type layouts to ensure there is room for everyone and that they can all see the speakers. Everything that has been agreed with the venue and any service suppliers, such as caterers, will need to be formalised in a contract that confirms the particulars of what has been ordered and includes the terms and conditions.

Think about it

One group of learners borrowed a whole theatre for a day and put on a fashion show. Another group organised their event for children in a local primary school. The local council allowed another group to put on a Christmas fête in a hall at the local Guild Hall. What kind of venues could you use for an event?

Date and time

The proposal will give suggested times and dates or will meet those determined by the customer.

Agenda

For a meeting or conference an agenda will be required. These will be prepared in advance and can be as simple as a sheet with times of speakers and activities and locations of seminars or meetings. For an exhibition, a full catalogue of exhibitors and their location within the venue will be provided. These catalogues can be sold to provide extra revenue. They sometimes carry advertising.

Booking methods

The customer needs to know when and how deposits and payments are to be made to secure their booking. They also need to be informed of the cancellation policy. Note the payment methods available in the booking form shown in Figure 17.4. How would you pay if you booked online?

Conference Booking Form 2011

The conference fee includes all meals, tea and coffee and evening events. Standard accommodation at one of the colleges can be booked using this form. Information about hotel accomodation is available from the Tourist Information Office.

Title _____ Name _____

Address _____

Email _____

Tel. _____ (wk) _____ (home)_____

Affiliation _____

Three-day conference fee (including lunch, dinner, tea and coffee)_____

    Full fee (£155)_____   Postgraduate fee (£125)_____

Conference accommodation:

Bed and breakfast (August 15) standard (£30) _____

Bed and breakfast (August 16) standard (£30) _____

Bed and breakfast (August 17) standard (£30) _____ Total_____

I am a vegetarian _____ Other dietary or access needs _____

For any further information about booking meals and accommodation please contact the conference organiser.

Payment

By cheque: Cheques should be made payable to Conference Services plc.

By credit/debit card

I would like to pay by Visa _____ If other, please specify _____

Card number _____ Expiry date _____

Issue no. (if applicable)_____ Security code _____

Name on card _____

Address of cardholder _____

Please debit from my account the sum of: _____

Signed _____ Date _____

Figure 17.4: Conference booking form

Equipment

At a conference the basic equipment needed is presentation material, that is, a flip chart and markers. Sometimes an overhead projector is needed but today many speakers arrive with PowerPoint® presentations on a laptop computer and they will expect a screen and laptop-compatible projector to be provided. They may also require internet access. It is usual to provide pens and paper for delegates and water should be on the table.

More sophisticated equipment, such as video-conferencing or computer networks, will have to be specially ordered.

At an exhibition or event, all kinds of special effects may be required from lighting to graphics. These could be provided by a specialist company.

Activity: Organising a conference

Make a list of all the equipment you would need for a conference in your school or college. You could ask your marketing department if they have any college pens or diaries that they could give you. If you wanted to have a display you might need to borrow boards or stands from your school or college.

Signage

Signs may be needed at various points around the building, particularly in venues where several events are taking place at the same time. Organisers should remember that signs may also be needed to guide people to a venue.

Refreshments and catering

Organisers will have a budget for catering. At exhibitions people will buy their own refreshments, but they will expect facilities to be provided. At conferences you would need to find out any special dietary requirements and cater for them. You should include times of refreshment breaks on your agenda.

Additional services available to delegates

As we saw earlier, the venue may not be able to provide everything needed or the organiser may just want something different. In that case the organiser will look to outside contractors to provide extras. They might order:

- flowers
- food and drink
- transport, for example taxis or buses to shuttle delegates from one venue to another
- accommodation – this might be provided at hotels near the venue in a separate contract
- use of a business centre or gym – may be on-site or nearby.

Promotion

Promotion could include any of the following:

- advertising
- direct marketing to exhibitors
- invitations to VIPs
- public relations
- discounts.

Unless the event is a very small conference or meeting, it will require publicity or advertising. The two are often used together in a campaign. The advertising for an event will, of course, have been planned in advance, and hopefully press releases will result in press interest and the press will turn up to the event. However, this should never be assumed and it is a good idea to put on some pressure by reminding the press a couple of days before that the event is happening.

Even if press do not attend, a photographic record of the event can be made and a further press release sent out with photos after the event. This would still be useful publicity. The photos can be posted on a website.

Direct marketing means contacting people from a mailing list or database and letting them know individually about the event. This could be by mail, email, text or social networking sites.

Special guests may be sent an invitation early in the marketing. Their acceptance can then be used as an incentive for others to attend the event.

Discounts might be given for block bookings from companies rather than individual bookings. Early bookings might also merit a discount.

Here are some examples of promotion for different types of events.

A conference for company staff

All this requires is an internal email or invitation for staff to attend. Posters and leaflets advertising the event can be distributed throughout the company.

A national conference for travel professionals

It is necessary to inform potential delegates of the event. This can be done by placing advertisements in professional travel journals. Press releases with information about the event can be sent to journals too. These have the benefit of generating free publicity – if they are used. A delegate's pack can be sent to each person with details of the location, accommodation and agenda. Pre-conference reading can be included.

A national trade exhibition, for example World Travel Market

As soon as one of these major trade fairs finishes, work begins on planning the next. The fair's website is constantly updated, giving information about dates and exhibitors. Press releases are sent out to all the travel trade press, particularly in the weeks leading up to the fair. These give news updates and information about competitions to entice visitors. Advertising is placed in travel trade journals. Mailshots are sent to all the people who attended the fair in the previous year with their pre-registration information.

A national consumer exhibition, for example Clothes Show Live

This is a very popular, successful show and therefore can afford a large advertising budget. Money is spent on television advertising, as well as press advertising. Mailshots are sent to schools and colleges who have previously sent groups to the show. In addition, a publicity team generates press releases and news items to create press interest. Celebrity presenters are an added attraction.

Activity: Promoting a charity auction

Prepare a press release for a charity auction which is being held at your school or college to raise money for cancer research. Use headed paper and include a picture that a newspaper could print. Make sure you have all the details of:

- what is happening
- where it is taking place
- the date
- the times
- contact details for further information.

Registration format

At a conference there is an attendance list which delegates should sign to confirm their presence. Badges should be provided for delegates as it cannot be presumed that they all know each other. Also, they will hope to network – which badges enable them to do more easily.

At exhibitions it is usual to collect all details of visitors. At a large event like the World Travel Market a system of pre-registration online or by post enables visitors to arrive with tickets. This means reception halls are not clogged with people filling in forms, although there is a provision for people to register on arrival as well.

Prizes and sponsorship

If prizes or awards are to be given it should be determined what form these will take and how much they will cost. Each award can be sponsored by an organisation. This brings good publicity for the sponsor and provides an award for a company or individual.

Evaluation

It is very important that the issue of evaluation is not left until the end of the event or conference. At this stage it is too late to decide how to evaluate the event. For this reason, decisions on evaluation and the criteria that will be used must be incorporated into the planning stages. Aims and objectives must be set at this early stage. Then, when the team of organisers meets after the event, it can go through every detail and analyse the event against the agreed criteria. The organisers will be very critical and look for areas which can be improved on next time.

Feedback methods

Questionnaires

Questionnaires are a useful tool for gathering feedback. They have to be prepared well in advance and the usual rules of questionnaire design apply. The organisers must determine who the respondents of the questionnaire will be, for example at a large exhibition it would not be feasible to ask everyone to complete a questionnaire but a sample could be completed.

Statistics

Quantitative information about numbers of visitors is easily acquired and allows organisers to make comparisons with the same event in previous years or with comparable events.

Feedback cards or forms

It is customary for delegates at a conference to fill in an evaluation form. The example shown in Figure 17.5 is from a seminar organised by local government to encourage sustainable business practice. You can see that the format is very simple but gives the organisers a clear idea of the success of the seminar.

Staff feedback

The organiser should consider using feedback from different groups of people and not just the organising team. In this way, different points of view are aired.

Clients or suppliers invited to an event, such as corporate hospitality, can be invited for their views on how it went. Of course, having been invited they can be expected to be complimentary but observation of behaviour and enjoyment during the event will give a good indication of how it is going. At an exhibition, visitors and suppliers can complete feedback forms provided around the venue. They will probably require different questionnaires as they will be evaluating different aspects of the exhibition.

The UK travel and tourism sector

Central City Hotel – 14th September 2010

Name: _____   Company: _____

Contact details: _____

1. Did the conference meet your needs?   Yes ☐   No ☐
If not, why?

_____

2. What sessions/activities/topics did you find the most useful and why?

_____

3. What sessions/activities/topics did you find the least useful and why?

_____

4. Please rate the following between 1 and 5
(1= excellent, 2 = good, 3 = okay, 4 = poor, 5 = very bad)

Please tick the appropriate box: 1   2   3   4   5
1. Booking arrangements
2. Presentations and content
3. Topic relevance
4. Effectiveness of the conference
5. Standard of delegate packs
6. Standard of catering and refreshments
7. The event overall

Would you be willing for us to contact you in the next few weeks
to discuss ways in which the conference could be improved?   Yes ☐   No ☐

Please add any further comments you have in the box below:

_____

Figure 17.5: A sample feedback form

Useful questions for evaluation

Meetings of planning teams following the event will aid a critical evaluation of its success. One of the first things they will want to consider is whether the objectives were met. Objectives relating to numbers of visitors are easy to measure. It is more difficult to measure issues such as 'raising awareness'. Delegates can be asked if they consider that the objectives of the conference were met on their feedback forms.

Other points for consideration include the following:

- Was the venue suitable and the event well designed?
- Were the roles and responsibilities allocated appropriately?
- Were legal requirements met?
- Was the budget met?
- How were individual performances and skills?
- Was the programme suitable?
- Was the evaluation system a success?
- What were the areas for improvement?
- What improvements are recommended?

3.3 Health and safety factors

The Health and Safety at Work Act 1974 lays out a duty of care towards members of the public visiting an establishment. Thus, a conference or exhibition organiser must ensure, so far as is reasonably practicable, that visitors are not exposed to health and safety risks. In addition, the Occupier's Liability Act 1984 places a duty of care on occupiers to see that a visitor will be reasonably safe in using the premises for the purposes for which they are invited, or permitted by the occupier to be there.

If an organiser brings in outside contractors to a venue, for example catering, then the organiser must make sure that the contractor complies with health and safety legislation.

The following are some of the points relating to health and safety that should be considered.

Risk assessment

The Management of Health and Safety at Work Regulations 1999 have specific requirements regarding risk assessment and it is necessary to carry out a risk assessment in relation to people visiting an establishment.

When carrying out the risk assessment the following points should be considered.

Who is at risk?
- people attending the event
- organisers
- outside contractors working at the event.

What are the possible hazards?

- tripping or slipping
- manual handling injuries
- bad housekeeping
- electrical problems
- fire hazards from heaters or smoking
- food hygiene.

How can the risk be minimised?

- remove the hazard, for example no lit candles, no blocked gangways
- minimise the hazard, for example provide fire extinguishers, provide training in lifting techniques.

An example of risk minimisation by an organiser is the Leeds Festival organised by Mean Fiddler. No campfires are allowed on-site, which reduces the risk of fire and is a condition of the festival licence from Leeds City Council. Patrols are carried out to make sure fires are not lit and there are fire observation towers.

What is the level of risk? Is it:

- very low
- low
- medium
- high
- very high.

A risk assessment form should be completed and kept.

Delegate numbers and flow

Every conference or exhibition room has a maximum capacity which should be displayed in the room. The capacity is determined by the size of the room and by ability to exit in a fire. A room with many fire exits will be allocated a larger capacity than a room with only a few. Organisers must make sure the maximum capacity is not exceeded and bear in mind that if there are many wheelchair users then the overall capacity is reduced.

Entrances, exits and reception areas must be able to cope with numbers of visitors arriving at the same time. Consideration should be given to the movement of people around the building, to toilets, dining rooms, etc. If necessary, people should be guided in smaller groups.

Fire safety

When designing the room layout make sure that everyone will be able to get out if necessary. Make sure that exits and gangways are not blocked and that there are no obstacles for people to fall over. Ensure that there are signs showing the fire exits and

procedures, and that both of these are made known to delegates at conferences.

Guidance on fire safety is provided by an HMSO publication called *The Guide to Fire Precautions in Existing Places of Entertainment and Like Premises* (known as the 'Yellow Guide').

Organisers have to consider access for people with impaired mobility or other special needs and should take account of the Disability Discrimination Act 1995, as well as fire safety advice.

Security

Delegates or visitors should have secure places to leave their belongings. Rooms should be locked when not in use.

Activity: Assessing the risks

Imagine you have invited a group of 15 eight-year-olds to participate in an afternoon of games in your sports hall. Carry out a risk assessment under the headings 'Hazard', 'Risk level', 'Safety measure', 'Who is responsible?'.

Evacuation

Evacuation only takes place in cases of emergency but if you are organising any event you must be aware of the evacuation route and be prepared to lead your delegates to safety. It is good practice also to warn people if there is to be a fire alarm test so that they do not get ready to evacuate when it is unnecessary.

Environmental factors

The comfort of delegates or visitors to an event or exhibition will be affected by the level of heating and ventilation. Many delegate feedback forms mention 'too hot' or 'too cold' in their evaluation, thus impacting on the success of the event. The room temperature should be set at an appropriate level and delegates in a conference room should be able to adjust the temperature to suit them.

3.4 Operational factors

Time constraints

Everyone involved in planning an event must know exactly what they are responsible for and work to agreed deadlines.

Preparation will vary depending on the type of event but will include:

- venue liaison and booking
- administration
- finance
- fundraising
- marketing
- catering
- contracting speakers
- planning layout, delegate flow, signage, etc.
- methods of gathering feedback for evaluation.

In addition, people will have particular responsibilities on the day of the event. These may include:

- welcome and registration
- setting up the room(s)
- food preparation
- guiding delegates and speakers
- taking photos
- meeting press
- hosting the event.

Timings

Timings for the event, conference or exhibition are needed, that is, the start and end times, or the opening times. For a conference, timings will be shown in the agenda. For other events they will be publicised in promotional material or advertising.

Minimum numbers

If too many people turn up on the day it may affect health and safety requirements so you must be aware of the maximum capacity of your venue. If too few turn up it will be too late to cancel so the event will have to carry on, but having too few people will have an impact on the success of the event.

Staff

At an exhibition, staff are needed to meet the visitors and establish their needs, and then to sell. At a conference, an administrator will be needed to register people and see to any last-minute issues. Catering staff are also needed. At exhibitions and events security staff are needed. If an exhibition has stands

booked from different companies each company will provide the staff for its own stand.

Contingency plans

The risk assessment will identify some hazards, but there are many things that can go wrong which do not fall into the category of hazards. When planning an event, conference or exhibition it is always best to think of everything that could possibly go wrong and prepare for it by creating a **contingency plan**. The most common problem at conferences is the late arrival or cancellation of speakers. Good planners confirm with their speakers the week before and the day before the conference and make sure times and transport details are confirmed in writing. It is such attention to detail that may prevent problems. At a very large exhibition it may not be so noticeable if one or two exhibitors cancel. However, exhibitors may have problems if their products, props or outside contractors let them down.

Key term

Contingency plan – a plan you have ready to deal with things that go wrong.

The contingency plan should be written and available. It allows organisers to check contingency procedures and gives them confidence. Organisers need to know when the contingency plans come into play, that is, what the trigger is. For example, if an event is to move indoors in case of rain, does a shower trigger the move or should you wait until it becomes a downpour? Absolutely every detail of an event should be written down and everyone should know where the plans are and what the timetable for the day is.

Equipment failure

Equipment should have been checked in advance but even so it can often go wrong. It is essential to have back-up for IT equipment. Most venues provide ICT facilities but you do need to check what is available and whether there is an extra charge. Sometimes wireless internet is available but delegates will need their own laptops to access it.

Activity: What if something goes wrong?

Think about each of the following problems and discuss with your group what you might do about them. Also think about whether a contingency plan or better planning would have helped. If so, what plans would have been set up in advance to avoid problems?

- You have organised a conference and half of your delegates haven't turned up. There is a traffic problem on the motorway and you think they will arrive later. In the meantime your first speaker is ready to begin.

- One of the delegates has a mobile telephone and has taken three calls by lunchtime in the middle of the conference.

- The conference has four key speakers and the third one hasn't shown up.

- One of the delegates is taken ill. He appears to be having a heart attack.

- You are holding a fashion show and plan to sell wine in the interval. You didn't realise you needed a licence and the health and safety officer at your college is refusing to let you sell it.

- One of the exhibitors at your tourism event has placed their stand in front of a fire exit.

- You are delighted when the press arrive to cover your event. Unfortunately, one of the exhibitors who had a big problem with their equipment is talking to the reporter at length.

Delays

Speakers may not turn up or may be delayed. You should always have a contingency plan for this. Either move another speaker forward and finish the day earlier or have a member of staff prepared to step into the breach with something. If suppliers fail to provide essential equipment you will need back-up. Checking everything over and over again prevents such delays.

Transportation

Delegates or visitors may be held up by transport problems. You have to decide whether to wait for latecomers or start on time. It is usually better to start on time rather than risk frustrating those who have arrived.

Weather

Poor weather can affect the success of an event. For example, heavy snowfall may mean that only 10 people turn up at an event for 40. The event may have to be held again at great cost. However, the original 10 can enjoy a very good day and learn a lot.

Activity: Proposal and costings

You work for the Institute of Travel & Tourism as an adminstrator. The Institute wants to organise a training event for travel agency managers in the South East of England. The brief is as follows.

- Event to take place on a Friday in June in a Central London venue.

- One main room to seat 50 cabaret style.

- One breakout room.

- Data projector and laptop required.

- 2 flip charts required.

- Lead trainers = 3.

- Travel agency managers to be invited = 50.

- Invited speakers = 3 x 30 minutes each.

- Workshops of 90 minutes led by trainers; each one will run twice so that the group can split into two smaller groups to attend workshops.

- Buffet lunch to be served in a restaurant.

- Coffee mid-morning and afternoon tea.

- Registration and badges required.

- A proposal for the event to be produced.

- Costings for the event to be produced.

Produce the proposal and costings and explain how they meet the client brief and how they take into account factors that may affect the event's success.

3.4 Costings

Calculations per delegate/attendee

Venues calculate rates for delegates/attendees on a day basis or on a residential basis. Such rates will usually include accommodation, meals and use of facilities if at a hotel. Conference organisers may add a percentage onto these rates to add to their profits and to apply for additional services.

The following extract describes events at a conference venue in the North of England in 2010.

The average event duration was 1.8 days, this is slightly higher than the national average of 1.6 days. The average daily delegate rate achieved by the venue for conferences was £39, the average 24 hour/residential rate was £145 and the average rate for banquets, dinners and receptions was £29. The average conference size was 35 delegates, slightly lower than last year when it was 38.

Exhibition space rates

When booking space at an exhibition, suppliers have to take into account the cost of stands and space. The best positions, for example at the top of escalators, cost more as do the larger stands. Companies have a budget allocated annually which must cover all the shows at which they wish to exhibit. This budget must cover the cost of hospitality on the exhibition stand as well as any props.

A holiday home company exhibiting at the National Park & Holiday Home Show has the following costs to consider:

- cost of stand
- wine and appetisers on the stand to offer to customers
- props inside the holiday homes
- purchase of garden chairs, tables and parasols to add ambience to the stand
- hire of greeters (to meet customers and direct them to sales personnel).

In addition, the company is likely to provide corporate hospitality in the evenings in terms of dinners out and entertainment.

Case study: Ernst Hotel

You are going to use the Ernst Hotel for a small conference to discuss the next year's business plan. You have 12 staff but it is not essential that they all attend. However, some may be upset if they are not invited. You have a budget of £2000 for the event. Table 17.1 shows the delegate rates charged by the hotel.

1 Decide whether it is to be a day meeting or a residential one and what you will offer the delegates.

2 Draw up a table showing how you have spent the budget.

3 Compare your plan with those of your colleagues.

Table 17.1: Conference and meeting facilities delegate rates for the Ernst Hotel

Week commencing	24-hour delegate rate	Daily delegate rate	Week commencing	24-hour delegate rate	Daily delegate rate
January			April		
Monday 01	£120	£50	Monday 02	£120	£50
Monday 08	£120	£50	Monday 09	£120	£50
Monday 15	£120	£50	Monday 16	£160	£50
Monday 22	£120	£50	Monday 23	£160	£50
Monday 29	£120	£50	Monday 30	£160	£50
February			May		
Monday 05	£140	£50	Monday 07	£120	£50
Monday 12	£140	£50	Monday 14	£160	£50
Monday 19	£140	£50	Monday 21	£160	£50
Monday 26	£140	£50	Monday 28	£120	£50
March			June		
Monday 05	£160	£50	Monday 04	£160	£50
Monday 12	£160	£50	Monday 11	£160	£50
Monday 19	£160	£50	Monday 18	£160	£50
Monday 26	£160	£50	Monday 25	£160	£50
Extra charges, charged per delegate: Use of gym £5, Production of programmes and materials £2.50, Car parking £1 per day					

Calculation of ticket costs

The second strand of revenue for exhibition companies is the entry fee. Exhibition organisers have to decide at what price to sell their tickets. Remember too that many business customers will not be charged for entry to an exhibition as their custom is precious and if they do not attend then the exhibitors do not want to be there. For example, at the World Travel

Market everyone who pre-registers gets in free. Of course, the organisers then have useful names and addresses for their future mailings. Some exhibitions are targeted at the public and in this case an entrance fee can be charged. The fee will depend on what customers will be prepared to pay and on how many visitors to an exhibition are expected. This is not difficult to calculate for an exhibition which is held regularly as previous visitor numbers are available.

Calculations of additional services

If the organiser wishes to provide transport or accommodation this cost must be added to the delegate rates when calculating final costs.

Budget and breakdown of costs

A budget must be realistic and include all costs and all sources of revenue. It should include an amount for contingencies.

Case study: Stand application form

The Stand Application Form for World Travel Market indicates the cost of space and stands. Those suppliers on a limited budget may opt to share a stand.

WTM 2010 Stand Enquiry

Your Company Details

Exhibiting Company

Title   First name

Surname

Job Title

Address

Tel   Fax

Mobile

Website

E-mail

(Please provide your email address so we can keep you informed about World Travel Market.)
If you do not wish your email address to be used by any of the following please tick the appropriate box.
○ WTM ○ other relevant Reed Exhibition Events ○ Other Companies approved by Reed Exhibitions

Stand Requirement

Our 2009 Stand No. was:

For 2010 I require _____ m² of stand space

We wish to register _____ exhibiting partners @ £69 each

Stand Packages

Option 1
○ Space Only at £310 per m²
You use your own suppliers to design and construct the stand to meet your requirements.

Doubledecker
○ Space only @ £54 per m²

Option 2
○ Shell Scheme at £367 per m²
Space plus basic exhibition.

Region

(Tick one)
I wish our stand to be located in the following region:
○ Africa   ○ Latin America
○ Technology & Online Travel   ○ Global Village*
○ Asia/Pacific/Indian Ocean   ○ UK & Ireland
○ Middle East/North Africa   ○ Caribbean
○ North America   ○ Europe & Mediterranean
* For international companies with global representation

Registration

○ Main Standholder registration   £315*
○ Main Standholder registration after 12th August 2010   £330

○ Stand Insurance   £100

*Includes Product + Services Gallery as part of the online Exhibitor listing for MSH & all EPs

Sponsorship

○ Tick here if you would like details of WTM sponsorship opportunities

Nature of Your Company Activity

○ Accommodation   ○ National Tourist Boards
○ Air Travel   ○ Regional Tourist Boards
○ Airports   ○ Technology Companies
○ Business & Financial Services ○ Ticketing Agents
○ City Tourist Boards   ○ Tourist Attractions & Entertainment Providers
○ Convention Bureau   ○ Tours
○ Destination Management ○ Trade Associations
○ Event Support Services ○ Training / Recruitment
○ Golf Related Services ○ Travel Agency
○ Ground Handling Services ○ Water Travel
○ Land Travel
○ Media

Option 3 Packages vary to include the below. For further details please contact the WTM sales team. Prices do not include VAT.

	120w Adjustable Spotlights	13 Amp 3 Pin Socket- 500w Max	Literature Rack	Standard Chairs	Lounge Chairs	Round Table	Coffee Table	Storage Unit	Waste paper bin
○ Package 2 - £850, 9-20m²	x3	x1	x1	0	x2	0	x1	x1	x1
○ Package 3 - £910, 9-20m²	x3	x1	x1	x3	0	x1	0	x1	x1
○ Package 4 £990, 9-20m²	x4	x1	x1	0	x2	0	x1	x1	x1
○ Package 5 £1,070, 9-20m²	x4	x1	x1	x3	0	x1	0	x1	x1

Figure 17.6: ExCeL pricing information and Stand Application Form

1 Who is selling the stand space?

2 What do you think is meant by sponsorship opportunities?

3 Explain the other services on offer.

4 Discuss your answers with your group.

(Source: World Travel Market www.wtmlondon.com)

Activity: Budget and breakdown of costs

Here is an example of a budget form for a travel and tourism conference.

Pre-conference budget

Conference title: _____ Date: _____

Organiser(s): _____

Expected Income
Registrations:
Non-members @ £30   Members/concessions @ £20
Speakers (consessionary rate for 2-day + conferences) @ £20
Sponsorship (state which bodies you have applied/are applying to)
Fees for stands @ £500 per exhibitor per day
Fees for programme advertisments £30 per ad
Other (please state source)
Total Projected Income £

Expected Expenditure
Cost of venue
Travel expenses for speakers
(give name of each speaker and where travelling from)
Hotel accommodation for speakers @ £90 per night per speaker
(only where agreed with the Institute and where strictly necessary; please name each speaker involved)
Tea/coffee/biscuits @ £1.25 per person per break
Lunch @ £6.50 per speaker per day
Administration costs @ £250 (1 day events)
Any publicity (please state nature and estimated cost)
AV technical support @ £35 per hour (weekdays)
Other (please state)
Total Projected Expenditure £

Total Projected Loss/Profit £

Signature	Print Name	Date

What other items would you add to the budget?
What other sources of income might there be?

Activity: Talent show budget

Produce a budget for a talent show at your school or college. The target audience will be parents and friends of the students. Estimate all the costs you will have and all the revenue. It is likely that you will be keeping costs as low as possible and using accommodation and facilities in your school or college as far as possible. Will you be able to charge for entry? How much will you charge?

You will have some expenses, for example you might want to serve refreshments. If you have no funds available for your event, consider fundraising activities like sponsored walks and cake sales. Don't forget to ask your school or college if they have funds allocated for student events.

Assessment activity 17.2

You and your colleagues are to put on a conference. The theme is to be 'Careers in Travel and Tourism' and you will invite all the travel and tourism learners at your college or school to attend. There must be at least 50 delegates. You may, of course, invite other learners if you wish. Although this is a group activity, all your evidence must be your own individual work and should record your own individual contributions to the conference. Remember to consider evaluation at the early stages and not just at the end.

Make sure that you cover the full range, referring to the content and assessment guidance in the unit specification for the detail required.

Task 1

Produce a full dated proposal for this event. **P4**

The following information will help you, although you may add any other details you think are appropriate:

- Objectives – to provide learners with information about potential employers, locations and types of jobs.
- Target market – all learners in the schools and colleges in the area who may be interested in entering employment in the next two years; you cannot expect them to pay to attend.
- Exhibitors – you will need to invite employers to attend; you will not have to pay them.
- Room layout – must allow visitors to look round all stands in safety; determine maximum capacity.
- Equipment – consider stands, tables, chairs for exhibitors, lighting.
- Catering – you should provide drinks and possibly lunch for exhibitors. You could have drinks and snacks on sale for visitors (consider contracting to your cafeteria).

- Planned promotional activities, including invitations to exhibitors with response forms, marketing to schools and colleges, press releases.
- Decoration of hall and signage needed.
- Budget needed.
- Programme for visitors listing exhibitors and location.
- Timings for the day.
- Operational factors.
- Health and safety considerations.
- Evaluation methods needed.

Task 2

Prepare costings for your event. These can be produced as an information sheet. **P5**

Task 3

Explain how your proposal and costings meet the brief. **M2**

Grading tips

P4 Make sure your proposal looks professional and has full detail.

P5 You need full costings stating whether they are for an individual or for a particular item.

M2 Say why you chose particular aspects of the proposal.

PLTS

Producing proposals for an event, conference or exhibition to meet a given brief will help to develop your skills as a **creative thinker**.

Functional skills

You will practise your **Maths** skills by selecting and applying a range of mathematics to find solutions, and by drawing conclusions and providing mathematical justifications to meet the budget.

Hayley Bevan
Events and Sponsorship Manager, FIA

Hayley, your job title sounds very interesting. Can you tell us what it's about?

My job is to arrange various seminars and conferences throughout the year for the Fitness Industry Association (FIA).

We have some Professional Development seminars throughout the year, which I organise with my team. Then there might be dinners such as our 20th anniversary dinner at the London Transport Museum.

How did you get the job?

I started with the company as a Programmes Co-ordinator, working on projects to get children active.

I managed a project called Go London that was located in Brent, promoting gym use to teenage girls. When the Manager position came up I applied and got it, making good use of my project management experience.

Are you responsible for any really big events?

The major event that I organise is an annual conference for the FIA. This year it's at the Reebok Stadium in Bolton. The aim of the event is to bring all suppliers and operators in the fitness industry together. It is a huge undertaking to organise as we have 700 delegates. It takes a year to arrange from start to finish. We need a venue that can hold the 700 delegates for two days, plus room to host a black tie dinner for 900 as extra people attend a ball on the second day. This ball incorporates an awards ceremony recognising excellence in the industry.

The event is sponsored so I have to find the sponsorship and secure the funding for the event, for example gym equipment suppliers might sponsor us. Once the sponsorship and venue are secured there is a lot of work to do arranging the marketing, invitations, delegate lists, details of programme and equipment needed. Everything has to be organised to deadlines.

Think about it!

1 What project management experience could you include on a CV or application form?

2 Have you arranged any events at school or college?

3 Have you arranged any events for friends?

Just checking

1 Explain the difference between a trade fair and a consumer fair.

2 Explain what is meant by corporate hospitality.

3 What kind of venue would be most suitable for a national exhibition?

4 Discuss the advantages and disadvantages of academic venues.

5 Explain what a roadshow is.

6 What services do conference organisers offer?

7 Comment on the impact of web-conferencing.

8 How is fire safety ensured in a venue?

9 What is the purpose of a risk assessment?

10 Think of five things that could go wrong at a conference.

11 What is meant by a delegate day rate?

12 Suggest some promotional activities for a national exhibition.

13 What is a contingency plan?

14 Why is it important that evaluation is considered at the planning stage of an event?

Assignment tips

- Find out about as many different local events as you can and see if you can attend them.

- Do not be shy about asking organisers at events about their work in planning.

- Ask friends and family about events, exhibitions and conferences they have attended for their work and what they were like.

- Think about when you have organised events for friends such as parties. What did you have to do to plan?

19 UK visitor attractions

Visitor attractions make an important contribution to the travel and tourism sector. They provide interest, excitement and activity for tourists when they visit a destination or when they venture out on a day trip.

In this unit you are going to find out about the different types of visitor attractions and the products and services they offer.

You will determine what it is that constitutes appeal to a visitor at particular attractions and consider how the appeal can be increased. You will also investigate the impact of the attractions on the wider community, in enhancing the appeal of the whole area and creating income and employment.

While studying this unit you will be encouraged to visit as many attractions as you can to aid your knowledge and understanding. You can easily visit attractions in your own locality but don't forget that you may be going on organised visits with your group or going on holiday with friends and family during your studies. Use these outings to take the opportunity to visit more attractions and compare their appeal. You are fortunate too in that almost all visitor attractions have their own websites full of information.

Some of them have prepared materials which you can download. Remember that such materials are meant to aid your research and cannot be submitted as your own work.

Learning outcomes

After completing this unit you should:

1 know the products and services provided by different types of visitor attraction
2 know the range and purpose of techniques used for visitor interpretation
3 understand the appeal of visitor attractions to different types of visitor
4 understand the importance of visitor attractions to the popularity and appeal of UK tourist destinations.

Assessment and grading criteria

This table shows you what you must do in order to achieve a **pass**, **merit** or **distinction** grade and where you can find activities in this book to help you.

To achieve a **pass** grade the evidence must show that you are able to:	To achieve a **merit** grade the evidence must show that, in addition to the pass criteria, you are able to:	To achieve a **distinction** grade the evidence must show that, in addition to the pass and merit criteria, you are able to:
P1 describe the products and services provided by one built and one natural visitor attraction **See assessment activity 19.1, page 134**	**M1** analyse how the products, services and interpretation techniques of a built or a natural attraction contribute to the appeal for two different types of visitors **See assessment activity 19.1, page 134**	**D1** evaluate the contribution of a visitor attraction to the popularity and appeal of a destination or area **See assessment activity 19.2, page 138**
P2 describe the purpose and techniques used for visitor interpretation at one built and one natural visitor attraction **See assessment activity 19.1, page 134**		
P3 explain the appeal of one natural and one built visitor attraction for two different types of visitors **See assessment activity 19.1, page 134**		
P4 explain why visitor attractions are important to UK tourism **See assessment activity 19.2, page 138**	**M2** compare the importance of two different visitor attractions to the popularity and appeal of a destination or area **See assessment activity 19.2, page 138**	

How you will be assessed

This unit will be assessed by one or more internal assignments that will be designed and marked by your tutor. Your assignments will be subject to sampling internally and externally as part of Edexcel's quality assurance procedures. The assignments are designed to allow you to show your knowledge and understanding related to the unit. The unit outcomes indicate what you should know, understand or be able to do after completing the unit.

Sally, 19-year-old BTEC National learner

I live in York, which is a city full of tourist attractions and very appealing to overseas visitors. Throughout school and college I have been taken on trips to local attractions. I have also been on visits with my family so I had a good knowledge already of what is around.

I chose my two attractions very carefully for my assessment. I wanted to know how many attractions people visit and where they are from, as well as wanting to get information about the attraction. It is easy to find out what the primary and secondary products and services are from leaflets and websites but getting visitor information is more difficult.

I found out that York Tourism carry out lots of research and have statistics on all aspects of tourism. I started with their website and found a lot of useful statistics. I also gave them a call to ask some specific questions and they helped me a lot. Doing this research helped me choose my two attractions, one was the famous Jorvik Viking Centre and the other one was the River Ouse. Of course, this was more challenging in terms of appeal as I had to consider the activities that take place on the river (e.g. boat trips) as well as the events and experiences on it and along it (e.g. the York Rivers Festival).

Over to you!

1 What attractions would you recommend to a visitor in your locality?

2 Can you guess what primary and secondary products and services are? If not you will find out in this unit.

1 Products and services provided by different types of visitor attraction

According to a survey carried out by iknow-uk, 6 in 10 British people can't identify Windsor Castle. About half didn't know where Stonehenge is. How much do you know about UK attractions?

Make two lists, one of all the UK visitor attractions you have ever visited and one of all the attractions within an hour's drive of your home. Are the lists the same?

Think about:

- the ones you visited further way – what was the appeal?
- the ones you didn't visit nearby – why not?

Discuss your findings with the whole group and compare notes.

Each of the national tourist boards of England, Northern Ireland, Wales and Scotland conducts an annual *Survey of Visits to Visitor Attractions* to monitor visitor and other trends.

The following is an extract from the definition of a visitor attraction. A visitor attraction is:

an attraction where it is feasible to charge admission for the sole purpose of sightseeing. The attraction must be a permanently established excursion destination, a primary purpose of which is to allow public access for entertainment, interest, or education; rather than being primarily a retail outlet or a venue for sporting, theatrical or film performances. It must be open to the public, without prior booking, for published periods each year, and should be capable of attracting day visitors or tourists, as well as local residents.

(Source: Survey of Visits to Visitor Attractions England 2008)

Note the main points of the definition:

- It must be feasible for the attraction to charge admission – but many are free.
- It must be permanently established – thus, for the purposes of the survey, events such as the Notting Hill Carnival would be excluded.

- It must have a primary purpose of entertainment, interest or education – thus, shopping centres are excluded even though they attract tourists.
- It must be open to the public for at least part of the year.
- It must attract tourists, not just locals.

The top five paid-admission visitor attractions in England in 2008 were:

- Westminster Abbey
- Kew Gardens
- Chester Zoo
- Windermere Lake Cruises
- The Eden Project.

The top five free-admission visitor attractions in England in 2008 were:

- British Museum
- Tate Modern
- National Gallery
- Natural History Museum
- Science Museum.

All the top five paid- and free-admission attractions given here are in England. Each of the UK's national tourist boards compiles its own separate figures on visitor attractions. You can find out what these are by visiting the websites of the national tourist boards. It is important to note that it is optional for attractions to provide figures for league tables, etc. which means that these lists are not definitive.

1.1 Products and services

Primary

Whatever the visitor attraction, the main reason for the visit is the **primary product or service**: if you visit a gallery it is to see an exhibition of art; if you go to a stately home it is to admire the beauty of the architecture and learn about its history; if you go to a theme park it is to have fun on the various rides; if you go to a countryside area it is to admire the landscape.

The primary product or service can change from time to time but rarely changes completely. If it were always exactly the same there would be little reason for visitors to go back. So, museums hold temporary exhibitions to attract people back and theme parks introduce new rides regularly for the same reason.

The primary product and service serves to attract visitors but is not always the main source of revenue. In fact, we have already seen that some of our most popular attractions are free to enter. These are usually museums and they do receive public funding but they also have commercial activities to raise revenue. Those attractions that we pay to enter often have special offers with free tickets, sometimes in conjunction with other companies, for example rail companies.

Think about it

If attractions are free, or often give away free tickets, how do they make money?

Key terms

Primary product or service – the main purpose of the visit, for example the exhibition in a gallery or the rides in a theme park.

Secondary product or service – products or services which add to the appeal of the attraction and are a means of revenue but do not provide the main draw. The main sources are shops and restaurants.

Dwell time – the length of time a visitor spends at the attraction.

Secondary spend – the money that visitors spend on the secondary products and services during their visit.

Secondary

The role of a **secondary product or service** is to provide the services that customers require during a visit to an attraction and to raise money from these services. There are several benefits of providing such services:

- They increase customer satisfaction during the visit.
- Visitors are encouraged to spend more time at the attraction so **dwell time** is increased.
- There is an increase in revenue from the **secondary spend**.

All visitor attractions have similar secondary products. They include:

- catering
- gift shops
- restaurants
- snack bars
- ice cream stands
- minor attractions that cost extra, for example special exhibitions
- children's activities
- photos.

Additional

Most visitor attractions offer guided tours and/or educational events and hire out rooms for business seminars, special celebrations and even weddings. Although such services are additional to the main product, they are a major source of revenue and visitor attractions try to make the most of these lucrative markets.

Visitor

These services include first aid, cloakrooms, parking and services for visitors with special needs.

1.2 Types of attraction

In general, visitor attractions can be divided into built or natural attractions. Built attractions include buildings, of course, and other constructions such as the London Eye or a theme park. Natural attractions include National Parks such as the Brecon Beacons and other areas of natural beauty.

We will look at some of the categories from the English National Tourist Board's *Survey of Visits to Visitor Attractions* and find some examples. We will consider their primary products.

Built attractions

Museums and art galleries

The most popular museums and art galleries in the UK are in London. We saw that many of them feature in the top attractions in England:

- Tate Modern
- British Museum
- National Gallery
- Natural History Museum
- Victoria & Albert Museum
- Science Museum
- National Portrait Gallery
- Tate Britain.

These all offer permanent exhibitions of artefacts and artworks but they differ according to the museum's speciality or leaning.

Of course, there are important museums outside London, such as the Kelvingrove Art Gallery and Museum in Glasgow and the Lowry Centre in Salford.

Historic properties

The following are some examples of the UK's most popular historic properties:

- Tower of London, London
- Edinburgh Castle, Edinburgh
- Windsor Castle, Windsor
- Roman Baths, Bath
- Stonehenge, Amesbury
- Chatsworth, Bakewell
- Tatton Park, Knutsford.

Why are historic properties, such as Chatsworth House, popular in the UK?

The Tower of London is managed by the Historic Royal Palaces Agency, who also manage other unoccupied royal palaces. The Agency is responsible to the Department for Culture, Media and Sport (DCMS).

Windsor Castle is one of the UK's royal residences and is held in trust for future generations, so the Queen cannot decide to sell it. The palaces – others are Buckingham and Sandringham – are royal homes, used for state functions and are also open to the public at certain times of the year. Windsor Castle is an official residence of the Queen and the largest occupied castle in the world.

Chatsworth House is a beautiful stately home and is the home of the Duke of Devonshire and his family. The house is a major visitor attraction in Derbyshire.

There are two important organisations that look after heritage in the UK. These are English Heritage and the National Trust. There is also a National Trust for Scotland and a Welsh Historic Monuments organisation.

Leisure/theme parks

According to Mintel Theme Parks (February 2010), the theme parks market grew by 2.4 per cent to £315 million in 2009. Admissions grew by more than 3 per cent to almost 14 million. It appears that theme parks have benefited from the recession as more people have opted to take days out at home rather than go on holiday abroad. The weather is the major factor affecting visits because theme park activities mainly take place outside.

About 60 per cent of a theme park's revenue comes from admissions, that is the primary product, and the rest from secondary products, such as food and retail.

Natural attractions

Nature reserves

Natural England owns or manages over 200 national nature reserves. The organisation acts as the government's advisor on the natural environment. The purpose of Natural England is to protect and improve England's natural environment and encourage people to get involved in their surroundings.

The organisation is responsible for increasing opportunities for everyone to enjoy the wonders of the natural world. You can find out more about what Natural England does at www.naturalengland.org.uk.

The following are some examples of popular country parks in the UK which attract more than a million visitors a year:

- Strathclyde Country Park, Motherwell, Scotland
- Ashton Court Estate, Long Ashton, England
- Upper Derwent Reservoirs, Bamford, England
- Drumpellier Country Park, Coatbridge, Scotland
- Fairlands Valley Park, Stevenage, England.

Local authorities manage country parks, for example North Lanarkshire Council is responsible for Strathclyde Country Park. They protect different types of landscape, such as woodlands, wetlands and lakes and the wildlife that inhabits them.

Entry to a country park and many of its activities is free, so visitors can go birdwatching, walking or cycling. However, there are some activities which are charged for to allow funds to be raised for further improvement to the park. Examples include watersports, hire of land and equipment, and accommodation on campsites. Country parks may charge for parking instead of having an entrance fee.

Is it important to encourage visitors to attractions like the Upper Derwent Reservoirs?

Gardens

The following are some examples of the UK's most popular garden attractions:

- The Eden Project, St Austell
- Royal Botanic Gardens, Kew
- Royal Botanic Gardens, Edinburgh
- Royal Horticultural Society Gardens, Wisley
- Botanic Gardens, Belfast.

2 Range and purpose of techniques used for visitor interpretation

Interpretation is part of the visitor experience and when it is done well it makes visitors feel enthusiastic and involved with the attraction. They will enjoy themselves and want to come back or tell their friends about the attraction. They will also stay longer and spend more money if they are enjoying themselves. You will now look at interpretation techniques and their purposes.

> ### Key term
>
> **Interpretation** – a means of imparting information to visitors so that their understanding and enjoyment of the attraction are enhanced.

2.1 Interpretation techniques and purpose

Displays

Static displays are not very exciting but do have a place, particularly in museums and galleries where people sometimes want to stand and admire pieces. Even so, basic interpretation will include signage, labels and information about the artist or the piece of work.

More exciting for the visitor are interactive displays where they can participate and make something happen. Children in particular like interactive displays and learn more through them.

For security, exhibits are protected by many means, from very sophisticated alarm systems in galleries to roped-off areas and glass. Vulnerable items like tapestries are also protected from light and flash photography. The purpose here is conservation.

Actors

One way of communicating art to visitors is through the use of creative writing or storytelling workshops or performances. These techniques allow the visitor to become connected and emotionally involved with the exhibition rather than just looking at it. Galleries and museums use these techniques constantly and advertise them in their programmes. The London Dungeon uses actors to help horrify the visitors!

The reason for using actors is that they can be entertaining and informative. Visitor attractions often have outreach objectives and actors can help to achieve these, perhaps by visiting a school and putting on a performance relating to the visitor attraction.

Interactive technology

With interactive technology things happen! Computers are used and exhibits do things – these kinds of exhibit are often used to explain scientific principles in a hands-on way. At the Imperial War Museum North, a series of interactive exhibits have been introduced. The Trench Action Station allows children to explore the terrible conditions for soldiers in First World War trenches through 'feely boxes' and smells.

Do interactive exhibits, for example those at the Imperial War Museum, give you a better understanding of the past?

Guides and tours

Guides can be written in the form of books, leaflets or maps. All are useful for visitors but personal guides have the opportunity to bring an attraction to life. Guides are usually very knowledgeable and at their very best are performers connecting the visitor to the attraction.

The following features of good interpretation should be taken into consideration when producing a written guide:

- It is targeted at the right audience.
- Each piece of interpretation communicates a clear message.
- It is fun, not dull and boring.
- It stimulates different senses.
- It is interactive.
- It doesn't have too much text.
- It is updated and maintained as necessary.
- It tries to be different.

Audio guides are increasing in popularity in visitor attractions. They consist of taped information, available through an individual headset, in different languages.

Audio guides have many benefits:

- The individual can tour the attraction at their own pace.
- They are cheaper than guides.
- The individual can elect to hear extra pieces of information at the touch of a button.
- Special sound effects can be included.

However, it is difficult for the visitor to ask questions when they are plugged into the tape and it can be a lonely experience being cut off from the other visitors.

Examples of visitor attractions using audio guides are Buckingham Palace and the Churchill War Rooms in London, Althorp in Northamptonshire and Milestones Museum in Hampshire.

The Milestones' Acoustiguide Programme for Primary Schools won an Interpret Britain award for its interpretation of the county's history. Acoustiguide is a brand of audio guide using a listening device which combines narrative, music and sound effects.

Guides can be entertaining but their main purpose is education.

Activity: Listen to the attraction!

Visit www.acoustiguide.com and find out the benefits of this type of guide. Make notes.

Acoustiguide claims to be an attraction in the way it uses an audio guide. Try to think of your experiences of using audio guides and decide whether you agree with Acoustiguide's claims.

Leaflets and maps

All visitor attractions produce leaflets about their products and services. These can be displayed in Tourist Information Centres (TICs) or in hotels, airports and so on, to get the attention of potential customers. Maps are often incorporated into leaflets to help visitors reach the attractions.

Curators

Curators are people who are on hand to give information about an attraction, usually in a historic attraction such as a stately home. They will be well-informed and able to answer questions.

Curators give information but also aid security and conservation as they can monitor the behaviour of visitors.

Signage

We are surrounded by so many signs that there is now a campaign to reduce them! However, signs are important at visitor attractions to show us the way to get to them and to help us round them. It is not only their information-giving quality that is important; signs need to fit in with the theme of the attraction.

In one Area of Outstanding Natural Beauty (AONB) in Sussex, 16 different kinds of signs were found. It was decided to design a completely new system and replace them all. New designs were developed in conjunction with the Guild of Sussex Craftsmen. These designs used local materials and built on the traditional style of Sussex countryside furniture. Then a new system of waymarking was developed which was designed to fit into the local landscape. The signs are made of rounded oak and give information such as designation, for example footpath, destinations or distances.

Case study: Activities at the Science Museum, London

Below are some extracts from the education programme at the Science Museum in London. Note all the different interpretation techniques used to enhance learning and enjoyment. Note also special events for children with special needs.

Centenary Journey

We've highlighted ten of our most amazing objects in a new trail through our ground-floor galleries. These ten Centenary Icons changed the future. Read their stories and imagine what life was like before they existed.

Which one is your favourite and why?

Download the free Centenary Journey trail and associated teachers' notes from:

www.sciencemuseum.org.uk/educatorsresources

Bugs Days

See Bugs! 3D and request places at the Hands-on Bugs! session to get up close and personal with creepy-crawlies from around the world.

Science in the News

This free journalism workshop gets students talking with experts, writing bite-sized text, backing up opinions with evidence and selecting images to create their own science news story.

The Enormous Turnip Storytelling

'A brilliant interactive show with fantastic presenters – well done.'

Farmer Giles uses forces and lots of pupil participation to pull up an enormous turnip.

Special Educational Needs Events

45 mins, 45 places per session

Students with Special Educational Needs are welcome at any time, but on particular days Launchpad is reserved for SEN groups, providing a calmer opportunity to engage with the hands-on exhibits and your own Explainer to accompany students around the gallery.

You can also request the Bubbles Bubbles Bubbles show tailored to the age and needs of your students.

(Source: http://www.sciencemuseum.org.uk/educators.aspx)

1 Study the extracts and describe all the interpretation techniques used.

2 Visit the Science Museum website and look for some current examples of use of interpretation techniques.

Activity: Defining terms

Think of definitions for each of the following terms:

- Primary product
- Dwell time
- Secondary product
- Interpretation
- Corporate hire
- Signage.

3   The appeal of visitor attractions to different types of visitor

Obviously, different types of attraction appeal to different people. Visitor attractions have to be aware of their target audience and direct their marketing efforts at the right groups. Sometimes there are attempts to target a new audience in order to increase revenue. This could be done by working with VisitBritain to encourage inbound tourists to come to an attraction or by targeting different groups of domestic tourists.

The different types of attraction were described earlier in this unit. Now you will consider the needs of the different types of visitor to whom the attractions try to appeal and study the features of attractions that might affect people's choice of visit.

3.1 Appeal and different types of visitor

We will look at the following in terms of appeal:

- Accessibility – location, opening times and 'Access for All'.
- Transport links – in terms of mode of arrival. Where possible, attractions will encourage their visitors to use public transport to lessen the impact of traffic on the local community.
- Range of products and services provided.
- Costs of visiting, such as admission charges and special offers.
- Image.
- Novelty.
- Type of visitor.

Visitors may be adults or children, visiting as individuals or groups. Visitors may be from the UK or overseas. We will look at some examples of appeal to different groups of visitors.

Overseas visitors

Overseas visitors make up an estimated 16 per cent of visits to English visitor attractions according to the Survey of *Visits to Visitor Attractions*.

Visitor attractions need to be aware of the country of origin of their incoming tourist visitors. This helps them to ensure that literature and interpretation are available in the relevant languages and that they

know where to market their products and services. UK visitor attractions that depend on inbound tourists suffered a drop in visitors in the early years of the twenty-first century. Overseas tourists, particularly North Americans, were deterred from travelling after 11 September 2001, due to fear of terrorism. Although there was recovery from that situation, a worldwide recession in 2008 and 2009 once again meant people travelled less.

Location

London is the most popular destination for overseas visitors and, of course, London attractions benefit. Other popular destinations include Edinburgh, Stratford, York, Oxford and Cambridge. While in these cities, overseas visitors take the opportunity to visit the local attractions.

What attractions could you take advantage of in a location like Oxford, e.g. the Radcliffe Camera? What about in York or Cambridge?

Opening times

Overseas visitors to the UK visit mainly in the summer. Besides being the main holiday season, the summer is when opening times are at their least restrictive, with many attractions opening every day and longer into the evenings.

Transport links

Overseas visitors require good transport links from gateway airports and ports. They are most likely to visit a particular destination first and then select visitor attractions in that area. Within London, overseas visitors are likely to depend on public transport and attractions must give clear directions and include Tube and bus stops in their literature.

Products and services provided

Those attractions with a worldwide reputation are likely to attract overseas visitors, as people prefer to see things they have heard about. Those visitors whose first language is not English will be looking for interpretation in their own language.

Cost of visiting

The price of entry to an overseas visitor varies according to the current exchange rate. In the early years of the twenty-first century the pound was strong against both the euro and the dollar so that overseas visitors from Europe and the USA found the UK expensive. By the end of the first decade, this situation had changed and the pound weakened. The result was a favourable exchange rate for European visitors who now found the UK much cheaper.

> **Think about it**
>
> Without doing any research at all, can you think of any attractions in Edinburgh which would appeal to you as a tourist there?

Groups (children)

Educational visitors are usually in groups, although the groups and their needs are very diverse. They may be children from primary schools or university students doing specialist courses. The Eden Project, for example, provides activities and learning materials for primary school children, GCSE and A-level students and special needs children. In addition, it holds sessions for teachers.

Educational groups are a very important client group for many attractions from theme parks to museums to educational projects.

> **Did you know?**
>
> The Eden Project welcomes about 250 children per day and some of them come from as far away as Scotland and France.

Visitor attractions often employ education officers and hold events to attract students, providing case studies and assignment materials. At Alton Towers and Chessington World of Adventures, student events are held that are linked to different vocational areas, such as Travel and Tourism or Leisure Studies. These events bring in revenue when the parks would otherwise be quiet and give them a reputation for helping in education.

Location

Primary school children are usually taken to local attractions. For other student or pupil groups the nature of the attraction is more important than the location.

Opening times

Educational visits take place mainly in term time. However, groups of children may be taken to visitor attractions at other times for party outings.

Transport links

Most domestic school and college visits take place via coach transport. It is the easiest and safest way (in terms of keeping tabs on people) of transporting a group. Group leaders of any kind of group will expect attractions to have access for coaches and adequate parking facilities not too far from the attraction.

Products and services provided

For educational groups, products and services must fit what is being studied. Teachers look for attractions which provide products, activities and learning materials linked to the National Curriculum. College students are taken to attractions which complement their A-level or vocational courses.

For entertainment, children may want parties or story-telling arranged.

Cost of visiting

Price is an important factor for this group as schools and colleges do not fund student visits except in cases of extreme hardship. Parents are expected to pay, therefore prices must be reasonable as transport costs will also add to the price. All attractions offer group price concessions.

Corporate groups

Corporate customers have different needs from other groups. They are interested in providing an experience for their customers or employees that is different, even unique. They will be using the visit to the attraction as an incentive for clients to buy their products or services, or for loyalty and high regard from their employees.

Location

This depends on the nature of the corporate event. International companies will host events anywhere in the world if it is appropriate. Theme parks are suitable venues for corporate entertainment or conferences. Small companies will look for a local venue.

Transport links

This is not so important for delegates who will be used to finding their way around, although good directions should be provided. Access may be a factor if the corporate customer wants to use the attraction to display their products. They will need space and delivery access.

Products and services provided

These are very important for corporate groups, although not in terms of the attraction itself. Catering, accommodation and possibly entertainment will be needed and should be of high quality. Visits to the attraction will be an added bonus for the delegates, not the main purpose of their visit.

Cost of visiting

Corporate packages are offered by attractions – the price is dependent on the facilities and services required and on the number in the group. Corporate customers, while expecting value for money, do not usually base their choice of venue on price alone.

Special needs

Provision for special needs

There are many examples of good practice in provision for people with special needs at visitor attractions. In the Science Museum example on page 130 we saw how special events are put on for children with special needs. At the Tate Gallery in London many talks and events offer interpretation for hearing impaired or visually impaired people.

> **Activity: Making attractions accessible to all**
>
> Visit the Eden Project website and find out how its interpretation techniques include provision for people with disabilities. Suggest other techniques that could be used and present your ideas to your group.

How does the Eden Project attract large numbers of school groups as well as adult visitors?

Location

Location is not as important as the suitability of the attraction to the person's interest and its access.

Accessibility

Accessibility is of vital importance for customers with special needs. If there is no access for people with special needs, they will not visit the attraction.

The Disability Discrimination Act now applies and should result in improved access and services for customers with special needs. New purpose-built attractions always have good access as it is factored into the design. Heritage attractions have greater problems as it is not always possible to bring modern access into old buildings. Advice is provided at www.direct.gov.uk/en/DisabledPeople/Everydaylifeandaccess/VisitingPlacesOfInterest

Products and services

These are important factors when choosing an attraction, depending on personal interest. Attractions should consider special needs customers when planning interpretation. There are many visual, audio and physical aids that can be included in interpretation.

Costs of visiting

Price is an important factor for groups who will need to keep costs down – special group prices will be expected.

Activity: What visitors like

Match the visitor types to the attraction feature which is likely to be most important to them.

Visitor type	Feature of attraction
Couple with twin toddlers	Lifts and wide passages
Japanese family visiting London	Quality accommodation and catering
Visitor in a wheelchair	Special working steam train day
Group of school children	Gallery holding Monet exhibition
Steam train enthusiasts	Activities based on the National Curriculum
Corporate customer wanting a two-day conference	Interpretation in foreign languages
Student studying Impressionist art	Family pricing, family friendly facilities

Assessment activity 19.1

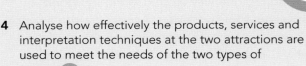

Your local newspaper has asked for your help in producing a supplement on local visitor attractions. It does not have the people to be able to assign a reporter to the supplement so it has invited students to prepare it. The supplement will be attached to the evening paper and also to the free weekly edition so it will achieve very wide coverage. The newspaper is read by local residents and also by a lot of inbound tourists who are interested in learning about the visitor attractions available. Some local people worry about the numbers of tourists visiting their local attractions and about the impact on the environment and on their society, so these issues will be covered in the supplement.

Your responsibility is to research two local visitor attractions, one **built** and one **natural**. You should make every effort to visit the attractions to carry out your research. Your work must be individual, although colleagues might be researching other attractions for inclusion in the supplement. You must provide information for the supplement as follows.

1 Give a description of the products and services provided by the two visitor attractions. **P1**

2 Describe the purpose and techniques used for visitor interpretation at each of the two attractions. **P2**

3 Explain the appeal of your two visitor attractions for a group of primary school children and a family of Japanese tourists. **P3**

4 Analyse how effectively the products, services and interpretation techniques at the two attractions are used to meet the needs of the two types of visitor. **M1**

Make sure that you cover the full range, referring to the content and assessment guidance in the unit specification for the detail required.

Grading tips

P1 Make sure you include primary, secondary, additional and visitor products and services.

P2 Besides making a visit to the attraction, if possible, use their promotional material and website to help with your research.

P3 Make sure you include all the following: location and transport links; opening times and costs of visiting; products and services provided; image; novelty.

M1 Make sure you are analysing, and not just describing, how the different factors appeal to different customers.

4 Understand the importance of visitor attractions to the popularity and appeal of UK tourist destinations

4.1 Importance, popularity and appeal

Attracting visitors from overseas

We know how popular the UK is with overseas visitors from research carried out in the International Passenger Survey and market intelligence from VisitBritain.

Research shows that one of the most important appeal factors to overseas visitors is culture and heritage. These are features of many of our visitor attractions in the UK.

Ten overseas markets make up 67 per cent of all overseas visits (see Table 19.1) so visitor attractions should be aware of these markets and make sure their marketing activity targets them.

Table 19.1: The UK's most important inbound markets in 2008

Top 10 visits 2008 (million)		% of all visits	Top 10 spend 2008 (£ million)		% of all spend
France	3.6	11.4	USA	2223	13.6
Irish Republic	3.1	9.6	Germany	1125	6.9
USA	3.0	9.3	France	1053	6.5
Germany	2.9	9.1	Irish Republic	983	6.0
Spain	2.0	6.2	Spain	815	5.0
Netherlands	1.8	5.7	Italy	809	5.0
Italy	1.6	5.1	Australia	769	4.7
Poland	1.5	4.7	Canada	522	3.2
Belgium	1.0	3.0	Netherlands	700	4.3
Australia	1.0	3.0	Poland	508	3.1

(Source: VisitBritain)

Activity: Visitor data

Study Table 19.1.

1. What is more important – numbers of visitors or how much they spend?

2. How does it help vistor attractions to know where most overseas visitors come from?

3. Produce two pie charts, one showing countries and their numbers of visits, the other showing countries and their spend. Remember in each case to calculate the percentage accounted for by 'other' countries before you produce the charts.

Visitor attractions can influence the numbers of overseas tourists they attract by working in partnership with VisitBritain to promote their attraction. VisitBritain invites businesses to place their products on their website so that interested visitors can find information and plan their holidays. In fact, VisitBritain says that it has over 40,000 tourism businesses on its websites. In addition, VisitBritain organises themed marketing campaigns which feature visitor attractions and again attract more visitors.

One way of increasing the spend of overseas visitors is to persuade them to stay longer. However, 43 per cent of visits to the UK are short breaks that do not leave a lot of time to visit many attractions.

Figure 19.2: Length of stay of visitors to the UK

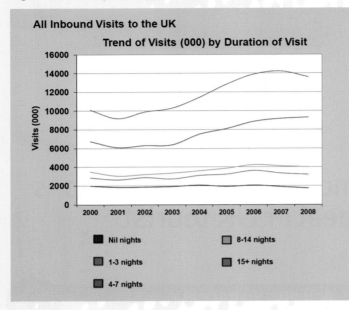

All Inbound Visits to the UK

Trend of Visits (000) by Duration of Visit

Legend:
- Nil nights
- 1-3 nights
- 4-7 nights
- 8-14 nights
- 15+ nights

Activity: Encouraging overseas visitors

What can be done to encourage overseas visitors to make longer visits to the UK? Discuss your ideas and consider what visitor attractions can do to help persuade visitors to lengthen their stay in the UK.

It is also useful for visitor attractions to be aware of the types of overseas visitors we receive in order to cater for their needs. Interestingly, VisitBritain reports that only 6 per cent of overseas visitors are traditional families – 20 per cent are spouse and partner without children and 40 per cent are lone travellers.

Think about it

Explain how visitor attractions can cater for lone travellers.

Stimulating domestic tourism

Visitor attractions provide a stimulus for UK residents to take a day out and visit them. As our country is small, people are often able to get to and from an attraction within one day. Where there are clusters of attractions, for example, in Edinburgh or York, they might be encouraged to take a short break and increase spend on accommodation and on food

and shopping. The importance of visitor attractions in stimulating domestic tourism is recognised by our national tourist boards. Besides their marketing campaigns and research carried out via the annual *Visits to Visitor Attractions* surveys, the boards monitor activities at a sample of attractions.

Recent research found that almost half of attractions held public events to stimulate visits. Another means of stimulating more visits was the introduction of membership schemes or season tickets.

Supporting the regeneration of areas

A visitor attraction can be the means of regenerating a whole area. This was the case with the Eden Project in Cornwall. Since its opening in 2001, it has attracted as many as 2 million visitors per year, settling at over a million in 2009.

The Eden Project makes a deliberate effort to source food, retail goods, plants and even electricity from local suppliers, thus supporting the Cornish economy. The knock-on spending, or **multiplier effect**, in the local economy from visitors who have come to Cornwall attracted by the Eden Project is estimated to be over £700 million since its opening.

Key term

Multiplier effect – where an initial amount of spending in one part of the economy, for example by an organisation investing, leads to increased spending by consumers.

In the UK, there are several other areas that have been regenerated and now attract tourists. Examples include the Salford Docks area with the Lowry Centre, and Covent Garden in London, where there are museums, shops and restaurants.

Contributing to the local and national economy

Creating employment

Visitor attractions create jobs. The Tate, for example, employs hundreds of people in its galleries in London, Liverpool and St Ives. In this kind of institution, many of these employees are highly skilled historians, conservationists, marketeers and administrators. They also need fundraisers, building managers and educators.

However, many visitor attractions have few permanent staff. Staff may be employed on flexible contracts so that they can be called upon as needed, posts may be seasonal due to winter closures and pay is often low for unskilled work. Associations like the Association of Leading Visitor Attractions (ALVA) are aware of these problems and are lobbying the government for action and investment in training. In addition, there are a large number of volunteers working in historic properties.

Visitor attractions provide investment in a local environment. The visitors generate wealth in the locality by spending their money in hotels, restaurants and amenities in the area, as well as in the visitor attraction. The Natural History Museum attracts more than 3 million visitors a year. In fact, in 2009 it welcomed its 25 millionth visitor since 2001 when entry became free. These visitors generate a lot of spending in London.

Promoting cultural exchange

The role of the UK's many galleries and museums is to conserve British culture so that it is there for future generations to see.

There can be no doubt that the British government supports the cultural aspect of the UK's public museums and galleries as they all receive funding via the Department for Culture, Media and Sport to varying degrees and take on the responsibility of protecting our cultural heritage.

The following extract from the Tate website explains how important this is:

> Tate Britain is the world centre for the understanding and enjoyment of British art and works actively to promote interest in British art internationally. The displays at Tate Britain call on the greatest collection of British art in the world to present an unrivalled picture of the development of art in Britain from the time of the Tudor monarchs in the sixteenth century, to the present day.
>
> *(Source: www.tate.org.uk)*

The Tate's collection now consists of over 65,000 works of art encompassing the national collection of historic British art from 1500 and the national collection of international modern art.

There is no point in having all these works of art unless the public goes to see them. Thus, it is also the responsibility of the museums to attract different types of visitor and explain the exhibits to them, that is interpret them. The Tate does this via an extensive programme of activities and entry to the Tate and to other public museums is free.

The Natural History Museum welcomes 125,000 school children each year, successfully introducing children to exhibits and learning.

Conservation

In some cases, visitor attractions suffer from their popularity. Historic buildings or sites can be subject to deterioration and erosion. In these cases, measures must be taken to protect the buildings by restricting visits or closing them for periods of time.

Stonehenge is a good example of the need for conservation. The site receives many visitors and the stones have suffered erosion and damage, so a means must be found to preserve it. It is one of the UK's most famous and oldest monuments and a World Heritage Site. However, too many visitors over the years mean it needs to be protected while still maintaining access for the public, who see it as part of their heritage. This is under way with the 'Stonehenge Project'. The project involves the building of a new visitor centre and the removal of roads from the site to restore the site to being a peaceful location. There are several organisations involved in the project, including the Department for Culture, Media and Sport, English Heritage (who manage the site) and the Highways Agency. This project is currently subject to funding (in June 2010 the public funding for the project was removed).

In the visitor centre there will be exhibitions and audio-visual presentations to help visitors enjoy and understand Stonehenge. There will also be shops, catering facilities and an education area. Those who wish to visit the stones will walk from the centre. Perhaps fewer people will visit the stones but still get a flavour of what they are about from the visitor's centre by taking a 'virtual tour'. The central circle of stones is already roped off and visitors are not allowed to enter this area. This is not surprising when you hear that some visitors actually chip off bits of stone to take home as souvenirs.

The number of visitors to an attraction can be managed by raising prices for entry or issuing **timed tickets** – this means visitors buy a ticket and can only enter the building at the time stated. Timed tickets are also used to reduce waiting times during peak periods at theme parks. Customers collect timed tickets for the popular rides and can get straight onto the ride at the time given on the ticket.

Key term

Timed ticket – a means to control the flow of visitors by issuing tickets that are valid between certain times.

Providing a learning environment

All major attractions and many smaller ones recognise the importance of attracting school and college groups. Day visits from learners are an important source of revenue and a valuable way of providing resources and experiences to support teachers in delivering the curriculum.

Assessment activity 19.2   **P4** **M2** **D1** **BTEC**

In this activity you will return to the supplement on visitor attractions that you are helping to produce for a newspaper and that you worked on in assessment activity 19.1.

You are being asked to write an article for the supplement that explains the importance of visitor attractions to tourism in general terms and then specifically looks at one destination and two of the attractions in or near that destination. You will then need to compare the importance of the two visitor attractions to the popularity and appeal of an area. This should be a detailed explanation with examples.

1 Write an introduction to your article explaining why visitor attractions are important to UK tourism. **P4**

2 Choose one area – for example, your town – and compare in the article, the importance of two visitor attractions to the popularity and appeal of that area. **M2**

3 Evaluate the contribution of one of your attractions to the popularity and appeal of the area. **D1**

Make sure that you cover the full range, referring to the content and assessment guidance in the unit specification for the detail required.

Grading tips

P4 Support your explanation with statistics and examples – use the VisitBritain website to help you.

M2 The area you choose must have at least two visitor attractions. It would be a good idea to choose a local area that you can visit easily. Statistics on visitor numbers will help support your findings. You should be able to get these from the attractions or from the Survey of *Visits to Visitor Attractions*. You can choose the same attractions as in assessment activity 19.1 if you like.

D1 You could consider factors such as impact on tourism as a whole in an area. For example, do visitors to the attraction go anywhere else to spend their money, and if not how could this be encouraged? Make judgements based on evidence such as statistics.

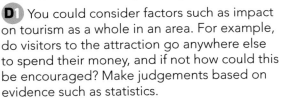

PLTS

You will demonstrate **independent enquirer** skills when you carry out research and evaluate the contribution of your chosen attraction to the appeal of the area.

Functional skills

By producing an article you will practise your **English** writing skills.

Chris Reed
Volunteer at a National Trust property

Chris is a semi-retired vicar who works as a volunteer at a National Trust property called Bateman's, a house formerly owned by Rudyard Kipling. The house is located in Burwash, East Sussex. It is a 17th century house with mullioned windows and oak beams. There is also a garden, a shop and a tea room.

Can you tell us what being a volunteer for the National Trust involves?

I work as a Room Guide. I work in different rooms in the house and I have to know about the history of the house, about Rudyard Kipling and about all the treasures in the house.

It is important that I engage with visitors and give them information. A steward's book is provided in each room with detailed information to help us explain things.

How often do you volunteer?

I have other responsibilities so I work once a fortnight but many people act as guides on a weekly basis.

What training did you receive?

I had to attend two induction sessions before starting volunteering. The first was a general induction on the work of the National Trust and the second was a more specific introduction to the work of a Room Guide. After that you shadow other guides until you build up enough knowledge of the property to be a guide by yourself.

Think about it!

1 Volunteering is interesting work and gets you invaluable experience:
   - Can you think of anywhere you could volunteer to work?
   - What knowledge and skills do you think you would need?
2 Find out about Bateman's at www.nationaltrust.org.uk/main/w-batemans
3 Find out about volunteering for the National Trust at www.nationaltrust.org.uk/main/w-trust/w-volunteering.htm

Just checking

1 Which are the most popular attractions in the UK?

2 What is meant by 'secondary spend'?

3 Why are some attractions free to enter?

4 Why is secondary spend so important in museums?

5 What is the primary product at a gallery?

6 What is meant by 'dwell time'?

7 What economic benefits can visitor attractions bring to an area?

8 How does the Eden Project support the Cornish economy?

9 Explain what a curator does.

10 Why are actors used in museums?

11 What do we mean by interpretation?

12 Describe three interpretation techniques.

13 Give an example of how a visitor attraction can promote cultural exchange.

14 Which 'appeal' factors are most important for school groups?

15 Which 'appeal' factors are most important for families?

edexcel

Assignment tips

- Completing the assessments for this unit could provide evidence for other units, for example Marketing or Customer Service. Make sure that you plan for this when you go on any visits so that you collect appropriate information.

- Visit as many attractions as you can to collect information for this unit and be able to recognise good practice.

- Your local Tourist Information Office may be able to help you by telling you which attractions in the area are the most popular.

- Your regional tourist board will have statistics on visits to attractions. You should be able to find these boards on the internet.

- You saw that the *Survey of Visits to Visitor Attractions* was referred to in this unit. Remember to look at the latest report.

- The VisitBritain website and the national tourist board websites have lots of information about attractions.

- Remember to look at information provided by English Heritage and The National Trust.

20 Hospitality operations in travel and tourism

Hospitality is central to the travel and tourism sector. It occurs both as an industry in its own right and as part of many other travel and tourism industries, such as visitor attractions, where hospitality is part of the overall visitor experience and helps to maximise income. Hospitality is the provision of accommodation, food and drink, and other services of this type.

In this unit you will find out who are the providers of hospitality in travel and tourism.

Hospitality and travel and tourism are closely intertwined and interdependent. For example, an integral part of some holidays is the provision of a hotel room and restaurant meals. Similarly, the hotel relies on travel and tourism services to deliver its guests to its premises. You will explore the different products and services offered by providers and look at what factors affect the provision.

Finally, you will develop your creative skills by planning hospitality provision for a travel and tourism organisation.

Learning outcomes

After completing this unit you should:

1 know the products and services offered by hospitality providers to meet customer expectations

2 be able to plan hospitality provision in a travel and tourism context

3 understand factors affecting hospitality operations in travel and tourism organisations.

Assessment and grading criteria

This table shows you what you must do in order to achieve a **pass**, **merit** or **distinction** grade, and where you can find activities in this book to help you.

To achieve a **pass** grade the evidence must show that you are able to:	To achieve a **merit** grade the evidence must show that, in addition to the pass criteria, you are able to:	To achieve a **distinction** grade the evidence must show that, in addition to the pass and merit criteria, you are able to:
P1 describe different types of hospitality providers and the products and services they offer to meet differing customer expectations **See assessment activity 20.1, page 152**	**M1** compare how two selected hospitality providers meet the expectations of different types of customer through the provision of products and services **See assessment activity 20.1, page 152**	**D1** recommend, with justification, new or enhanced products and services that could be provided by a selected hospitality provider to complement current provision **See assessment activity 20.1, page 152**
P2 produce a plan for hospitality provision in a travel and tourism context **See assessment activity 20.2, page 153**	**M2** explain how the plan for hospitality provision meets the needs of the travel and tourism organisation's customers **See assessment activity 20.2, page 153**	
P3 explain how internal and external factors affect hospitality operations in travel and tourism organisations **See assessment activity 20.3, page 156**	**M3** assess how hospitality operations in travel and tourism organisations have responded to internal and external factors **See assessment activity 20.3, page 156**	

How you will be assessed

This unit will be assessed by one or more internal assignments that will be designed and marked by your tutor. Your assignments will be subject to sampling internally and externally as part of Edexcel's quality assurance procedures. The assignments are designed to allow you to show your knowledge and understanding related to the unit. The unit outcomes indicate what you should know, understand or be able to do after completing the unit.

Martin, 19-year-old BTEC National learner

When I started this unit I was wondering what it had to do with travel and tourism. I hadn't chosen to do a hospitality course! In the very first class we were told about the links between hospitality and tourism and how most tourist attractions and providers had to think about hospitality.

My group came up with the example of a visit to Alton Towers. If we went by train we would buy refreshments at the station or on the train. Even though we went to Alton Towers for the rides, we would be buying lunch and drinks and lots of ice creams. We remembered that there was a hotel at Alton Towers too so we could even stay the night – though we couldn't afford to. It made me think that most tourism organisations had to provide food and drink at the very least.

Part of the unit is planning some kind of hospitality. I decided to plan a spa and café area to attach to the college leisure centre. I worked on this with my friend and it was good fun. We looked at lots of brochures and were able to measure up the area we wanted to use. We came up with a decorating scheme and we added lots of luxurious touches like huge fluffy towels and scented candles everywhere to our plans.

Over to you!

1   What kind of hospitality do you think you would be able to plan? Think about what is on offer in your school or college.

2   What about a gym or leisure centre you attend? Maybe you will be able to work with a local hotel and plan a new bar area?

1 Products and services offered by hospitality providers to meet customer expectations

1.1 Types of provision, products and services

The nature of the hospitality business is that small, independent companies characterise the hotel, restaurant, bar and pub market. In contract food services and visitor attractions, the opposite is true and the market is dominated by a few large companies. For example Compass, a food service provider, dominates contract food services.

When we think about hospitality in our homes we think about providing people with a welcome and offering them food and drink and possibly a place to stay. This is exactly what hospitality means in hotels, restaurants,

etc. However, the food, drink and accommodation vary according to the specific needs of the customer. For example, a vegetarian needs to be offered an alternative to meat, families might expect children's meals, cots and extra beds to be provided. As we take a more detailed look at different types of hospitality provision, we will take an overview of their products and services.

Hospitality provision as a main business

First we'll look at where hospitality is the main focus of a business, that is, the provision of accommodation and food. Providers whose main business is hospitality include hotels, guest houses, motels, holiday centres, campsites and caravan parks.

What would you look for in choosing a hotel?

Hotels

A hotel is an establishment that offers accommodation and food and drink to anyone who is fit to receive these services and is willing to pay for them. Many hotels also provide leisure facilities, conference and banqueting facilities and business services.

There are over 40,000 hotels in the UK. This figure incorporates all sizes of establishment, including guest houses. Most are independent but there are also several large groups, as Table 20.1 illustrates. Whitbread is the largest group with more than 500 hotels. Note that the table rates the hotels by size not by revenue or profit.

Note also that, although figures are accurate at the time they are compiled, they change quickly as companies dispose of assets and buy different ones.

Table 20.1: Top 20 UK hotel brands

	Company	Number of hotels	Brands	Number of rooms
1	Whitbread Hotel Company	518+	Premier Inn	36,000+
2	InterContinental Hotels Group	256	*InterContinental (1), *Crowne Plaza (18)*, Holiday Inn (116)*, Express by Holiday Inn (120), Staybridge Suites (1)	34,530
3	Travelodge Dubai International Capital	333+	Travelodge	23,150
4	Accor Hotels	130	*Sofitel (3), Novotel (31), Mercure (29), Ibis (50), Etap (12), Formule 1 (5)	18,952
5	Hilton Hotel Corporation	71	Hilton (69), *Garden Inn (1), *Doubletree (1)	15,610
6	Best Western	285	Best Western	15,305
7	Marriott International	52	Renaissance (2), Marriott (48), JW Marriott (1)	11,436
8	Wyndham Worldwide	107	*Days Inn (25), *Days Hotel (10), *Ramada (65), *Ramada Encore (6), Wyndham Grand (1)	10,589
9	Carlson Hotels Wordlwide	40	*Radisson (11), *Park Inn (19), Park Plaza (8), *Country Inns and Suites (1)	7,725
10	De Vere (AHG)	62	De Vere Hotels (12), Village (20), Venues (30)	7,310
11	Thistle Hotels	35	Thistle (32), Guomon (3)	7,040
12	Britannia Hotels	33		7,000
13	The Rezidor Hotel Group	31	†Radisson SAS (11), †Park Inn (19), *Country Inns and Suites (1)	6,034
14	Choice Hotels International	75	*Clarion (3), *Comfort (14), *Quality (45), *Comfort Inn (13)	6,020
15	Ramada Jarvis Hotels	43	†Ramada (43)	4,900
16	Jurys Inns (Quinlan Private and Oman Investment Fund)	17	Jurys Inn	4,538
17	Millennium Copthorne Hotels	20	Millennium (7), Copthorne (13)	4,496
18	Macdonald Hotels	51	Resorts (5), Associate hotels (6)	4,369
19	Mitchells & Butlers	116	Innkeepers Lodge (91), †Express by Holiday Inn (25)	4,250
20	Shearings Hotels	49		3,932

* Some or all franchised to another operator   † Franchised hotels

(Source: www.caterersearch.com)

Approximately 22,000 hotels and guest houses are registered with the tourist boards, as are 16,000 bed and breakfast establishments. The rest are unregistered. The major groups have a lot of influence on the hotel business.

Did you know?

A lot of hotels are run by their owners and the average size of a hotel is 20 rooms.

The core products of hotels are accommodation, that is, hotel rooms, and food and drink. Of course, within that there is a vast range. Hotels may offer basic rooms, executive and deluxe rooms or suites, and family rooms, all at different rates.

In a hotel, the size of the kitchen and restaurant will depend on the size of the hotel and number of guests.

Some hotels have several restaurants open to guests and to the public; others do not have restaurants but only a breakfast room. A hotel which caters for families would have family rooms or adjoining rooms, children's facilities, and special meals and meal times. We will look at a specific example in the next section.

Bars may be found in hotels, restaurants or nightclubs or exist in their own right. Bars need cellar attendants to run the cellar and bar staff to serve the customers.

Budget hotels

Budget hotels cater for visitors on short stays or who are travelling. Their core product is accommodation. They have fewer facilities than other hotels, for example there aren't many staff, perhaps just one person on reception and no room service. There are no luxuries and usually no catering facilities, although en-suite bathrooms are provided and there is often a breakfast room and café. Families and people with disabilities are catered for, but only in terms of accommodation and access.

This sector is growing because customers realise that the budget hotel sector gives excellent value for money in convenient locations.

Budget hotels are such good value that they enjoy a 90+ per cent occupancy rate. Premier Inn is the UK's leading budget hotel brand, with more than 500 hotels, including one at County Hall, London, on the south bank of the Thames near Westminster and the London Eye.

Guest houses

Usually the difference between a hotel and a guest house is one of size. Most guest houses are family run and only have a few rooms. They are often situated in large houses that would originally have been intended for families.

The core products that guest houses provide are the same as those of hotels except that it is very unlikely

Case study: Alternative Hotel Group

You may not have heard of the Alternative Hotel Group (AHG) but it is the parent company behind several prestigious brands. These include the De Vere Hotel group which was bought by AHG in 2006 for just over a billion pounds. The De Vere chain includes 62 hotels and conference venues in the UK.

Malmaison and Hotel du Vin are also hotel brands under the AHG umbrella. The group owns the Village chain of hotels and the Greens health and fitness chain. Although hotels represent the core business, AHG also has:

- Greenall Distillery.
- MWB Business Exchange, which provides office space either on a serviced lease basis or on an ad hoc basis to cater for meetings.
- Searcy, which provides catering at several well-known venues including the National Portrait Gallery, The Pump Room in Bath and the Champagne Bar at St Pancras station.

- Liberty of London, a famous department store in London's Regent St.

1. What were the reasons for the Alternative Hotel Group buying De Vere?

2. 'Most of AHG's companies are hospitality based.' Do you agree? If so explain why. If not explain why not.

3. How does the health and fitness chain fit in with the core business?

4. What are the reasons for including a department store in the portfolio?

5. Explain the differences between the different hotel brands by comparing the facilities, service and rates of an average room in each type of hotel.

that a full restaurant service is offered. In fact, whereas a hotel usually does provide food and drink to some extent, some guest houses might not provide any. However, many guest houses supplement their income by providing evening meals for guests, often to order.

Many guest houses have rooms with private bathrooms, and lounges for guests to sit in if they wish.

Holiday centres

These may be camping and caravan parks or purpose-built sites with accommodation, entertainment and leisure facilities. Examples include Pontins, Butlins and Center Parcs. They often offer self-catering accommodation.

Many people prefer self-catering accommodation for the extra freedom it allows them in deciding when and what to eat. Self-catering also allows a greater level of informality on holidays.

Generally, self-catering properties are suitable for people who want to be independent and do not expect to have the services that would be provided in a hotel, such as entertainment, bars and restaurants. However, many holiday centres have blocks of self-catering accommodation in which all the facilities of a hotel are available but in addition kitchens and cooking facilities are provided.

Campsites and caravan parks

The UK Caravan Parks and Campsites Directory shows that there are more than 2500 caravan sites, parks and campsites in the UK.

Camping and caravanning have become an important sector of the tourism industry both in the UK and throughout Europe. Camping has changed a lot over the years and campsites have become much more sophisticated and offer many more facilities than they used to.

A wide range of accommodation and food services is on offer at some large camping and caravanning sites, including a range of luxury accommodation, bars, restaurants, takeaways and supermarkets.

Hospitality as an additional service

Sometimes businesses offer hospitality to give added value to the range of products and services they provide, but it is not the main focus of their business. The primary purpose of their business may be to transport passengers or to entertain. The revenue gained from customers spent on hospitality in these cases is known as secondary spend. We are going to look at some examples of organisations who offer hospitality as a secondary focus.

Airlines

It is evident that the primary business of an airline is to transport passengers from one place to another. Traditionally, airlines offer hospitality to their customers to enhance the customer experience on board the aircraft. The hospitality would take the form of meals and drinks.

Today full-service airlines still offer this hospitality and it is included in the price of the ticket. Passengers on a cross-Atlantic flight from an airline such as Virgin or British Airways might expect a choice of meal, an afternoon tea or breakfast depending on time of day and free drinks, including alcohol. The catering is provided by a contract food supplier and is specially packaged for airline use.

Low-cost airlines, such as Ryanair, also offer hospitality in the form of snacks and drinks but passengers pay for whatever they choose and this is an important source of revenue for the airline. Thus the purpose of the hospitality for this type of airline is to make money as well as to offer a service.

Would you expect a full range of facilities at a campsite/caravan park?

Conference and exhibition centres

There are several purpose-built conference and exhibition centres in the UK. These include the NEC in Birmingham, and Earls Court, Olympia and ExCeL in London. Visitors attending exhibitions will be there for a few hours and will expect to be able to buy food and drink. Hospitality is also essential for exhibitors as they may choose to entertain clients within the exhibition area. Again, the hospitality provision is a source of revenue for the exhibition centre.

MENU

Salmon & Vegetable Kebabs with Soy & Ginger

Tandoori Chicken Spring Rolls with Cucumber Mint Yoghurt

A Selection of Open Sandwiches on Ciabatta Bread

Brie Cheese, Leek & Button Mushroom Tartlets

Chicken Satays Brushed with Oriental Plum Sauce

Potato Wedges Flavoured with Garlic & Oregano

Sour Cream & Chive Dip

Broccoli & Brie Puffs with Lemon & Herb Mayonnaise

Figure 20.1: Example of a finger buffet for conference delegates

Exhibition venues are also used for conferences and catering must be provided for delegates. A catering manager is available to advise conference organisers on menus and catering provision. Menus may range from finger buffets to full dinners.

Attractions

Restaurants, bars and cafeterias are usually provided in visitor attractions. They add appeal to the attraction and encourage visitors to stay longer and spend more money. They are an important source of secondary revenue.

Hospitality at attractions helps keep guests there longer and the management hope that the longer they stay the more money they will spend, not just on hospitality but in the shops and on photos, etc. Some attractions have extended their hospitality provision to the opening of hotels. Alton Towers has two hotels which are themed and help attract visitors to the park.

1.2 Customer expectations

Each type of customer has different expectations. First we will take an overview of these in general terms and then we will look at them in relation to specific types of customers. Expectations are in the following areas.

Level of service

Of course service is important to everyone but those who are spending a lot of money or corporate customers expect an even greater level of service.

Range of products and services provided

The products and services expected range from the core products mentioned in the first section of this unit to extras such as spa facilities, theatre and restaurant booking, and children's facilities.

Location

Location is of the utmost importance. For travellers the location must be convenient, and so they tend to choose hotels and budget hotels on major routes and at airports. Business customers look for city-centre hotels or those located near exhibition centres like the NEC in Birmingham. People on holiday may be looking for a beautiful setting, perhaps with sea views.

Availability

Consolidators like Lastminute.com and Expedia display lists of available hotels or restaurants on their websites in response to specific searches by location and dates. Customers choose the venue on the basis of what is available in their price range.

Accessibility

Accessibility is particularly important for disabled visitors who might need ground floor rooms and special facilities.

Quality

Many customers are looking for specific standards. They may be guided by reviews such as those at Trip Advisor, word-of-mouth promotion or the classification awarded to the facility.

Speed of service

This factor is more important to some customers. For example, restaurants serving pre-theatre dinners or those in airports are aware that customers have time commitments.

Level of hygiene

No matter what grade the hotel or facility, hygiene is vital to customer satisfaction. A poorly cleaned bathroom or public washroom will result in discomfort and complaints from customers. Most hospitality providers now expect cleaners to check public washrooms every hour to ensure they are clean and tidy. Hygiene is also important and is subject to legislation in kitchens and restaurants. Hospitality providers can expect to be inspected by health and safety inspectors who will consider general cleanliness and hygiene.

Value for money

Customers do not expect luxury if they have paid only £15 for a Travelodge room, for example. However, even at this price, they will expect a clean room with a comfortable bed and bathroom facilities. Sometimes customer expectations may exceed what can reasonably be expected at the price paid and the provider has to manage such a situation with tact and diplomacy.

Classification

Classification systems help customers assess the level of service and quality to be expected from a hospitality provider. Reputable companies such as the AA, Michelin and tourist boards may recommend hotels and restaurants and award ratings, such as Michelin stars, for restaurants. These are helpful for the public when making a choice of hotel or restaurant.

Star ratings

A wide range of properties, from hotels and guests houses to serviced accommodation and campsites, is assessed and marketed under the National Quality Assurance Schemes (NQAS – the star rating schemes).

Hotels are given a rating from one to five stars: the more stars, the higher the quality and the greater the range of facilities and level of service provided.

Activity: Investigating facilities

- In groups, ask 100 people to rank the hotel facilities shown in Table 20.2 in order of importance. Compare your results with those given in the table.

- Investigate the facilities provided for families at a local hotel. Assess how far they meet the needs of families. Perhaps you can arrange a group visit.

1.3 Customer types

Different types of hospitality are targeted at different kinds of customers. Examples of customers are:

- families
- solo travellers
- corporate
- special needs
- groups.

First take a look at Table 20.2. It shows the most important facilities selected by 1000 internet users aged 15+ in a survey for Mintel in 2008.

Table 20.2: Most important hotel facilities, November 2008

	%
Swimming pool	37
Quality restaurant	35
Satellite or cable television in the room	31
Internet provided	30
Flexible mealtime	26
Spa	25
Hotel bar	23
Gym	22
A safe in the room	20
Electronic/late checkout	15
Beauty services (e.g. hairdresser, massage)	14
Children's facilities (e.g. playground, playroom, baby monitoring facilities)	14
High-quality complimentary toiletries	14
Additional accessories (e.g. bathrobes, slippers, shoe polish, branded toiletries)	14
DVD/MP3 dock in room	12
Other sports facilities (e.g. tennis, squash)	11
Electronic/in-room check-in (i.e. without having to go through paperwork at reception)	11
Electronic games (e.g. Playstation)	11
Golf course	10
None of these	28

(Source: GMI/Mintel)

Families

Hotels often offer special deals for families. Examples are free accommodation for children sharing their parents' room and meal offers for children. A swimming pool and children's playroom are appealing to families.

Solo travellers

People travelling on their own are often business travellers but may be single people on holiday. Unfortunately this type of customer usually fares worst in hotels and restaurants. Single rooms are often small and in the worst location and they are more expensive per person. Single people in restaurants may also be given small tables which are poorly placed. Many tour operators and travel agents are trying to improve facilities for solo travellers, by arranging rooms without single supplements and offering the means of meeting other people for group holidays. However, these measures do not help business travellers. Women solo travellers sometimes have special facilities, such as women-only floors and enhanced security features. Many hotels now offer TV dinners for solo travellers – a table for one in the restaurant with a personal television and headphones.

Corporate

Corporate customers may be individuals using the hotel as a base to attend meetings elsewhere. They expect to be offered business services, internet access and food at convenient times for their business needs, as well as a comfortable room. They also expect a good restaurant and bar where clients can be entertained. Many hotels now recognise that business customers often require leisure facilities and provide a gym or fitness centre and sometimes a pool. Often these are free for all residents to use.

Corporate customers may be attending a conference. This will be organised by the hotel's conference and banqueting manager. The conference business is very lucrative and the conference manager has targets to meet and must encourage conference business.

Hotels produce sales literature aimed at the conference market and offer delegate packages per day or per number of days. Corporate entertainment is another service offered by venues, as the Newmarket racecourse case study shows.

Special needs

Special needs usually relates to the services required by those who are physically disabled. Hotels are aware of their obligations under the Disability Discrimination Act 1995 and 2005 and most extend a welcome to guests with special requirements. A series of symbols is used to illustrate the extent of wheelchair access and some hotels provide rooms adapted for disabled users.

A charity, Tourism For All, is concerned with accessible tourism enquiries. It works with tourist boards and is accredited to inspect accommodation in the UK against National Accessible Scheme Standards. These standards were revised in 2002.

Case study: Newmarket racecourse

The prime business of Newmarket racecourse is to provide a venue for racing, with facilities for race-goers. You might be surprised to learn that races take place on only about 40 days per year. As there are two racecourses at Newmarket, this means that there are a lot of facilities whose use would not be maximised if they were not used for some other purpose. Newmarket racecourse is therefore offered for all sorts of hospitality use including conferences, weddings, parties and corporate events.

On race days a series of packages is available for corporate clients. A business can invite its customers to watch the races from an executive box where they will be able to eat, drink and place bets without leaving the box. Those with larger parties to entertain can hire their own marquee.

Find an example of another corporate hospitality package. You might find an example at a venue in your own locality. Otherwise search on the internet. Consider looking at theatres, visitor attractions and sporting venues.

Special needs may also refer to special requirements of customers, for example a special celebration like a wedding. Weddings can take place almost anywhere these days and hotels are keen to promote the use of their premises for wedding ceremonies as this means they will be very likely to host the reception also. This dovetails very well with conferences as most weddings are at weekends and most conferences are during the week. Wedding customers can have the services of a wedding coordinator. Some weddings are booked and planned a year in advance and the wedding coordinator will offer a range of packages including menus and drinks, evening buffet, master of ceremonies and even advice on wedding etiquette.

Groups

Groups of customers may be corporate groups, as we have already discussed, or they may be groups of leisure travellers, for example learners going on a residential study trip.

What special occasions can hotels cater for?

Activity: Group expectations

Consider the expectations of a group like yours for a study trip. What particular needs would you have? What kind of accommodation would you require? What facilities and level of service do you expect? What kind of bars and restaurants would you visit? Discuss this with a partner, make notes and then share your findings with another pair.

Activity: Types and expectations

Try this simple activity as an introduction to customer types and their expectations. Match up the customers in the table below to the most suitable form of hospitality and give the reason you think it is suitable.

Customer	Type of hospitality	Reason for choice
Jemima is a stockbroker – she is treating her boyfriend to a birthday dinner	A hotel belonging to a large chain situated at the edge of a city by a major road junction	
Joe is taking his twin 11-year-old boys away for a weekend for a summer treat	The Oxo restaurant, a smart expensive restaurant in London	
A property company wishing to put on a weekend exhibition about Spanish second homes	A city centre youth hostel	
A group of 200 doctors attending a conference about the latest research into airline passenger health	A university campus in the Easter period	
A group of students visiting Manchester for educational reasons	McDonald's	
A group of four young mothers who are taking a week away from their families for a rest and pampering	Splash Landings Hotel at Alton Towers	
Panday is six years old – her parents are taking her and six young friends out for tea	A spa resort in Majorca	

Assessment activity 20.1

P1 M1 D1 **BTEC**

When you left college with a BTEC National qualification you found a job at a hotel in London belonging to a major chain. You were accepted onto their management trainee programme and have so far worked in two of their hotels. You are currently working in the marketing department where it has been decided to produce a monthly newsletter to be distributed to hotel staff throughout the group. The aim is to improve communication between management and staff and use the newsletter to inform staff of company policy and educate them about industry issues. The newsletter has to be of interest to staff at all levels from cleaning and waiting staff to managers.

The first edition of the newsletter will introduce some issues relating to the hospitality business.

You are to produce an article for the first edition. You should consider the layout of the article and how it might be illustrated.

1 Describe different types of hospitality providers and the products and services they offer. Explain how providers meet the needs and expectations of different types of customer. **P1**

2 Draw up a comparison of how two selected hospitality providers meet the expectations of different types of customer through the provision of different products and services. Write up your findings as a chart with detailed explanatory notes and discuss your work with your tutor. **M1**

3 Recommend new or enhanced products and services that could be provided by one selected hospitality provider. **D1**

Make sure that you cover the full range, referring to the content and assessment guidance in the unit specification for the detail required.

Grading tips

P1 You must describe at least two providers where hospitality is the main role and at least two which are secondary. Make sure you include a wide range of products and services for each organisation.

M1 Make sure you are not merely describing the products and services but are identifying and explaining the differences and similarities.

D1 Your recommendations could be targeted at a new type of customer or they could relate to an existing provision for current customers.

D1 You need to clearly justify your proposal in relation to the needs of different types of customers.

PLTS

By analysing and evaluating information and including that which is relevant for your article, you will be developing your **independent enquirer** skills.

Functional skills

To produce your article you need to enter, develop and format information to suit the purpose of the article, which will help you practise your **ICT** skills.

2 Planning hospitality provision in a travel and tourism context

2.1 Hospitality provision and context

You need to decide what kind of hospitality provision is required, for example catering, accommodation or a spa facility. You also need to decide on the context. This means the type of organisation or location that you are going to plan for (e.g. for an attraction, travel agency, Tourist Information Centre, festival, or event).

2.2 Plan

Part of your assessment includes planning hospitality provision. You will probably choose something quite small and manageable to design. You might design catering provision or accommodation for a hotel that needs a refurbishment, or your plan could be in a leisure club or for a cinema or airline. There are many possibilities. Whatever your plan you will need to consider:

Theme

Think about whether you need to follow a corporate design or brand – do you need to have consistent colours and features so that customers can easily recognise the brand?

Furnishing

Furnishing forms part of the design and may relate to current trends, for example many bars now provide comfortable leather seating to encourage customers to linger – and buy more products. In restaurants, the furnishings will be more formal to allow people to eat in comfort at the tables. Think about light too. Will you have natural or artificial light?

Level of service

In catering, this will range from self-service for passengers in a hurry to a full waitered dining service for those with more time and money. Another important factor in terms of service is the hours of trading that may be demanded. With accommodation think about how much luxury you are prepared to offer.

Location and size

These will depend on budget and your target market. The service you wish to offer will impact on size. If you want to have live music, for example, you will need space for this. If you are relying on passing trade you need to be located somewhere with good footfall.

Name

Having an established brand means the name is already known and recognisable. You need a name that is easily remembered and says something about the product.

Layout and customer flow

These are related as the layout determines the customer flow. Remember that layout covers both front of house (that is, the areas the customer can see and use) and back of house (this means, for restaurants, the kitchen and preparation areas).

Products and services

Products and services will vary according to the type of provision you plan. Coffee bars offer a range of good-quality fresh coffees and pastries and sandwiches. Restaurants may offer a fixed menu (table d'hôte) and an à la carte menu. Accommodation could be basic or have a whole range of extra services from room service to facilities in the room, such as wifi or expensive toiletries.

Assessment activity 20.2   **P2** **M2** **BTEC**

Imagine that you are opening a small coffee and juice bar in a new or refurbished airport.

1   Produce a plan for your bar considering all the factors outlined in the text. Decide on its name. Draw your plan on graph paper. It does not need to be to scale. Describe the features of all aspects of your plan. **P2**

2   Explain how your plan meets the needs of the airport authority and the needs of the passengers at the airport. **M2**

Make sure that you cover the full range, referring to the content and assessment guidance in the unit specification for the detail required.

Grading tips

P2 Make sure your plan shows the location of your provision, customer flows and layout of your provision. Don't worry you won't be assessed on your artistic ability.

M2 You should explain your plan, focusing on the reason for inclusion of all aspects of the design. Your reasons should be linked to the organisation's customer types, that is, the airport staff and customers.

PLTS

You will be generating ideas and exploring possibilities when you plan your coffee and juice bar, demonstrating your **creative thinker** skills.

Functional skills

You will enter and develop information when you organise information of different types, e.g. images and text to produce your plan. This will help you practise your **ICT** skills.

3 Factors affecting hospitality operations in travel and tourism organisations

The success of a hospitality provider is affected by several issues both internal and external. These can be assessed by means of **SWOT** and **PEST** analysis, terms which you may recall from other areas of your course, particularly marketing.

> **Key terms**
>
> **SWOT** – analysis of the Strengths, Weaknesses, Opportunities and Threats of an organisation. Strengths and weaknesses are internal, threats and opportunities may be internal or external depending on their nature.
>
> **PEST** – analysis of the Political, Economic, Social and Technological factors affecting an organisation.

3.1 Internal factors

Products and services offered

The range of hospitality products and services offered is determined by management and, as we have seen, varies to meet the expectations of particular customers. The range is subject to change as customer needs are not static and change according to fashion and current trends. These, in turn, are part of the external environment of the organisation.

Brands

This can be an internal factor as large groups have many different brands and may be in competition with each other. For example, Accor Hotels offer brands at different market levels – the Ibis, the Mercure and the Sofitel hotels – targeted at different types of customers. However, a customer travelling to London has all these brands open to them, so the brands are in competition to an extent.

Pricing strategies

Again, prices are pitched at the needs and expectations of different customers. However, all hotels measure their success by an average room rate achieved. This means the revenue achieved by the hotel divided by how many rooms they sold.

Last-minute deals are always offered in hotels as an empty room does not make any money. Always ask 'Is that your best price?' when you make a late booking for a hotel. The rate will often be reduced.

Promotional strategies

You have studied promotion on your BTEC course and so you are aware of the complexity of planning strategy. This will be undertaken by head office in the case of a group but local promotions might be undertaken by local management with a set budget. Smaller establishments, such as independent restaurants or guest houses, undertake their own activities and they are likely to consist of fairly simple things such as promotion through the local tourist office or placing local advertising. Many establishments choose to have their own websites and they may update and host these themselves or employ web managers, depending on their expertise.

Location

The location affects hospitality operations as a convenient location should mean good customer flow and high occupancy rates. Restaurants must either be of such high repute that customers travel specifically to them or else they must be in convenient town-centre locations.

Image and appeal

Customers choose a hospitality provider on the basis of its reputation. A brand is built up over a period of time by having high levels of service and good quality products. For restaurants, popularity is affected by reviews. Once it is established, bookings flow and the restaurant is able to command high prices and be discerning about who is allowed in.

Sometimes, several of these internal factors are combined to attract customers and increase profitability. Hilton is one of the world's most famous hotel chains. It offers a range of different packages. However, sometimes these packages need to be adapted to appeal to local customers. An example is the provision of murder mystery breaks at its hotel in Dartford Bridge; these include a three-course dinner along with the entertainment.

3.2 External factors

Legislation

In some companies the Human Resources department is responsible for ensuring legislation is complied with. The department needs to be aware of the latest legislation, as new legislation might make it necessary to set up special training to ensure staff comply with it, or changes to legislation might affect recruitment. Examples of such legislation include the Disability Discrimination Act 1995 and 2005, which makes it unlawful for providers of goods, facilities or services to discriminate against members of the public on the grounds of disability. This also relates to employment.

Smaller organisations, for example guest houses, may use organisations such as their local Chamber of Commerce or Business Link to help them ensure they comply with legislation. They must be aware of health and safety legislation, fire regulations, food regulations and licensing laws.

Economy

The UK hotel industry turns over about £27 billion per year but is affected by economic issues, including exchange rates, which impact on tourist arrivals. When the pound is strong against the dollar and the euro, tourists are less likely to visit the UK as they find it expensive. Fewer visitors results in rooms being let for lower rates and in lower room-occupancy levels.

In addition, the domestic economy affects bookings. People are less likely to take leisure breaks and eat out when their disposable income is reduced through factors such as higher interest rates or increased taxation.

Availability of skilled workforce

Much of hospitality work is part-time. This might be a good thing in terms of flexibility for employees but the work is also low paid and often seasonal. Employers are allowed to top up wages with tips so that the minimum wage is met, in spite of strong criticism from trade unions. The employers argue that food and accommodation are often provided for workers and that this should be taken into account when setting wages.

> ### Did you know?
>
> According to the People 1st State of the Nation report 42 per cent of hospitality work in hotels and 50 per cent in restaurants is part-time – compared with only 25 per cent across all industries.

These factors cause recruitment difficulties and jobs are often taken by those who have difficulty finding work in other sectors, such as refugees and people with few basic skills, or those for whom English is a second language. Having workers who have problems communicating in English, or lack other basic skills, impacts on customer service and hotels and restaurants often have to keep people lacking such skills away from customer-facing activities, giving them, for example, kitchen work. Even there, a lack of English may cause other problems as instructions on catering and kitchen products cannot easily be read.

As there is a high turnover of staff in this sector there is a need for constant training to cover existing and replacement staff. However, if good quality training were available it would be expected that staff retention would improve. Some businesses, encouraged by organisations such as **People 1st**, have understood this and managed to reduce staff turnover and recruitment costs by providing relevant training.

> ### Key term
>
> **People 1st** – the Sector Skills Council (SSC) that represents the hospitality, leisure, travel and tourism sector on skills matters, to optimise skills funding and to identify and endorse suitable training provision.

Other organisations encourage training, for example the British Institute of Innkeeping has developed a qualification which will eventually become a requirement for new pub tenants.

Many organisations offer on-the-job training leading to work-based learning qualifications in hospitality and catering.

Competition

New businesses open and close as organisations merge or dispose of assets. These factors affect hospitality providers as they can mean more or less business.

Accessibility

If a hospitality provider is not accessible, it will not attract business – a restaurant off the beaten track has to be excellent to warrant a difficult journey. Accessibility does not just relate to location. Some restaurants are deliberately exclusive, for example The Ivy in London and often are not generally accessible.

Proximity to markets

Proximity is closely linked to accessibility. A coffee bar must be centrally located for passing trade. Hotels are often near motorways, airports or exhibition centres to attract business people.

Current trends

Customers' expectations change according to current trends. These may be legally imposed, such as the smoking ban, or be related to health or fashion, for example the desire to eat more healthily. Hospitality providers must be aware of trends and provide products and services in anticipation of them.

Assessment activity 20.3   **P3** **M3**   **BTEC**

Joshua Kintuck runs a pub in a small village in Suffolk. His partner is Spanish and a superb chef. She specialises in Catalan dishes, particularly fish dishes. Over the last ten years she has built up a reputation and people flock from far and wide to eat in the pub. On Friday and Saturday nights it is impossible to get a reservation without booking weeks ahead.

Although the business is successful, it is not an easy life as the Kintucks take only one day off a week and rarely find time to visit their grown-up children. Besides running the business and ordering and preparing the food, they have to hire and train staff. To attract staff, Mrs Kintuck advertises in a London listing magazine. She has had some excellent young people who have come to the UK to learn English. She has trained them as much as she has time for, particularly in food safety. Unfortunately, they do not always stay very long as there is a limit to the attractions of the countryside. This leads to a further round of recruitment and basic training. Some of her staff are from outside Europe and Mrs Kintuck has found it difficult to understand all the regulations regarding the employment of non-Europeans.

Another problem facing the Kintucks is the change in licensing laws. They still close promptly at 11 p.m. and do not wish to open longer. Although the law, which came into force in November 2005, does not mean they are forced to open longer, they are under pressure from a few customers to do so.

They are also worried about the smoking ban, but they have provided more outside tables and gas heaters and haven't noticed any change in custom.

1 Explain how internal and external factors impacting on the pub/restaurant business in general affect their operations. **P3**

2 Assess how pubs and restaurants have responded to internal and external factors affecting their operations. **M3**

Present your findings orally to your group.

Make sure that you cover the full range, referring to the content and assessment guidance in the unit specification for the detail required.

Grading tips

P3 You should explain at least two internal and two external factors affecting hospitality provision in general and then demonstrate your understanding by explaining how selected factors affect this business.

M3 You should focus on the actions that hospitality providers have taken as a result of internal and external factors, following on from **P3**. You should research real examples. Copies or examples of promotional material could be included to support assessment.

PLTS

By exploring issues from the perspective of the pub owners, you will be practising your **independent enquirer** skills.

Functional skills

In presenting your findings to your group and practising speaking skills by making an effective presentation, you will be developing your **English** skills.

Gemma Fisher

Event Coordinator, Hotel

Your hotel caters for a lot of weddings – how important is that for the hotel?

What I always try to remember is that the bride has spent a year planning this day and it has to go well. All the staff understand how important the occasion is even though we have wedding functions every week.

Can you describe a typical wedding and the duties of the banqueting staff on the day.

The first thing we do in the morning is put the red carpet at the front of the hotel ready for the bride and groom's arrival.

In the function room we lay out the tables according to the plan that the couple has agreed with our banqueting manager. We have menus and place cards to put on the tables. Sometimes we have little novelties or keepsakes provided by the bride to put on the tables as well. When the guests arrive we serve welcome drinks in the function bar and they have photos taken outside in the gardens. Then it's time for the line up. This is where the couple welcome their guests in a line. The meal is served when everyone's at their table. We use silver service and serve the top table first. After the meal, we present the cake and the bride and groom cut it. During the speeches we take the cake away and cut it properly.

Do you have to do anything in the evening?

After the meal there may be an evening party. We clear the room and everyone goes away to their rooms or the bar for a while. We prepare the room for a disco and buffet.

Think about it!

1 Are you the type of person who likes working with customers?

2 Are you able to present a positive professional image for very long hours?

3 What would you feel about working when other people are enjoying themselves?

Just checking

1 Give three examples of hospitality provision as a main business.
2 How do airlines provide hospitality?
3 Which is the largest hotel group in the UK?
4 Discuss three issues currently impacting on hospitality businesses.
5 Why is room service important?
6 What is a budget hotel?
7 How does location affect a restaurant's operations?
8 What are the issues about skilled workforce in hospitality?
9 Name the sector skills council for hospitality.

Assignment tips

• Find out what hospitality provision is available in your area and see if you can visit.
• If you are near an airport look at what is provided there in terms of hotels and catering.
• To keep updated about what is happening in the hospitality industry look at www.caterersearch.com

Credit value: 10

26 Researching current issues in travel and tourism

The travel and tourism sector is always affected by current events and issues that arise either within the sector or in the external environment. Travel and tourism companies continually have to react to changes and issues and it is vital that managers have a high level of awareness of issues affecting their business.

In this unit you will have the opportunity to develop knowledge and understanding of an issue that is currently affecting travel and tourism. In doing so you will develop your research skills and gain an understanding of research methodology. You should be able to make links with other units that you have covered in your programme.

You will be introduced to useful information sources to help you with your research and you will be taken step-by-step through the planning and research process. This unit differs from other units in that it is assessed at Level 4 rather than Level 3.

Learning outcomes

After completing this unit you should:

1 understand methodology for researching complex current issues affecting the travel and tourism sector

2 be able to conduct research into complex current issues affecting the travel and tourism sector

3 understand impacts of complex current issues on the travel and tourism sector.

Assessment and grading criteria

This table shows you what you must do in order to achieve a **pass**, **merit** or **distinction** grade, and where you can find activities in this book to help you.

To achieve a **pass** grade the evidence must show that you are able to:	To achieve a **merit** grade the evidence must show that, in addition to the pass criteria, you are able to:	To achieve a **distinction** grade the evidence must show that, in addition to the pass and merit criteria, you are able to:
P1 explain methodology for researching a complex current issue affecting the travel and tourism sector **See assessment activity 26.1, page 170**		
P2 plan and carry out research into a complex current issue affecting the travel and tourism sector **See assessment activity 26.2, page 180**	**M1** explain how the proposed research plan enables exploration of a complex current issue **See assessment activity 26.2, page 180**	
P3 present a detailed analysis of results from research into a complex current issue affecting the travel and tourism sector **See assessment activity 26.2, page 180**	**M2** conduct independent research into a complex current issue, using at least four different types of sources of information, showing awareness of limitations of sources **See assessment activity 26.2, page 180**	**D1** evaluate the research undertaken and recommend improvements to own research skills in the future **See assessment activity 26.2, page 180**
P4 discuss how a complex current issue impacts on the travel and tourism sector **See assessment activity 26.3, page 182**	**M3** communicate information about a complex current issue clearly, concisely and coherently using specialist vocabulary, making connections and synthesising arguments **See assessment activity 26.3, page 182**	**D2** use findings from research into the complex current issue to recommend actions for the travel and tourism sector **See assessment activity 26.3, page 182**

How you will be assessed

This unit will be assessed by one or more internal assignments that will be designed and marked by your tutor. Your assignments will be subject to sampling internally and externally as part of Edexcel's quality assurance procedures. The assignments are designed to allow you to show your knowledge and understanding related to the unit. The unit outcomes indicate what you should know, understand or be able to do after completing the unit.

Sanjay, 21-year-old BTEC National learner

This unit is challenging as it means working at a higher level than the other units. It also means you work by yourself on a research project. I was worried about this but I found out that it didn't mean I wouldn't get any help. I was able to do my research and write up the project independently but I could still talk over my ideas and any issues with my tutor.

I want to go to university after this course so learning how to do research properly really will help. I've already written about my project in my personal statement. I knew how to use Google and other search engines before I started but now I know how to use other sources of information and how to be sure that my information is valid. I learnt how to use Harvard referencing. I know I have to do this at university too.

Over to you!

1 How do you think knowing the best ways of doing research will help you?
2 Have you heard of Google Scholar? Take a look and see how it differs from Google.

1 Methodology for researching complex current issues affecting the travel and tourism sector

Set off

Looking at the issues

As a group, choose one issue that is currently affecting travel and tourism. Think of as many different sources of information on this issue as you can. Examples include all the different daily newspapers, the television news, web news, trade press, travel and tourism news websites.

Divide into pairs, with each pair taking a different source. Then you and your partner should research the issue from your assigned source. Reconvene and discuss the similarities and differences in reporting. Discuss why differences occur.

In this section we will discuss research methods, look at key terminology used in the field of research and consider appropriate methods for your own research. We will also begin to consider the types of issues in travel and tourism that would be suitable for you to research yourself.

1.1 Research methods

Intervention

Research that includes intervention will influence a respondent's behaviour or thoughts in response to the research. These methods are generally to be avoided as they affect the objectivity of the research. You may use intervention in terms of prompts when you need to help respondents remember key points in a discussion.

Non-intervention

Non-intervention research methods are entirely to do with objective observation, for example where there is no intention or possibility of influencing results. You should aim to use a non-interventionist approach.

Action research

This is an interventionist approach to research. It is based on investigating your own practice, usually with a small team of colleagues. It considers an area of working practice and seeks collaborative solutions to improve it. You might be able to use this approach if you have a work placement and a suitable issue to investigate in the workplace. It is unlikely that you will choose to use it for your research for this unit.

1.2 Research sources and data

Research sources can be **primary research** or **secondary research** and the data collected from these sources can be **qualitative data** or **quantitative data**.

Key terms

Primary research – research carried out for the first time by you. It includes any surveys or interviews you do.

Secondary research – research which someone else has done and which you are using to help you with your project.

Qualitative data – data about opinions and reasons for doing things. These are harder to interpret than quantitative data but can be very rich and informative.

Quantitative data – data that consist of facts and figures. These are easy to measure but do not always tell us why things happen.

We will look more closely at different research methods so that you will know how to use them and be able to choose appropriate ones when you are ready to start your own project.

Researching from secondary sources

You must:

- be clear about what you are to find out
- know where to search for information
- be able to assess the validity of the source
- be able to cross-reference information
- be clear about what you want to find out.

It is worth spending some time on this preparation stage: identifying the objective of the research. Research is time-consuming and it is easy to get sidetracked, so make sure you know what you are looking for. If you have completed your research plan properly, you will know what you are looking for. You will also have had an opportunity to discuss your plan with your tutor. Ask questions and clarify anything you are unsure about. Make a list of the different things you need to find out. Write down key words to help your search.

Know where to search for information

Decide which information sources to use. When searching on the internet, remember to choose a search engine such as Google. You can search for images and news stories and can search their directory or the web. The directory differs from the web in that it is human edited and sorted into categories.

Be as specific as you can with your key words in order to narrow your search. If you want to search for an exact phrase put it in inverted commas. You might notice some of your results are termed 'sponsored results'. This means those companies have paid to be listed and may come up first. Remember that search engines provide help if you get stuck. Look for the help link on the main page.

When you are collecting information, organise it as you collect it. If you are making notes from the internet or a book, group all the notes relating to a particular topic together. If you are photocopying or printing, highlight the relevant points immediately and organise topics together.

A list of secondary sources of information for travel and tourism is given on pages 174–175.

Assessing the validity of a source

You need to make sure that your source of information is accurate, up to date and unbiased. It is important to do this with every source but it is more difficult to assess internet websites, as anyone can set up a website and they may not always represent objective information.

Use the following criteria for deciding whether your source is valid.

Who wrote it?

Are they qualified to write it? For example, you can be pretty sure that a textbook is written by a highly qualified person! A letter in a newspaper complaining about a package holiday may not be valid – it only represents one person's experience. Newspaper articles tend to be more trustworthy but again can reflect the paper's politics and opinions, so be careful.

What is the purpose of the information source?

If you are researching from holiday brochures or sales literature, remember the purpose is to sell, so they are biased in favour of certain products. They certainly will not tell you if there was an outbreak of food poisoning last season. A publication such as *World Travel Guide* is considered more reliable than brochures, as it is based on factual information as an aid to the travel trade and is not trying to sell.

Is the information up-to-date?

When was the information written? If it is a web page how often is it updated? If it is not up to date don't use it. Of course, if you are researching a topic that does not change, such as the development of tourism in the UK, then an older textbook will still be useful.

Does the author give sources of facts and figures?

You need to check this as you too need to quote sources. You may be able to go back to the quoted source and check for accuracy.

Does the author seem to be biased in their presentation of information?

You will recognise bias when you have experience of using different sources. Initially it is difficult to recognise but you can practise by reading several different newspaper accounts of the same event.

Activity: Validity of information

Assess the validity of the following three pieces of information. Comment on the type of current research issue they would be useful for. Make notes on your findings and discuss them with your colleagues.

1 Fledgling publishes its monthly passenger traffic figures, including load factors, within the first five working days of the month (note that these figures are an example only).

Table 26.1: Passenger traffic in January–March 2009/2010

	Passengers			Load factors		
	2009	2010	Rolling 12 months	2009	2010	Rolling 12 months
Jan	1,464,762	2,198,657	36,445,987	72%	70%	80%
Feb	1,538,425	2,233,091	36,998,023	76%	75%	80%
Mar	2,040,881	2,843,687	38,001,554	81%	70%	81%

2 New provisional figures from the International Passenger Survey – the key monitor of international tourism to the UK – highlight the very real challenge facing Britain's inbound tourism industry as international travel suffers from the impact of the global economic downturn. The figures demonstrate the scale of the task facing the industry and that people won't just travel to Britain because sterling is weak.

> The figures show that in the first three months of 2009, overseas residents made 6.3 million visits to the UK and spent just over £3.1 billion. Before adjusting for inflation, there is no change in spending compared to January–March 2008, while the number of visits has fallen by 13 per cent. Sterling was on average 29 per cent weaker against the US dollar and 16 per cent weaker against the Euro in March 2009 compared to March 2008.
>
> *www.tourismtrade.org.uk*

3 The following is an extract from a holiday brochure.

> Siblu parc Le Bois Dormant offers a special kind of holiday. This beautiful parc, located in one of the best seaside resorts of the Vendée, offers both a relaxing retreat together with a lively break.
>
> Le Bois Dormant feels spacious and well-thought out. The holiday homes are spaced out across the parc, but not too far away from the hub of activity around the pool and restaurant area. The outdoor pool complex offers something for everyone, from a main swimming pool, to waterslides, a toddler splash pool and even a spa bath.
>
> The bar and restaurant terrace offer lovely views over the pool if you want to stop for a quick snack – the pizzas come highly recommended! Away from the pool is an outstanding sports complex, together with a multi-sports pitch where the youngsters can be kept entertained with regular football and basketball tournaments.
>
> If you're in search of evening entertainment, then head over to siblu parc Le Bois Masson, situated just across the road, and make the most of their full programme of events:
>
> - fantastic sports facilities
> - spacious and attractive parc
> - superb beaches – 1.5 miles from the nearest beach
> - great for golfers
> - wide range of accommodation.
>
> *(Source: Siblu brochure 2009; © Siblu)*

Case study: Checking information

P&O Cruises sees 2011 booking improvement

Date Posted: 10 Jul 2009 | Category: P&O Cruises News

Anybody doubting the strength of the cruise industry may want to look at the advanced booking figures for vessels from P&O Cruises and Cunard Line.

The cruise lines revealed that reservations for sailings in 2011 for round the world cruises are 47 per cent ahead of this time last year.

Some 2,044 holidaymakers have booked up for the cruise trips in two years time, compared to the 1,385 individuals who booked for 2010 last year.

Nigel Esdale, managing director of P&O Cruises, said:

"The appetite to take that 'once in a lifetime' voyage is far from in decline and for many experienced cruisers a world voyage is becoming a regular winter holiday experience."

P&O Cruises is also set to provide passengers with an action-packed host of options for 2011, with four ships setting sail to various locations around the globe. Starting from Southampton, the ships will stop at 89 ports in 46 countries, according to Mr Esdale.

P&O Cruises head to a variety of regular locations including the Caribbean, South America and the Middle East.

Written by Chris Smith

(Source: www.iglucruise.com, 10 July 2009)

Copyright©Iglucruise.com

1 Think of three different ways you could check the information given in this extract.

2 Remember to keep details of your sources as you do your research.

Be able to cross-reference information

Cross-referencing is a means of checking that the information is correct. It is more important if you are not absolutely certain that your original source is accurate. For example, you may have found some figures quoted on a tour operator's website and you may not be certain that they are up to date or accurate, so you look for a second source of the same information to check the figures. The second source could be official statistics or other tour operators' findings.

Researching from primary sources

A research project should not rely on secondary sources. You should carry out some original research of your own. You need to decide what type of primary research you want to do at the planning stage and incorporate it into your plan.

The most appropriate research methodologies for your project will be:

- interviews
- focus groups
- questionnaires.

Interviews

A formal interview is very structured, with a list of prepared questions to be asked. It is similar to carrying out a questionnaire on a one-to-one basis or with a small group.

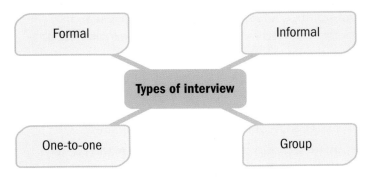

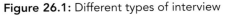

Figure 26.1: Different types of interview

An informal interview allows more scope for the interviewee to develop the flow of the interview. You still need to prepare a list of topics that you want to cover in the interview but you can be flexible about what order they are covered in and if the interviewee suggests an issue that they consider particularly relevant you can include it in your discussion. Where this is done with a group it develops into a focus group.

In terms of your research project you are likely to find that an informal interview is more appropriate if you are speaking to an 'expert', such as a manager of a visitor attraction or a tour operator. The expert will bring points to the discussion that you may not have previously considered. This is most likely to be on a one-to-one basis.

On the other hand, if you are interviewing ordinary consumers you may want to use a formal approach if it is one-to-one, as the interviewees will depend on you to direct the interview. If you still prefer an informal structure consider carrying out a focus group.

Focus groups

A **focus group** is very useful if you want to find out consumer attitudes or perceptions about a company or service. For example, you might hold a focus group to find out attitudes towards booking holidays with travel agents.

Key term

Focus group – a small number of people (up to about 15) who are bought together in a moderated meeting to talk about a specific product, service or issue.

It is also a technique that you can practise and develop during the course of your project. This research method is used extensively in consumer marketing. How do you carry out a focus group?

* Decide what kind of people should be invited, for example if your project is about attitudes to flying on low-cost airlines, you must invite people with experience of travelling on these airlines.

* Invite a group of people (between 6 and 12) to a pre-arranged venue. Focus group participants are often paid but you are unlikely to pay them. However, you might offer refreshment as an incentive to attend.

* Prepare a list of discussion points but be prepared to be flexible – the discussion should flow from the interviewees. If it goes completely off track, you will have to pull it back. This is where experience helps.

* In a focus group an extrovert personality can easily dominate discussion. Try to bring in quieter members.

* Record the discussion – you cannot take notes and lead the session. You will need a tape recorder or a scribe. Ask a friend or colleague to help you. You can reciprocate for them.

The following are some useful techniques that an interviewer can use in running a focus group.

* Playing devil's advocate – this means that the discussion leader deliberately takes an opposing point of view to a participant in order to stimulate a strong defence and further discussion.

* Sophisticated naivety – the leader pretends not to understand a participant's point in order to get them to expand on it.

* Closed-book technique – participants in a focus group are aware they are taking part in research and may not choose to reveal too much of their real opinions. The closed-book technique is used to formally bring the focus group to an end. The leader thanks the participants and puts their papers away or turns off the tape recorder. The leader should be listening intently at this point as the participants will relax and may, in speaking to the leader or as asides to each other, reveal some interesting attitudes when they think they are no longer being recorded.

Think about it

Imagine you are researching into day trips taken by your colleagues. Can you think of some possible focus group topics for this research issue?

Questionnaires

Questionnaires are useful means of getting information from a large number of people. Remember you can use them in an informal interview if you choose. Refer to Unit 5 on Marketing, in Student Book 1, for guidelines on designing a questionnaire.

Activity: Asking the right questions

Design a questionnaire that can be used to find out the frequency of using internet booking for flights among your friends and family. You need to find out:

* whether they book flights

* how they book flights

* how often they use the internet to book flights

* why they use the internet to book flights.

Pilot your questionnaire with your colleagues and then amend it in the light of their constructive criticism.

Carry out the questionnaire with at least 20 people and analyse the results. Prepare a short report on your findings. Include graphs and tables to illustrate your findings.

1.3 Travel and tourism sector

Now that you are more knowledgeable about research methods, you can begin to consider what kind of issues in travel and tourism you might want to research. Before you do that, Figure 26.2 provides a reminder of the industries within travel and tourism.

Figure 26.2: The components of the travel and tourism sector

Remember that your research issue must relate to the travel and tourism sector in general or to one of its industries.

1.4 Types of current issue

We will look at some current examples of issues affecting the travel and tourism sector. Issues could relate to:

- changes in demand for products and services
- current affairs
- the environment
- health.

You may find one of these of particular interest to you and then decide to study it in greater depth. You can, of course, choose a completely different issue as long as it relates to travel and tourism.

It is important to spend some time considering possible issues for research as you must determine whether sufficient information is available in order to do your research properly.

The following example relates to changes in demand for products and services.

Are package holiday sales in decline?

This topic might have been brought to your attention by a news item or feature in one of your news sources. The following extract comes from *Travel Weekly*.

Package holiday market still 'huge', says Mintel
(12 March 2009)

The decline of the package holiday has been exaggerated and the market remains huge although it has stagnated compared with an overall rise of 13% in overseas leisure travel since 2003.

That is the conclusion of market analyst Mintel's latest survey of the trade, revealed exclusively by Travel Weekly.

And while package sales have not kept pace with the rise in independent travel, revenue from packages hit a record last year when income from the sale of independent holidays declined.

Mintel reports package sales stabilising around 19 million to 20 million a year since 2003, estimating total sales last year at the lower end of the scale.

But that is easily in line with the decline in capacity, with Thomas Cook chief executive Manny Fontenla-Novoa estimating 25% has been taken out by the two major groups since 2006 and Mintel forecasting there will be 20% fewer package holidays available this year than last.

Sales of independent holidays rose from 21.7 million in 2003 to 27.2 million last year, according to Mintel, leaving packages at just over 41% of the overseas holiday market – although the trade's share is greater when its share of independent sales is included.

At the same time, the value of package sales rose from £9.6 billion in 2003 to £11 billion last year. The value of independent sales also increased, from £10.1 billion in 2003 to almost £13.2 billion in 2007, but then suffered a marginal fall last year to £13.1 billion.

So while packages account for 41% of holiday sales, they make up 46% of total revenue – up from 44.5% in 2006.

Mintel notes: "Independent travel has grown 25% over the last five years as the package market has flattened. However, the package industry still sold 3.5 million more trips last year than a decade earlier."

It adds: "Despite the growth of single-component sales and dynamic packaging, the pre-packaged product remains the staple segment for travel agents."

(Source: www.travelweekly.co.uk)

At first view this looks like a suitable topic for further research. Why? It gives a good overview of the topic including:

- a controversial point of view
- quotes from major market players
- statistics to interpret and analyse
- clues about where to look for further information.

What factors are impacting the appeal of package holidays?

Think about it

At this stage you have not chosen your topic – you are considering different topics as potential research issues. You still need to find out if more information about the chosen issue is accessible.

What next? How will you find out what further information is available on this issue?

1. Look at other sources and see if any of them are reporting on this trend. Print out or save relevant articles for analysis. Remember to start your bibliography by noting all sources in detail.

2. Read the text and see what clues there are for further research possibilities. List them with notes:

* Mintel – can I access their research data?
* Can I get other stats on how many package holidays are sold?
* Can I get stats on the rise of independent travel and dynamic packaging?
* How many people use the internet to book holidays?
* What about the increase in tailor-made holidays?
* Can I find out more about Thomas Cook?

3. Armed with your list you are ready to appraise what information is available. Be prepared for this to take an hour or two even at this stage. You will find other information later. At the moment you just want to know if there is sufficient information available for you to do a good research job on the issue.

Remember

Restrict your research to the internet and readily available sources at this stage. You do not have time to write to companies or do interviews with people before you select your research issue. If you don't know how to do internet research, refer back to page 163.

Assuming you did this initial research, the text below shows what you might find.

* Can't access Mintel's data on the internet – may be able to access it through a library.
* Lots of other news articles are available on the increase in dynamic packaging, e.g. on Travelmole.
* A quick Google search shows that there are several sites with information about numbers of package holidays sold. Bookmark these for revisiting later.
* Official statistics are available online at www.statistics.gov.uk.
* Last week, internet monitoring firm Hitwise reported that visits to UK travel sites were up 14 per cent in the first week of this month, compared with the same period last year. Travel websites, which are regularly among the most popular sites in the UK, accounted for one in every 20 visits to the web in the UK. This can be followed further.
* Found a BBC news item with figures on low-cost flights – will follow up that too.

From this initial research we can see that the 'decline' of package holidays is a suitable issue to research further. Each tranche of research leads to further possibilities and relevant statistics are available.

Remember to track your research – it is very easy to find a useful source and then lose it! Use the 'Favourites' listing on your PC or a hard copy notebook.

Activity: What's happening out there?

In order to understand current affairs, you need to find out what is happening in the world and how it affects travel and tourism. For this activity you will need all of one day's newspapers. Sunday newspapers are ideal as they report on a whole week.

Work in small groups and go through one of the newspapers to find examples of natural incidents/political change/interest rates rising, etc. Mark up each article with a few notes on how you think it impacts on travel and tourism.

When you are ready, present your articles and discuss them with your group. You may have found an issue that you would like to explore further.

The case study below relates to current affairs and environmental concerns.

Case study: Researching the impact of pressure groups

Tourism Concern's policy on working with industry

Most organisations working in tourism would acknowledge that their activities are not yet fairly traded nor sustainable. Tourism Concern welcomes the opportunity to work with any organisation willing and capable of change so long as this reflects our mission and does not compromise our values.

Tourism Concern's mission is to make sure tourism always benefits the local communities. We work in a number of different ways, primarily campaigning. Our integrity and independence are fundamental to achieving our mission and to providing a credible service to those organisations we work with.

When entering into a working relationship with an organisation Tourism Concern will respect the confidentiality of any information obtained through that relationship. No confidential information will be used by Tourism Concern in their campaigning activities.

Tourism Concern is committed to campaigning against exploitation in tourism. It is essential to our independence and integrity that there be no influence or preferential treatment expected or given should an organisation with which we are working be involved in activities against which we are campaigning.

Tourism Concern will work with organisations:

- That have a genuine commitment to continuous improvement on their social performance including active approval and continued commitment at senior management level.

- Where there are measurable improvements as a result of the changes they have implemented within the communities in which they operate.

- That will not behave in such a way as to compromise the reputation of Tourism Concern, or have any negative impact on Tourism Concern's core activities.

(Source www.tourismconcern.org.uk)

1   Imagine your research project is about the impact on travel and tourism of environmental pressure groups.

2   Suggest a hypothesis for this project – you may want to consider the issue in relation to just one sector of travel and tourism to narrow your research.

3   List the further types of information that might be useful.

4   Suggest at least five sources for this information (use the list on page 174 to help you).

5   Carry out some initial research and decide whether this is a viable issue.

Assessment activity 26.1

P1 BTEC

You work for a travel and tourism marketing organisation which conducts research for and on behalf of industry members. The company has been invited to contribute research findings to a series of workshops at the World Travel Market. Although the company will not be paid for this work, it is a prestigious event and may result in new business.

Staff have been asked to carry out research on a variety of current issues affecting the industry. Each member of staff will present their findings orally at one of the workshops. You have been given several weeks to prepare for your presentation and you have also been asked to present a workshop on research methods.

Prepare for your first workshop. You are to explain different methods that can be used to research a current issue in travel and tourism. You must cover at least two research methods and all the different kinds of sources and data covered in this unit. Present the advantages and disadvantages of each method. P1

Make sure that you cover the full range, referring to the content and assessment guidance in the unit specification for the detail required.

Grading tips

P1 Ensure you include primary and secondary methods and consider both qualitative and quantitative data from several sources. Give your reasons why the chosen methods would be effective.

PLTS

By researching different methodologies and sources of data, you will be practising your **independent enquirer** skills.

Functional skills

By reading and summarising information from different sources, you will be developing your **English** reading skills.

2 Conducting research into complex current issues affecting the travel and tourism sector

2.1 Research plan

Once you have done your initial investigation and selected a current issue for research you are ready to write your **research plan**.

This is completed before you start your project and provides a useful summary of what you are going to do. Your tutor will expect to see this to ensure that your chosen issue is suitable for research and that you are sufficiently prepared to begin your project.

Key term

Research plan – an overview of, and rationale for, the research project.

The research plan should contain the following elements:

- **Title** – this sums up what your study is about.

- **Hypothesis** – the statement that you are going to test or investigate.

- **Terms of reference** – this gives some background to the project, explains the context (that is, a description of events that led to this issue arising in travel and tourism) and describes why the issue is important.

- **Aims and objectives** – this section covers what you hope to achieve and the limitations of the project. Limitations ensure that you do not make your project so broad that your research does not address a specific issue.

- **Planned outcomes** – this section explains what you expect the results of your research to be.

- **Research methodology** – this section explains how you are going to conduct your research and the methods to be used to collect your data. The different methods that you might use for your research will be covered later in the unit. You might wish to refer to that section briefly now to help you write your research proposal.

- **Sources of information** – when you did your initial research to test the suitability of your current issue, you bookmarked useful websites and you noted relevant sources of information that you wanted to revisit. List these now and include any others which have since occurred to you.

- **Task dates** – these should be detailed in your plan so that you are not tempted to leave all your research until the last minute.

- **Review dates and monitor** – the review dates will indicate both formal and informal reviews. You should review your progress yourself and adjust your plan accordingly. In addition, you should arrange tutorials to monitor your progress. This is important as it is easy to go off track and waste time researching irrelevant points.

- **Contingencies** – back-up plans: perhaps an alternative source of information if one fails or a different research method.

- **Ethical issues** – this relates to confidentiality, types of question to be asked, and how and when the research will be carried out. You must make sure that you adhere to the Data Protection Act 1998 when storing personal information.

- **Evaluation** – Did your methods work? How will you know whether your research project has been successful? What will you measure it against? Did you achieve your objectives? Did you use appropriate sources of information? What would you do differently next time?

Example of a research plan

Now we will look at the research plan in more detail and consider an example.

Title: A study of the package holiday market and factors contributing to its decline.

Hypothesis: Package holidays sales are in decline.

Terms of reference: Several news reports in travel and tourism trade publications have indicated that sales of traditional package holidays are in decline. If this is so, the impact on the industry is of great importance as it would affect the core business of tour operators and travel agents. This research project will test whether the assertion is true by looking at available data and

will assess the reasons for decline, if they can be found. It will also consider if, and how, tour operators are reacting to the issue of decline in package holidays.

Aim: To investigate the possible decline of traditional package holiday sales.

Objectives

- To determine whether sales of traditional package holidays are in decline.
- To determine if specific package holiday destinations are in decline.
- To assess reasons for any decline.
- To investigate the reactions of tour operators to any decline.

The research will be limited to sales of outbound holidays from the UK. Domestic tourism is excluded from the research project.

Planned outcomes: Sales of package holidays are in decline because increased use of the internet means that travellers can easily book their own flights and accommodation. Research as described will prove or disprove this.

Research methodology: Secondary research will be carried out using the sources of information listed in this proposal. The research will include analysis of available statistics.

Primary research methods will include:

- A focus group with people who are intending to book holidays this year – discussion will centre on whether they will be booking a package holiday or another type of holiday.

- An interview with a tour operator to find out if its data suggests package holidays are in decline and to ask what its strategies are for addressing this. This will be an informal interview with unstructured questions.

The data will be analysed and a report produced on the findings. Interview records and notes and tapes from the focus group will be available with the report.

Sources of information

- Mintel – data given in *Travel Weekly* article.
- Statistics on package holidays taken from the Office for National Statistics.
- Travelmole.com – archive search.
- www.guardian.co.uk/technology

- Low-cost airline websites for information on increases in passenger numbers.
- www.hitwise.co.uk for information on booking of holidays.
- Local tour operator to be approached for interview (name and address).

Contingencies

- Look for other sources of statistics in case Mintel is not available.
- Find an alternative tour operator to interview.
- Look at other news websites such as e-tid.com if Travelmole does not have sufficient information.
- Allow plenty of time for research.

Ethical issues

- Ensure that the tour operator is reassured about use of its name (i.e. the name will not be used).
- Agree ground rules with focus group participants.

Evaluation

- Arrange tutorials at regular intervals to review progress.
- Ask a colleague to read the work.
- Evaluate regularly against objectives.

Activity: Evaluation of the project

You should consider different ways of evaluating your work and reflecting on what you have achieved, and how you achieved it, so that you learn from the experience for future research projects.

Below are some aspects of the project that you can include in an evaluation.

1 Did my plan help me? How?
2 Did I stick to my planned deadlines?
3 Did I choose suitable research methodologies? Why were they suitable or not?
4 Did my sources of information produce sufficient, relevant information?
5 What other sources could I have used?
6 Were my findings presented in a logical way supported by relevant data?
7 Was my referencing correct?
8 Were my conclusions valid?
9 Did I produce viable recommendations?
10 To what extent did I work independently?
11 What would I do differently next time?

Agreeing your plan

Once you have completed your research plan, you should have an opportunity to talk it through with your tutor on a one-to-one basis. It is better to get your initial research plan agreed with your tutor before producing it in too much detail. Your tutor should give agreement to your research plan before you continue.

Adding timescales

Once you and your tutor have agreed your plan, you are ready to refine it and add timescales. Your plan will be a working document and undoubtedly will change. This is fine as long as you write changes on the plan and they do not mean that you end up trying to do all the research at the last minute. You will need to discuss why and how your plan changed in your evaluation at the end of the research project. You will be expected to say how you dealt with problems that occurred in doing your research, so make sure you note them as you go along.

Your plan gives you a structure to work to, enabling you to make sure you have covered everything and that it is presented in a logical order.

When working out timescales allow time for writing up the project and for completing an evaluation. Include regular meetings where your tutor can check on your progress and discuss any problems that occur.

Timescales for research plan: Are package holiday sales in decline?

The following timescales have been assumed for this plan.

- The school/college is running a semester timetable so this unit is timetabled for half a year or 15 weeks.
- The first three weeks have been spent introducing the unit, deciding on a research issue, completing initial research and the research proposal for the chosen issue.
- Week 4 is spent on one-to-one tutorials to assess the research proposals and allow students to write their research plans.
- This leaves approximately ten weeks, allowing for contingencies and evaluation at the end.

Notes on the plan

- All the objectives must be covered in the plan.
- Each objective must link to the research methodology you are going to use to achieve that objective.

- The plan includes both primary and secondary research.
- Timescales are clear.
- There is scope to record changes to the plan.

Table 26.2 shows what the plan might look like. This one runs over several weeks. Yours will be adjusted to fit your timescales A plan always changes as time goes on so a column is provided to allow for this.

Table 26.2: An example research plan

Week	Objectives	Research method	Sources of information	Changes to plan
1	Determine if sales are in decline (there are conflicting views on this)	Secondary research Analyse statistics and produce relevant graphs and notes	*Travel Trade Gazette* (TTG) and *Travel Weekly* archives Mintel statistics as given in the TTG article Search www.statistics online Research low-cost airline websites	
2	Determine which particular package holiday destinations are in decline, if any	Secondary research Write up notes on findings – keep relevant articles/statistics for appendices	Trade mags archives as before	
3	Start to assess reasons for possible decline	Secondary research Categorise possible reasons and write up notes on supporting evidence	From trade sources including Travelmole and e-tid websites	
4	Assess reasons for decline	Add primary research plan focus group by inviting friends and family to participate – set a date for the focus group and arrange room and time Borrow tape recorder to tape discussion	Focus group	
5	Assess reasons for decline	Carry out focus group Transcribe tape or make detailed notes from tape Analyse findings and write up	Focus group	
6	Assess reactions of tour operator	Telephone local operators to arrange interview Prepare questions (informal interview – primary research)	Tour operator	
7	Assess reasons for decline	Secondary research – find out about internet booking	Hitwise website	
8	Assess reactions of tour operator	Primary research – carry out interview and analyse findings	Tour operator	
9		Start writing up report Mop up research for any checks to be made		
10		Finish writing up report – check appendices and referencing, write bibliography		
11		Evaluate the report and the methodologies used		

2.2 Sources of information

There are hundreds of sources of information available to you. These include:

- books
- journals
- newspapers
- websites
- television programmes
- published research papers
- official statistics
- questionnaire results.

When you select an issue for a project you must be certain that sufficient data is available for you to research your topic in depth and reach an appropriate level of analysis. This means you have to do some initial research to check on sources and find out exactly what kinds of information are available.

To help you with this initial research, and to get ideas on a range of topics, you should use some or all of these resources. This particular list consists of resources which report on news and events related to travel and tourism.

News sources

Online news information

- www.travelmole.com – a news and resource centre for the travel industry.
- www.thisistravel.co.uk – published by Associated New Media, the publishers of the Mail newspapers. It is aimed at consumers but is a useful source of news.
- www.e-tid.com – e-tid.com is a business travel news digest covering all sectors of the travel industry, from aviation and tour operating to hotels and cruises.
- www.travelwirenews.com – home of eTurboNews, whose aim is to present a fair and balanced coverage of the ongoing issues that concern the travel trade. This is an international newsletter and has subscribers in 230 countries.

You can subscribe to all of these news websites at no cost. Subscription means that you will be emailed regularly with travel and tourism news items. You will also be able to access the archives of information and past features on the websites.

Trade magazines

These are an excellent source of news. The magazines can be subscribed to in hard copy or you can access them online. Your library may have some of them. If you access them online you will have to register but registration is free.

- *Travel Trade Gazette* (www.ttglive.com)
- *Travel Weekly* (www. travelweekly.com)
- *Caterer & Hotelkeeper* (www.catereronline.com)
- *Leisure Opportunities* (www.leisureopportunities. co.uk)
- *Attractions Management* (www. attractionsmanagement.com)
- *Leisure Management* (www.leisuremanagement. co.uk)

Newspapers

Read a quality newspaper regularly. Although the travel sections are important, you should be reading all of a newspaper, as many international and national news events impact on travel and tourism, for example any incidences of terrorism or natural disasters in an area can affect tourism.

All the Sunday newspapers have travel supplements. Newspapers can be accessed online but some of them charge if you want to search the archives. You do not have to pay to search recent editions. Guardian.co.uk is a particularly useful source of travel features and it is free to register.

Once you have regular access to these news sources – and read the bulletins – you will find that your topical knowledge of travel and tourism improves immensely.

You will find that some news stories develop over days and weeks and have even greater impact on the industry. You will find it easier to choose an issue for your research project with your increased knowledge.

It is a good idea to select two or three initial ideas for your project as it may be that further information, particularly statistical information, is not easy to access. There is not room here to list all possible sources for all types of travel and tourism issues. Table 26.3 gives some general sources of online information and in the case studies later in the unit you will find some examples of sources of information for specific issues.

You will have come across many of the sources in the table before and indeed you will have used many of them.

Table 26.3: General travel and tourism sources on the internet

Information about tourism in the UK – a useful introduction	www.visitbritain.com
Department for Culture, Media and Sport	www.culture.gov.uk
World Tourism Organization	www.world-tourism.org
Customer comments about service on airlines and in airports	www.airlinequality.com
Columbus online world travel guide	www.worldtravelguide.net
Locations and addresses of tourist offices worldwide	www.tourist-offices.org.uk
Spanish Tourist Office	www.spaintour.com
French Government Tourist Office	www.franceguide.com
News about visitor attractions from the British Association of Leisure Parks, Piers and Attractions (BALPPA)	www.balppa.org
Tour operator – My Travel website (part of Thomas Cook)	www.mytravel.com
Company website for the Thomas Cook group – also has a history section	www.thomascook.com
Website for the First Choice group of tour operators (part of TUI group)	www.firstchoice.co.uk
Group website for TUI – parent company of Thomson – the tour operator	www.tuitravelplc.com
Website for the organisation representing the Association of Independent Tour Operators	www.aito.co.uk
Website for ABTA – The Travel Association	www.abta.com
UK Foreign Office travel advice	www.fco.gov.uk
Information on technology in marketing travel and tourism	www.eyefortravel.com
Information on reservation and distribution systems – particularly news sections	www.travelport.com www.sabre.com
International Civil Aviation Organization (ICAO)	www.icao.int
The UK Civil Aviation Authority (CAA)	www.caa.co.uk
Air Transport Users' Council for the UK	www.auc.org.uk
Official site of Scotland's national tourist board	www.visitscotland.com
Official site of Northern Ireland's national tourist board	www.discovernorthernireland.com
Official site of Wales's national tourist board	www.visitwales.com
Cruise information service provided by the Passenger Shipping Association	www.discover-cruises.co.uk
British Airports Authority	www.baa.co.uk

Activity: Exploring useful websites

A package is available on the internet which introduces you to travel and tourism resources. Visit www.vts.intute. ac.uk/tutorial/travel to go through a teach-yourself tutorial which will allow you to practise your internet information skills. On your way round you will be able to collect sites of interest and keep them for future reference.

You might begin by brainstorming a whole list of possible research topics and then selecting two or three for further exploration. Some researchers find mind mapping is a useful starting point to determine whether a research topic has further potential. All you need is a piece of paper with your potential topic written in the middle. From this you write notes indicating all the possible approaches and sub-topics arising from this issue.

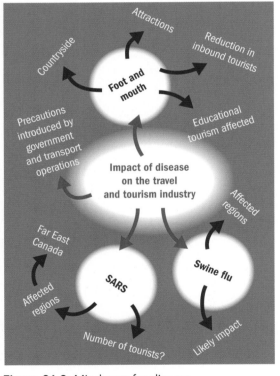

Figure 26.3: Mind map for disease

2.3 Referencing

References are a list of sources from which you have made direct quotes or extracted data. Everything you cite in your report should be listed once alphabetically by author in your reference list. The bibliography is a list of all sources that you have used to carry out your research, not just those you have quoted. It should be written in the same way as the reference list.

Harvard referencing system

The Harvard referencing system (also known as the name and date system) is the one that is conventionally used. In the text you should cite your source using the name of the organisation or individual who published the material you are quoting from or otherwise using, together with the name and date of the publication in which you found it. Quotes in text should be preceded by a colon and indented within the main text. Do not use quotation marks. The author, year and page number should follow the quote.

Example:

Company aims vary, particularly according to whether they are profit-making or non-profit-making. A profit-making company must make money to stay in business and to satisfy the shareholders, who, after all, have invested in order to make money.

(Dale, 2010, p.65)

In the reference list at the end of the text you should include the name(s) of the author(s), the date of publication, the title of the chapter or article, the title of the book or journal and the publisher. You will find this information on the title page of the book or document you are using. In a book this is inside the front cover.

Example:

Dale, G. (2010) BTEC *National Travel and Tourism Book 1,* Pearson Education Ltd

You must include newspapers and websites as well as books and journals.

For sources from the internet you name the author or editor of the page, if known, followed by the year. The title follows in italics with online in brackets (online), the publisher, then available from with the web address and the date you accessed it.

Example:

Guide to the Harvard System of Referencing 2007 (online), Anglia Ruskin University, available from: http://libweb.anglia.ac.uk/referencing/harvard.htm (accessed 3rd May 2010).

There are many study skills books and websites which explain how referencing should be done.

You should start thinking about how to present your research project at the planning stage. Your tutor may have a preferred method of presentation, such as a written report, but most are flexible. If you have an innovative idea for presentation discuss it with your tutor. Here we look at some methods of communicating your findings and presenting your information.

2.4 Communicating findings
Presenting your own and others' arguments

Your work must be objective; it must try to present all sides of an argument. In fact, you should not decide where you stand on a particular issue until you have finished doing your research and looked at all the arguments.

Summarising data

When you do research you end up with a lot of data. You cannot present all this data to an audience; it would be too boring and too difficult to understand. It is your job to summarise the data and make it easy for the audience to understand it. Present the summary in a visual way to aid comprehension.

Drawing conclusions

Once you have looked at the arguments and analysed your research findings what are the conclusions? Draw out key points from the findings. It will help you to remember that conclusions give meaning to the data. Look for links between sets of data.

Example:

Research shows that arrivals to Cape Verde (a Portuguese colony off the coast of West Africa) are increasing. There are now direct charter flights servicing the islands from the UK. There is an obvious link between the introduction of the charters and the increase in visitors.

What informed conclusions would you make about arrivals in Cape Verde?

Engaging your audience

You want your research findings to be read so consider how to present them. If you are going to present orally look at the tips in the next section. If you are going to present in a written format, consider layout, use of colour and language.

2.5 Appropriate media to communicate findings

You might choose to use one of the following four ways of communicating your findings.

Extended document

This should be of sufficient length to cover in detail all the elements of your plan. The information must be structured in a logical way and you must make sure that spelling, punctuation and grammar are accurate. Get someone else to proofread your work for an extra check once you have read it yourself.

Group discussion

This is a difficult medium to use unless you are very experienced. You have to be able to control the group discussion while still being able to put forward your arguments in a structured way. You could use it by carefully planning the discussion around your key points and being prepared to halt discussion and move on to your next point. It is a useful means of getting feedback on your research findings.

Oral presentation

You may decide to present your work orally. You will still have to do a lot of written work to keep track of your research, analyse findings and draw conclusions. However, you will not have to produce a full written report. Instead you can use your research findings to plan a presentation. From your notes you will plan a presentation which includes the following elements:

- **Introduction** – description of the research issue, the aims and the methodology chosen. You will also tell your audience what is going to be covered in the presentation.
- **Findings** – divide this into sections and make sure that the different sections are flagged up to the audience by using bullet points on an overhead projector or PowerPoint® slides, or by introducing each section verbally. You should use cue cards to

remind you of the key points you want to make in each section. Practise your presentation so that you are not totally dependent on the cue cards and you are not tempted to read from them.

- **Visual aids** – your presentation will be of greater interest if you support it with visual aids. You may choose to produce a PowerPoint presentation which can include charts and pictures. You may use a series of overheads or handouts. If you use handouts give them out at the beginning or the end but not when you want your audience to listen to you. They will get distracted by the handout and you will lose their attention.
- **Conclusions** – draw attention to the main conclusions from your findings.
- **Recommendations** – if these are appropriate, discuss these last.
- **Questions** – unlike a written report there is an opportunity with an oral presentation to invite your audience to seek clarification or expansion of points. You can limit the time for questions if you wish. If you get a question that you cannot answer, throw it open to your audience as in 'Thank you for that question, who would like to comment on that?' Thank your audience at the end.

Report

This written method is often easier than an extended document, as it has a very clear structure to help you.

How to write a report: structure

The following elements should be included in a report.

- **Title page** – you should always put the full name of your research project on the first page, along with your name and the date.
- **Contents page** – you can compile this at the end or as you go along. Ensure page numbers are given for each section. There is a system in Word which will do it for you if you want to use this.

- **Introduction** – this section explains the research issue and the aims of the report. You should also give an overview of the research methodology used. In a formal report this is headed 'Terms of reference' and will give more detail on the what, why and how.

- **Findings** – this is the main part of the report and is where you summarise all the research findings from both your secondary and primary research. It is where you present the main results from your research and analyse all the data that you collected. You may include description, facts, tables, graphs and quotes, as long as they are referenced.

- **Conclusions** – having presented all your findings you should draw some conclusions. This will be a series of important points resulting from your research.

- **Recommendations** – these are not always required but if so should be presented as a series of points for action resulting from the conclusions.

- **Use of appendices** – you can attach information, statistical data and pages from the internet in appendices. They should be labelled Appendix 1, 2, etc. and attached to the back of your work. They must be referred to in your work. For example, in your report you might state 'Statistics show that Paris is the most popular short-break destination – see Appendix 1'. Sometimes the reader needs to see the statistics or graphs and charts as they read the report as they are important to understanding a point. In this case, include them in the main body of the report and quote the source.

Note that reports can be informal or formal. An informal report is arranged under headings without numbering. A formal report has a system of numbering headings and then subheadings. The introduction is numbered '1'. The findings are numbered '2' and each subsection 2.1, 2.2, etc. The conclusions are numbered '3'. Recommendations, if included are numbered '4'.

2.6 Appropriate conventions to communicate findings

Whatever method you choose to present your work you must consider the following points.

Use of vocabulary

- Use the correct terminology for travel and tourism, for example 'arrivals' and 'receipts'.

- Use terms and vocabulary that can be clearly understood by your audience.
- Use correct spellings.
- Vary your sentences and choice of words.

Grammatical expression

Reports are always written in the third person. This means, for example, that you do not use 'I found that …'. You say 'It was found that …'.

Use correct grammar – if in doubt, look it up or ask.

Emphasis

Emphasis refers to the weighting and placing of key words and terms that you use to support your points in your report. For example, in the conclusion section you will probably put your strongest conclusion first.

Structure

- Have a clear purpose to the work.
- Clearly introduce your topic.
- Use report structure to help you if you find extended documents difficult.
- Have an introduction and a conclusion.

Logical sequence

- Each paragraph or section of a report should deal with one topic.
- Link one topic to the next.
- Do not jump around topics.

Plagiarism

Everything you write must be in your own words. It is unacceptable to copy from another source unless it is a direct quote. This must be acknowledged with details of the source and the date. If you do copy directly from a source without acknowledgement, this is called plagiarism and is very serious. In extreme cases it may result in legal action being taken against you.

Activity: Preparing your findings

With a partner, prepare for a presentation on the increase of air passenger duty on flights. Use appropriate conventions to convey findings.

Use appropriate sources of information and use a standard referencing system, such as Harvard.

Remember when carrying out research:

- Plan well – don't just browse at random.
- Check the validity of your sources.
- Never plagiarise.

- Present your work in a logical way with appropriate headings.
- Use appendices and always refer to them in the main body of your report.
- Add a bibliography.

Assessment activity 26.2

(P2) (P3) (M1) (M2) (D1)  BTEC

Remember the scenario you met in your first assessment activity? You are contributing to workshops at the World Travel Market. For your second workshop you must choose an issue that currently affects the travel and tourism sector. You may choose one of the examples in the unit if you like.

1 Produce a research plan which can be used to investigate your chosen issue. (P2)

2 Explain to your boss/tutor how the plan enables exploration of your chosen issue. This can be done orally or in a written document. (M1)

3 Carry out research into your chosen issue. (P2)

4 Use at least four different types of sources of information. (M2)

5 Produce a sheet on the limitations of your sources, that is what you could not find out from them. (M2)

6 Analyse the findings from the research carried out. (P3)

7 Carry out an evaluation of the research undertaken and recommend improvements to your own research skills for the future. (D1)

Make sure that you cover the full range, referring to the content and assessment guidance in the unit specification for the detail required.

Grading tips

(P2) Make sure your research plan addresses everything listed in the unit research plan. Include both qualitative and quantitative sources.

(P2) You must carry out, and not just plan, the research. There must be evidence of referencing, using Harvard or another accepted method.

(M1) Make sure you explain why the research methods chosen are suitable for the issue you want to explore.

(M2) 'Different types' means websites, trade journals, books and official statistics, for example, not four different websites. You need to show that you have worked independently and you must have used primary and secondary sources, qualitative and quantitative data.

(D1) Be specific about what you would do differently next time.

PLTS

Planning and carrying out research, and presenting a detailed analysis of results from research, into a complex current issue affecting the travel and tourism sector will help to develop your skills as an **independent enquirer**.

Functional skills

By selecting and using appropriate sources of ICT based information to carry out your research, you will be practising your **ICT** skills.

3 Impacts of complex current issues on the travel and tourism sector

In this section we will consider some more examples of current issues affecting travel and tourism. This time you will look more closely at the impact of these issues. You should be ready to conduct your own research and may already have determined the issue you want to research.

Issues can impact on the industry, or a sector of it, in various ways.

- Loss of customers – because of a terrorism issue in a particular country or a long-term health scare.

- Development of new markets – due to new technology in travel allowing easier access or tourism development in a country.

- Loss of revenue – due to decline in customers as they choose different destinations or book by other means.

- Changing demands – due to environmental awareness. For example, many travellers are concerned about the impact of their travelling on destinations and wish to visit those which have sound environmental policies or travel with a responsible tour operator.

- Additional costs – due to fuel surcharges or increases in taxation.

- Changes to products and services – due to decline in popularity of existing resorts, for example mainland Spain.

Several of these impacts can result from only one issue. Here are two examples.

Case study: One issue – big repercussions

1. Travellers unaware of new US visa rules

Travelsupermarket.com carried out some research that showed that most people do not know about the online visa waiver requirements introduced in January 2009 in the US. The survey polled 2000 travellers and 57 per cent had no idea that there was a new procedure.

Of those polled 37 per cent thought the online system was of benefit to travellers and thought that other countries should follow suit.

Those who haven't got organised and applied for the online visa may arrive at check-in and find they are not allowed to fly.

A visa is valid for two years but needs to be applied for online at least 72 hours before flying. If someone has a criminal record they should plan well in advance as the visa may be refused and an embassy visit will be needed.

A further requirement that people may not be aware of is that passports must have at least six months remaining in order to travel to the US.

For both examples:

1 Identify the issue and explore it further.

2 Explain the impacts on the travel and tourism sector.

2. Ash Chaos

In April 2010 the authorities in the UK closed all airspace for six days. This was due to an eruption of an Icelandic volcano leading to clouds of volcanic ash affecting airspace. The consequences of such blanket closure were that airlines and tour operators claimed to lose millions of pounds in revenue. In addition, airlines had a duty of care to provide food and accommodation for stranded passengers under European law (Regulation 261). The UK's two major tour operators, TUI and Thomas Cook between them had more than 100,000 passengers stranded. The companies had to continue to provide for these customers' extended holidays and repatriate them when airspace reopened.

The heads of the two companies joined with airline heads, including Virgin's Richard Branson, to criticise the government response to the crisis. They said there was no clear reason for the closure of airspace and that the repatriation effort was left to carriers rather than government. They claimed that the government should have ensured that the industry responded in a consistent and responsible manner to the crisis and that some low-cost carriers had failed to recognise their duty of care to passengers.

3 Provide a comprehensive analysis of the issue, combining and recognising different points of view.

4 Use your findings to recommend actions for the travel and tourism sector.

Assessment activity 26.3

(P4) (M3) (D2)   :BTEC

Present your research findings from the research you carried out for the World Trade Market workshop in assessment activity 26.2, explaining how the chosen issue impacts on the travel and tourism sector, remembering your audience of professionals at the World Travel Market. (P4) (M3)

Evidence must be clearly reasoned and explanatory. (P4)

Use findings from your research to recommend actions for the travel and tourism sector. (D2)

Make sure that you cover the full range, referring to the content and assessment guidance in the unit specification for the detail required.

Grading tips

(P4) (M3) (D2) Make sure you use appropriate vocabulary and other conventions in your presentation.

(P4) You can present your findings orally or in written format.

(M3) You must communicate clearly, concisely and coherently using specialist vocabulary, making connections and synthesising arguments.

(D2) You must have clear, justified recommendations for action on the researched issue.

PLTS

Discussing how a complex current issue impacts on the travel and tourism sector will help to develop your skills as an **independent enquirer**.

Functional skills

By making an effective presentation either orally or in written format, you will be practising your **English** speaking and listening skills.

Harry Figgis
Customer Service Director for a tour operator

Harry has been working in his current role for 5 years. Before that he was the Customer Service Manager for a low-cost airline.

Harry, you must have had a very busy time in April, 2010 when the volcano in Iceland erupted and called a halt to air traffic because of the ash cloud.

We did have a very difficult time. We established an Ash Crisis Team. Everyone was called in from off days and leave to deal with the problems it caused. We had holidaymakers all over Europe whom we couldn't get home as there were no flights for them. We also had customers here that we had to contact and tell them that they couldn't go on holiday.

How did you deal with the customers?

I divided my staff into teams. One team handled extending hotel accommodation for our customers. This wasn't as straightforward as you might think as we did not know from day to day how long the air closure would be.

Another team contacted all customers due to fly in that week and offered refunds or alternative holidays. This was problematic too, as we didn't have much spare capacity to offer them.

The third team was responsible for hiring coaches to transport customers in Spain to Calais where we were able to bring them back by ferry.

It sounds like an expensive operation.

In a lot of cases customers' insurance polices will pay for the costs of disruption but otherwise we are covering them. It has made a huge difference to our profits this year as it has cost us millions. However, we think that those customers who usually go on DIY holidays may, in future, opt for a package knowing we will look after them if anything goes wrong.

Think about it!

1 Find out what events occurred in April 2010, following the eruption of the volcano and write a brief account that you can relate to a classmate.

2 What protection is given to customers who have booked package holidays?

3 What happened to those who were stranded and had not booked packages?

Just checking

1 What is the difference between quantitative and qualitative data?

2 Give two sources of travel and tourism statistics.

3 How can you track your research?

4 What is 'action research'?

5 What should be included in a research plan?

6 Why do you need a research plan?

7 Give two examples of research methodologies.

8 When would you use a focus group?

9 Why do you need to assess the validity of an information source?

10 Think of two ways to communicate your findings other than a written report or oral presentation.

11 What is the referencing system that is commonly used called?

12 What is plagiarism?

13 Why do you need to do an evaluation when you have completed your project?

Assignment tips

- Agree your research issue with your tutor!

- Make sure that the issue you research is current, i.e. that it is happening now.

- Use a range of sources, electronic and printed.

- Sign up to travel and tourism news websites and get news sent to your email address – particularly useful are www.travelmole.com, www.e-tid.com and www.eyefortravel.com.

- Remember, as always, to read *Travel Weekly* and *Travel Trade Gazette*.

- Quality newspapers will explain events in terms of their impact on travel and tourism.

Glossary of key terms

A

Active listening – the process of demonstrating to another person both verbally and non-verbally that the information is being received. It is done by maintaining eye contact, nodding and agreeing in appropriate places.

Adhoc contract – the tour operator pays only for the rooms that they have taken.

Allocation contracts – the tour operator buys an agreed number of rooms (or flights).

B

Bond – a financial guarantee to refund travellers if the travel company collapses, provided by a bank or insurance company.

Bonding – an amount of money to cover the cost of reimbursing/repatriating tourists in the event of tour operator failure.

C

Charter flights – flights rented by a tour operator to fly for short seasons to holiday destinations. Small operators can group together to charter a flight.

Contingency plan – a plan you have ready to deal with things that go wrong.

Contract – a legally binding exchange of promises or agreement between parties that the law will enforce.

D

Dwell time – the length of time a visitor spends at the attraction.

Dynamic packaging – accommodation, travel and other services are separately researched and put together in a package for the customer.

E

E-brochures – electronic versions of tour operator information of the type that traditionally appears in print.

F

Fixed contract – if the accommodation (or flights) are not sold, the owner is still paid.

Focus group – a small number of people (up to about 15) who are brought together in a moderated meeting to talk about a specific product, service or issue.

G

Gateway ports – ports that provide a major link to other countries or access to destinations within a country for trade or passengers.

H

Horizontal integration – two companies at the same level in the chain of distribution merge or one takes over the other. For example in 2009, TUI Travel, parent company of Thomson Cruises took over Island Cruises.

I

Interpretation – a means of imparting information to visitors so that their understanding and enjoyment of the attraction are enhanced.

M

Multiplier effect – where an initial amount of spending in one part of the economy, for example by an organisation investing, leads to increased spending by consumers.

O

Office of Fair Trading (OFT) – the government office set up to oversee trading practices of organisations and individuals in the UK.

Off-peak seasons – the least busy times.

OTE (On Target Earnings) – often seen in advertisements for jobs, this means that you can expect to earn the stated figure if you meet the set targets. The basic salary may be only half this amount.

P

Package holiday – a holiday including at least two elements of transport, accommodation and other services, for example the services of an overseas representative.

Passenger crew ratio (PCR) – gives the number of crew in relation to passengers; the higher the crew number in relation to passengers, the more likely the customer is to get superior service.

Passenger manifest – a list or record of passengers.

Passenger space ratio (PSR) – compares the total public space to the passenger capacity the more space there is in relation to the number of customers, the more spacious the ship is likely to feel.

Peak seasons – the busiest times, coinciding with school holidays.

People 1st – the Sector Skills Council (SSC) that represents the hospitality, leisure, travel and tourism sector on skills matters, to optimise skills funding and to identify and endorse suitable training provision.

PEST – analysis of the Political, Economic, Social and Technological factors affecting an organisation.

Ports of call – ports that the ship visits and the passengers can take a shore excursion if they wish; they have to get back on before the ship sails again!

Preferred partner – an arrangement between companies where they promote each other's products or services.

Primary product or service – the main purpose of the visit, for example the exhibition in a gallery or the rides in a theme park.

Primary research – research carried out for the first time by you. It includes any surveys or interviews you do.

Q

Qualitative data – data about opinions and reasons for doing things. These are harder to interpret than quantitative data but can be very rich and informative.

Quantitative data – data that consist of facts and figures. These are easy to measure but do not always tell us why things happen.

R

Research plan – an overview of, and rationale for, the research project.

S

Scheduled flights – flights which run to a set timetable throughout the year. Timetables are adjusted for winter and summer seasons.

Secondary product or service – products or services which add to the appeal of the attraction and are a means of revenue but do not provide the main draw. The main sources are shops and restaurants.

Secondary research – research which someone else has done and which you are using to help you with your project.

Secondary spend – the money that visitors spend on the secondary products and services during their visit.

Shoulder seasons – the slightly less busy times either side of the peak season.

Subsidiaries – companies which are more than 50% owned by another company, known as the parent company.

SWOT – analysis of the Strengths, Weaknesses, Opportunities and Threats of an organisation. Strengths and weaknesses are internal, threats and opportunities may be internal or external depending on their nature.

T

Timed ticket – a means to control the flow of visitors by issuing tickets that are valid between certain times.

Trade fair – an exhibition held for people working within a particular industry. It gives an opportunity for people to meet and do business together and see what new products and services are on offer.

U

Upselling – refers to selling a more expensive product or adding options to a product being sold. It is most likely to occur in the selling of excursions, perhaps by selling a full day rather than a half day, or by selling more than one excursion to a customer.

V

Vertical integration – companies merge or one takes over the other at different levels in the chain of distribution, for example Thomson has an airline, a tour operation business, a cruise line and retail agents.

W

Web-conferencing – a system that allows two or more people in different locations to link up and communicate by video over the internet.

Index